ARABIA FELIX

Also by BERTRAM THOMAS

ALARMS AND EXCURSIONS IN ARABIA (*Bobbs-Merrill.* 1931)

Contributed to:

Royal Geographical Society:

> (I) March 1929, 'A Camel Journey through the South-eastern Borderlands.'
>
> (II) January 1931, 'A Journey into Rub' al Khali.'
>
> (III) September 1931, 'A Camel Journey across the Rub' al Khali.'

Royal Asiatic Society:

> (I) October 1930, 'The Kumzari Dialect of the Shihuh Tribe of Musandam.'
>
> (II) October 1931, 'Burton and the Rub' al Khali.' (Burton Memorial Lecture.)

Royal Anthropological Institute:

> (I) June-December 1929, 'Among some Unknown Tribes of South Arabia.' (Orientalist Congress. Oxford, 1928.)
>
> (II) December 1931-June 1932, 'Anthropological Observations on South Arabians.'

Royal Central Asian Society:

> (I) Vol. XV, 1928, 'The Musandam Peninsula and its Inhabitants—the Shihuh.'
>
> (II) Vol. XVIII, 1931, 'Across the Rub' al Khali.'

SANDS OF ARABIA FELIX.

ARABIA FELIX

ACROSS THE "EMPTY QUARTER"
OF ARABIA

by

BERTRAM THOMAS

O.B.E. [Mil.]; formerly Wazir to H.H. the Sultan of Muscat and Oman, sometime Political Officer in Iraq, and Assistant British Representative in Trans-Jordan. Founder's Medallist of the Royal Geographical Society; Burton Memorial Medallist of the Royal Asiatic Society; Gold Medallist of the Royal Geographical Society of Antwerp; and Cullum Medallist of the American Geographical Society, New York

WITH A FOREWORD BY
COLONEL T. E. LAWRENCE
[T. E. S.]

AND AN APPENDIX BY
SIR ARTHUR KEITH, F.R.S., M.D.

CONTAINING ALSO
MAPS, CHARTS, DIAGRAMS, AND
ILLUSTRATIONS COMPLEMENTARY
TO THE TEXT

NEW YORK
CHARLES SCRIBNER'S SONS
1932

TO

SIR ARNOLD WILSON, K.C.I.E., C.M.G., C.S.I., D.S.O.

TENACIOUS IN COUNSEL, SWIFT IN ACTION
TO WHOSE ADVICE AND ENCOURAGEMENT
IN THE YEARS 1918-1931
MY JOURNEYINGS IN ARABIA OWE THEIR INSPIRATION
THIS BOOK IS DEDICATED
IN ADMIRATION AND GRATITUDE

'He set my feet upon the rock and ordered my goings.'

Ps. xl. 2.

CONTENTS

CONTENTS

[vii]

CONTENTS

[viii]

CONTENTS

[ix]

CONTENTS

[x]

CONTENTS

LIST OF APPENDICES

[xi]

CONTENTS

LIST OF ILLUSTRATIONS

[xiii]

LIST OF ILLUSTRATIONS

[xiv]

LIST OF ILLUSTRATIONS

ILLUSTRATIONS FOR APPENDIX I

By Sir Arthur Keith, F.R.S., M.D., etc., and Dr. W. M. Krogman, Ph.D.

younger men died of their duty, directly; and that is why Thomas must come down to me.

I suppose no new Sixth Former can help feeling how much his year falls short of the great fellows there when he joined the school. But can the sorry little crowd of us to-day be in the tradition, even? I fear not. Of course the mere wishing to be an Arabian betrays the roots of a quirk; but our predecessors' was a larger day, in which the seeing Arabia was an end in itself. They just wrote a wander-book and the great peninsula made their prose significant. (Incidentally, the readable Arabian books are all in English, bar one; Jews, Swiss, Irishmen and What-nots having conspired to help the Englishmen write them. There are some German books of too-sober learning and one Dutch.) Its deserts cleaned or enriched Doughty's pen and Palgrave's, Burckhardt's and Blunt's, helped Raunkiær with his Kuweit, Burton and Wavell in their pilgrimages, and Bury amongst his sun-struck Yemeni hamlets.

Our feebler selves dare not be Arabians for Arabia's sake—none of us save Rutter, I think, and how good, how classical, his book! The rest must frame excuses for travelling. One will fix latitudes, the silly things, another collect plants or insects (not to eat, but to bring home), a third make war, which is coals to Newcastle. We fritter our allegiances and loyalties.

Inevitable, of course, that these impurities should come. As pools shrink they stench. Raleigh could hearten my ancestor—'Cozen, we know but the hand's-breadth of our world'—but since him Arctic and Antarctic, the wastes of Asia and Africa, the forests of America have yielded their secrets. Last year I could have retorted—'There is but a hand's-breadth we do not know'—thinking of that virgin Rub' al Khali, the last unwritten plot of earth big enough for a sizable man's turning in twice or thrice about, before he couches. However, only these few paragraphs of mine now stand between appetite and the tale of its conquest. To-day we know the whole earth. Would-be wandering youth will go unsatisfied till a winged generation lands on the next planet.

Few men are able to close an epoch. We cannot know the first man who walked the inviolate earth for newness' sake: but Thomas is the last; and he did his journey in the antique way, by pain of his camel's legs, single-handed, at his own time and cost. He might have flown an aeroplane, sat in a car or rolled over in a tank. Instead he has snatched, at the twenty-third hour, feet's last victory and set us free. Everything having been once done in the slowest fashion we can concentrate upon speed, amplifying the eye of the tortoise by the hare's and the bird's. All honour to Thomas. The Royal Geographical Society itself forgives, bemedals its supersessor . . . also he has an O.B.E.

I will not say how much I like this book, lest the publisher dig out the odd sentence for his blurb. Thomas let me read the draft, and I then did my best to comment usefully; once remarking that the tale was good enough for his journey—no faint judgment, set against what I think the finest thing in Arabian exploration. As he tells it, the achievement may read easy, because he is a master of every desert art. Here once more is the compleat Arabian traveller enshrined. Not twice but twenty times his tiniest touches set me remembering that wide land which I liked so much, twenty years ago, and hoped never to feel again. Thence, I suppose, the reason of my writing him this use-

less foreword; that and my understanding of his risks.
Only by favour of a propitious season could this very rare
individual, after infinite care and tact in preparation, have
gambled his life upon the crowning solidarity which the
desert owes to Ibn Saud, and won through. Thomas is as
fortunate as deserving.

T. E. S.

PREFACE

IN the preparation of this book I have made no attempt to collate the scanty scientific observations of earlier travellers in adjoining regions which may, or may not, have some scientific bearing upon the problems I have touched upon. To have done so, indeed, would have been beyond the scope of a personal record. Hence the reader is spared an impressive bibliography. My endeavour has been to set forth as a straightforward narrative the things that I saw and heard, and the experiences that befell me. If in the fulfilment of that task I have fallen short of standards that have been set me by my predecessors in the sphere of Arabian travel, I would plead that the narrative has been written amongst many other preoccupations in the few months since my return from Arabia. Where, in recording conversations and folk stories, Arabic, Mahri or Shahari words are used, I have transliterated them in accordance with the local dialects in which they were spoken, and have eschewed the Arabic lexicon.

I am indebted to Sir Arthur Keith who, in association with Dr. W. M. Krogman, has contributed a valuable Appendix to this work, not only for much kindly encouragement, but for a synthesis of my anthropological observations and measurements, by which they come to have a scientific meaning.

I have to thank the Royal Geographical Society for much assistance in collating my astronomical observations on this and on previous journeys, and in the preparation of the map which accompanies this volume; and especially the President, Admiral Sir William Goodenough, the

Secretary, Mr. A. R. Hinks, and the Map Curator, Mr. A. S. Reeves.

Dr. W. T. Calman and other members of the staff of the Natural History Museum, South Kensington, have been good enough to permit me to publish as an Appendix their notes on the specimens I collected.

The laborious task of reading the manuscript has been undertaken by friends—Aircraftman T. E. Shaw (Colonel Lawrence), who has been so good as to contribute a foreword; Professor H. A. R. Gibb, to whom I am also grateful for a number of valuable comments and suggestions; Mr. R. W. Bullard, H.B.M.'s Consul-General at Leningrad and formerly H.B.M.'s Consul at Jeddah, and Sir Arnold Wilson, my former chief in Mesopotamia. But for their advice and help it would not have been possible for me to have passed this book through the Press without considerable delay.

BERTRAM THOMAS

EAST INDIA UNITED SERVICE CLUB,
ST JAMES'S SQUARE,
December 12, 1931.

INTRODUCTION

ARABIA FELIX! Strange that the epithet 'Happy' should grace a part of the earth's surface, most of it barren wilderness where, since the dawn of history, man has ever been at war with his environment and his neighbour. Yet there can be no mistaking the classical geographers. To Strabo, Pliny, and Ptolemy, the term Arabia Felix served for the entire peninsula south of the Syrian desert (Arabia Deserta) and the mountains about Sinai (Arabia Petræa). True, the term consorts ill with the horrid wastes of Rub' al Khali that form no small part of Arabia, but there lies in the central south, bordering the Indian Ocean, a land at once of rare physical loveliness and of ancient fame. If there be any region in Arabia entitled to the epithet 'Happy,' other than the Yemen, whose glories were well known to the ancients, it is this province of Dhufar, an Arcadia of luxuriant forests that clothe steep mountains overlooking the sea, of perennial streams and sunny meadows, of wide vistas and verdant glades. Here, according to the writer of Genesis, Jehovah had set the limit of the known world 'as thou goest east unto Mount Sephar'; hither came the ancient Egyptians for frankincense to embalm their sacred Pharaohs; here, may be, were hewed the pillars of Solomon's Temple, if indeed Dhufar be not the site of Ophir itself, and the traditional market for ivory and peacocks' feathers.

I have attempted to set down in the pages that follow a narrative of my recent camel journey across Rub' al Khali, and of my researches in this fair province of Dhufar, the gateway of that journey, and to me the true Arabia Felix of to-day.

The virgin Rub' al Khali, the Great Southern Desert! To have laboured in Arabia is to have tasted inevitably of her seduction, and six years ago when I left the Administration of Transjordan for the Court of Muscat and Oman I already cherished secret dreams. The remote recesses of the earth, Arctic and Antarctic, the sources of the Amazon, and the vast inner spaces of Asia and Africa, have one by one yielded their secrets to man's curiosity, until by a strange chance the Rub' al Khali remained almost the last considerable *terra incognita*, which is surprising considering the great antiquity of settled Arabia, the border lands of which touched the early civilisations of Egypt and Babylonia.

Yet Arabia has remained the forbidden land. Throughout the centuries scarce twenty European explorers have been able usefully to penetrate to her inhospitable heart. For this there are two main reasons. First, lack of rain and the merciless heat of the Arabian desert permit of but scattered and semi-barbarous nomad societies, which are at such perpetual war that, even for themselves, life is insecure. Secondly, the religion of these desert men, at least in practice, is fanatical and exclusive. From time to time they hold it virtuous to enforce Islam with the sword. In Arabia proper all European visitors have been individual men, and only once in all her history, and that in Roman times, has she—the then supposed Eldorado— excited the cupidity of European invaders, so that among her inhabitants, left so severely to themselves, insularity, bigotry, and intolerance are indigenous growths with a long pedigree. Hence an area equal to half the superficies of Europe had remained a blank on our maps.

INTRODUCTION

It had fascinated Richard Burton, who in 1852 offered his services to the Royal Geographical Society for the purpose of what he termed 'removing that opprobrium to modern adventure,' but he succumbed to official obstruction and never put his plans to the test. I enjoyed advantages. Thirteen years of post-war service in various political capacities on three sides of Arabia enabled me to acquire a peculiar knowledge of tribal dialects and of Arab ways, and to become acclimatised. I had addressed myself for years past to two problems—how to find an avenue of approach to the interior and how to cultivate the tribes there. As a Minister of the Council of the State of Oman, my name came to be known throughout southeast Arabia; it was because I was the Sultan's Wazir and because of the cordial relations existing between the Ruler and myself that I was brought into personal touch with the most influential Arabs of that part. Hence a general attitude of tolerance towards me, an Englishman and a Christian, without which I could never have dreamt of moving off the beaten track.

Then, too, I knew the mind of authority and so avoided the pitfall of seeking permission for my designs. Was not the lesson of Burton before me? The British official attitude, with which, let me add, I am in general sympathy, is, in view of the anarchy that normally prevails in Desert Arabia, inimical to exploration. The good official must avoid responsibility and commitments, and to learn of, and not forbid, an expedition implies tacit authorisation. So my plans were conceived in darkness, my journeys heralded only by my disappearances, paid for by myself and executed under my own auspices. Throughout my service in Muscat I elected to spend my summers there, to save

ARABIA

Far are the shades of Arabia,
Where the Princes ride at noon,
'Mid the verdurous vales and thickets,
Under the ghost of the moon;
And so dark is that vaulted purple
Flowers in the forest rise
And toss into blossom 'gainst the phantom stars
Pale in the noonday skies.

Sweet is the music of Arabia
In my heart, when out of dreams
I still in the thin clear mirk of dawn
Descry her gliding streams;
Hear her strange lutes on the green banks
Ring loud with the grief and delight
Of her dim-silked, dark-haired Musicians
In the brooding silence of night.

They haunt me—her lutes and her forests;
No beauty on earth I see
But shadowed with that dream recalls
Her loveliness to me:
Still eyes look coldly upon me,
Cold voices whisper and say—
'He is crazed with the spell of far Arabia,
They have stolen his wits away.'

WALTER DE LA MARE

[xxix]

ARABIA FELIX

I: A PROPITIOUS START
AND AN EARLY CHECK

IT was midnight of the 4th-5th October 1930. The little Arab port of Muscat lay asleep. Only one of its inhabitants, albeit Prince amongst them, Saiyid Sa'id bin Taimur, had, in the absence of his father the Sultan, been taken into my confidence and made privy to the activities of the beach. There, a *badan* (small country rowing boat) was hauled close inshore and my faithful servant Muhammad bore to her his master's mysterious boxes, his gun and camel saddles. I was secretly embarking on my long-cherished ambition to unveil the unknown southern Arabian desert. To-morrow, the news of my disappearance would startle the bazaar and a variety of fates would doubtless be invented for me by imaginations of oriental fertility.

H.M.S. *Cyclamen* lay twinkling in the inner anchorage, and I went alongside to collect a mascot which Pemberton, her pilot, who had just been supping with me, would, he had said, leave with the 'hand' on watch. Thence my Baluchi boatmen, sworn to future secrecy, pulled on into the open sea. The brilliant light of the full moon allowed immediate introduction to my mascot—it was Walter de la Mare's poem, 'Arabia'—and, of more immediate importance, I could reassure myself of the contents of the cable in my hand:—

's.s. *British Grenadier* arriving 6.0 a.m. Sunday three miles off-shore-Muscat—Master.'

The dark mass of the 10,000-ton oil tanker came

[1]

looming up. A flag which I flew by arrangement did its work; I was quickly transhipped, and the *British Grenadier*, homeward bound, was on her course again ere four bells had struck, bearing me away from Muscat.

I planned to be landed at Dhufar half-way along the southern coast of Arabia if weather conditions at the end of this south-west monsoon season would permit, or failing that, to be dropped into the first Arab dhow we encountered. Next day the freshening wind slightly reduced our speed, and the prospect of making Salala in daylight grew doubtful. To 'stand off' all night was not to be entertained, and so it was an Arab dhow that we made for when we saw one. Her crazy little dinghy came alongside in response to our siren; Muhammad and I, dressed in Arab kit, slipped over the side and down the pilot ladder. My boxes made a precarious load, but she was equal to our demands, and carried us safely over the long undulations of the swell to the anchored dhow. The *British Grenadier* signalled 'good luck' and went forging ahead, soon to be hull-down in the grey watery solitudes where the sun had set.

The Arab captain of *Fath as Salaam*, for that was the dhow's name, shook his head when I spoke of landing; he had, in fact, quite other views. A ground swell, even in the mildest weather, runs vigorously along these gently shelving beaches, and sends huge rollers crashing inshore. A whaler or other English-built boat would surely capsize and break up, but the local *banush* (of sewn timbers), craftily handled by the fisherfolk, comes riding safely through, despite moments when it seems to stand giddily on end and one looks on apprehensively, knowing that the

A COCO-NUT GROVE AT DHUFAR: AN ILL-ASSORTED PAIR AT THE WELL.

sea, a boiling cauldron in the vicinity, would show small mercy to a swimmer.

Mindful of my chronometers, I persuaded the captain, after much argument, to make for Risut, a sheltered bay down the coast. Two hours after the lug had been bent and hoisted, it still flapped listlessly, while the unchanging view of the white fort and mosque, midst a coco-nut grove backed by the blue Qara Mountains, which constitutes all that is to be seen of Dhufar from the sea, showed that we had scarcely moved one way or the other.

A playful whale helped to beguile the moments—a ponderous dark green monster that came and lay alongside us like a submarine beside its parent ship, proud to prove itself not much smaller than the *Fath as Salaam*. It seemed to me perilously friendly as it dived just under us, to rise but a few feet away and break surface with a snort, before sinking heavily again, with a little wash and a multitude of bubbles to mark its going. Nor were our sailors unconcerned. With an eye on our dinghy, which lapped about astern of us, they kept up a frightening din by drumming empty kerosene tins. The wind freshened to deliver us, and by noon we came close hauled to Risut[1] where I landed.

And so into the saddle. We hugged the shore till we passed Auqad (Abkid), a small village in the plain, and thence rode along the edge of a coco-nut palm grove to make the fort of Dhufar at sunset on 8th October. Here,

[1] The adventurous Portuguese of the sixteenth century, in their day the most gallantly ruthless of Europeans in Asia, thought Risut worthy of their steel and blood; a flight of steps and some ruined fortifications still stand memorial to them. To-day Risut is the only possible seaplane base on this stretch of central south Arabian shore for some hundreds of miles during the summer monsoon months.

[3]

very tired after a sleepless twenty-four hours, I was to occupy my old room in the keep. But it was not a kindly night. Mosquitoes were legion and a swarm of yellow hornets were building themselves a house in the rafters above: a tiny insect, too, invisible as a sandfly but not less of a torment, took toll of my blood.

Salala knew of my presence: it must not know of my plans. Secrecy was imperative. To disclose them would be to invite hostility and the news would spread abroad, as all news spreads in illiterate Arabia, with the speed of the telegraph and unauthorised accretions that would not disgrace a London evening newspaper.

Where was Sahail the Rashidi? So much for a Badu's pledged word. I had heaped riches on this member of my last year's caravan and made a secret agreement that he should meet me at Salala in this mid moon of *Rabi'a al Awwal* with a camel party to take me into the great sands. He had sworn that only death would prevent his coming. Devious enquiries showed that he had not been heard of in Dhufar since he had gone off to his tribe with the two hundred dollars and a dagger—immense fortune— I had secretly given him then. If this and the promise of more had failed to bring him to fulfil a solemn promise I despaired of my prospects. The Rashid to which he belonged is the only genuine tribe of the Southern Sands, and without their assistance any dream of a crossing were vain.

The desert news in Dhufar was bad. War! The Rashid and the Sa'ar were fighting, the former my hoped-for friends, the latter their powerful hereditary enemies of the northern Hadhramaut—an ancient blood-feud. It followed that the immediate hinterland was menaced by raiders or

[4]

worse. It seemed that Sahail with the best of intentions might be unable to raise a party of his fellow-tribesmen to run the gauntlet to the coast for me. His tribe would either be engaged in offensive operations in the Hadhramaut or have withdrawn themselves for refuge into the depths of the sands. Here was a deadlock. For me the door to the sands seemed bolted and barred.

I could see no way out. Two Rashidi tribesmen, Ma'yuf and Khuwaitim, had come to Dhufar for the frankincense harvest, and I sent for them, for though without camels and out of touch with the tribe, they might yet be knowledgeable. However, it is difficult to gain an Arab's confidence without giving him yours, and it would have been perilous to show my hand prematurely, so we conferred daily for some days till I gathered that the Rashid tribe might be distant a month's march anywhere from north to west, and certainly indisposed to leave their sandy sanctuary.

I should be obliged in the happiest event to arrange a separate caravan, if I could, to take me to some water-hole on the edge of the sands (there were but three possible ones) and trust to the Rashidis' ability and willingness to come there to meet me and carry me forward. But the unpleasant experience of my journey of the year before had taught me the limitations of mountain caravans, of men's alarm for themselves and their camels even when there was no war in the air. The acting Governor to whom I dared reveal only this part of my plans tried cajolery, but there is no compelling authority in these mountains and I detected an undercurrent of hostility that would have made it madness to embark with such allies into the desert. My ambitious plans so carefully laid

[5]

II: AT DHUFAR: ANARCHY, TREACHERY AND HOSPITALITY

BELOW my window in the fort the palm-fringed beach shelved down to the sea. At anchor rode a dhow just arrived, eager from Basrah, with the first fresh cargo of this season's dates, announcing, by her gay bunting and firing of her muzzle-loading mortar that she was no stranger to Dhufar.

Along this seaboard the province of Dhufar[1] extends from Hadhbaram to Dharbat Ali. It consists of a massif 3000 feet high running right down to the sea on east and west, and retreating in the centre, to embrace the crescent-shaped maritime plain of Jurbaib.

Judged by Arabian standards it is a province favoured by Providence. It owes a unique climate to the 'Indian' south-west monsoon, which here makes a preliminary call and during the summer months sprinkles these mountains with a drizzling rain so that the region flows with milk and honey. Just over the mountain divide flourish the famous frankincense groves of Arabia. This precious product, sent to the temples of India, wins back rice and cloth, coffee and spices for its owner's booths, and has been the prosperity of Dhufar through the ages, though it were well not to confuse it with the Dhufar of Arrian near Sana' in the Yemen, a mistake made by Abul Fida'.

The two main settled tribes of the province are the Qara in the mountains, where they live by raising herds and

---

[1] The word Dhufar has also a more limited application. It sometimes stands for the capital of the province merely, that is, a group of three villages, Salala, Hafa and Al Husn, in a way corresponding with the Badu habit of the sands where Hofuf is called only Hasa, and Doha, Qatar.

the rewards of frankincense; and Al Kathir, who fish and farm and trade from villages in the plain. For the rainy months of summer when the seas are too stormy to be usable by native craft, there is a general exodus[1] from the plains to the mountains, where frankincense groves require harvesters and milk is in abundance.

Well water is plentiful, generally at a fathom's depth round the villages, and but for the paralysing hand of a wayward tribalism, artesian wells would probably make the whole plain blossom. Beneath the coco-nut groves wells, mostly served by slaves, bulls or camels, minister to fields of lucerne, sugar cane, plantains, wheat, millet, cotton and indigo. A sixteenth share of each crop must go as taxes to government, whose coffers otherwise receive only a nominal 5 per cent. share of the mountain produce. Here prevails the 'good old rule, the simple plan, that he shall take who has the power, and he shall keep who can,' and if the Sultan's writ runs strong along the coast, in the mountains it is a doubtful and variable quantity.

Ethnologically, Dhufar is as much an enclave as it is geographically. Tribal tradition is one of anarchy—of long internecine strife, alternating with short periods of sporadic government. No recorded history is to be found among the natives, though I was at pains to enquire from every literate resident. But illiteracy is general, and only the old Qadhi could tell a coherent though disconnected story of Dhufar's past. The people, composed of warlike and rival tribes, have always found law and order irksome.

---

[1] This movement finds a parallel in two other seasonal movements of man in south-east Arabia—the migration to the gardens for the ripening date-harvest of Oman, and to the Trucial coast for the summer pearl fisheries.

They love unfettered personal liberty more than life, and glory in their hereditary wars. The alternative of an extraneously imposed authority has in the past been acceptable to them only by force, or else as the lesser evil after periods of exhaustion and, as the lessons of one generation had to be relearned by the next, no dynasty has been able to entrench itself.

Historical landmarks are few. They begin in post-Islamic times with the ruler Muhammad bin Ahmad al Mingowi, whose ruined capital lies on the lagoon of Khor Ruri.[1] Mingowi is an ancient name that comes more readily to these people's lips than any other, and almost every ruin in the country is ascribed to him.

After him, in A.D. 1279, came Salim bin Idris al Habudhi. Driven by drought from his native Hadhramaut he put into Dhufar, first to covet, then to conquer it. In the sixteenth century rose Saif al Islam al Ghassan, a scion of Sana', whose palace was the citadel of Balid, to-day the most extensive ruins of the Dhufar plain. A hundred years of tribal anarchy was ended by a Kathiri master of the land, followed by yet another age without a name, lasting for the whole of the eighteenth century. An independent Saiyid, revered son of the Prophet, raised his standard successfully in the first years of the nineteenth century and endured for twenty-five years until the Qara killed him.

---

[1] The ruins about Khor Ruri—Husn Mirahadh and the entrance of Inqitat (Bent's Khatiya)—occupy the probable site of the ancient port of Moscha of the Periplus (Ptolemy's Abyssapolis as suggested by Bent). The Arab geographers give Murbat as the site of the ancient seaport and capital of Dhufar, which lasted until the tenth century of our era. Modern Murbat is twenty miles to the eastward of its prototype, which was here. And Murbat in the Shahari tongue is Sik, which would appear to preserve the important radicals of the name Moscha.

THE SULTAN'S FORT.

Fifty years later, about 1880, the scene was braved by Fadhul bin Aliyowi, a Hadhramauti, who came claiming authority from the Ottoman Government, but he could not maintain himself and was expelled.

Then it was that the people of Dhufar turned to the Ruling House of Muscat to take over their country. Though that was scarcely more than fifty years ago, Al Sa'idi influence grew to its present considerable proportions, and if there is no part of the Sultanate to-day where authority is wielded with more difficulty, nowhere is authority wielded more salutarily. Yet the foundations were laid in blood. That story is worth the telling, not so much as a sketch of recent history, as for the light it sheds on the psychology of tribal governors and governed in remoter Arabia.

Saiyid Turki bin Sa'id, the grandfather of the present Sultan, was the Ruler of Muscat to whom the Dhufaris had turned for protection. Now Turki had a slave, one Sulaiman bin Suwailim, a man in whom he reposed complete trust; he had manumitted and exalted him to be Counsellor, and Commander-in-chief of his forces—not an impossible destiny for a slave in Arabia. Sulaiman enjoyed an immense prestige among the tribes of Oman for his personal qualities. He was fearless, unscrupulous and strong. If the lawless reputation of the Dhufaris was deserved, no lesser man could be expected to establish Muscat influence, with the little backing Muscat could give. Sulaiman, therefore, it was that the Sultan sent to Dhufar as his first *Wali* (Viceroy).

Did not the Ruler habitually address his slave as *abana* (our father)? said my informant, an old pensioned soldier who had come to Dhufar in those far-off days with the

[11]

original Army of Occupation and remained ever since. 'Abud bin 'Isa was a Nejdi, a fine old veteran with brown flashing eyes, a heavy jowl and large ears that showed he was no South Arabian. Like many of his kind, to Omanis known as *ahl al gharb* (people of the west), he had left his native country as a boy to come and take service in the army of the Muscat Ruler, lured thither by the attractions of the pay—three dollars a month to a Badu of Inner Arabia was in those days a glittering reward. And this mercenary army was a pillar of strength to the Ruler of a country riven by rival claimants to the throne; it was not merely of good fighting stock, but of unswerving allegiance because unaffected by local loyalties.

Eighteen of these Nejdis arrived with the Wali Sulaiman to occupy Dhufar. It was a small force, but it enabled a start to be made, and before the arrival of the Omani garrison of a hundred askaris, Sulaiman had taken in hand the building of a fort-prison at Salala on the Omani model, impressing slave and *dha'af*[1] labour for his purpose.

But the vigour of his activities, to which had been added the collection of taxes, was not to tribal liking and discontented murmurings soon arose from among the Qara. A man of less resolution would have been intimidated. Sulaiman was not to be deflected; his acts knew no moderation, he behaved arbitrarily. Now came a challenge. One of his soldiers was ambushed and murdered at Hamran, where a picket had been placed over the water. But even

---

[1] *Dha'af*. Dhufar has a caste system below the noble rank of tribesman. Thus there are the *Bahara* and *Dha'af* as well as the slave community. The *Dha'af* (literally, 'weak,' though the connotation corresponds with the *Baiyasira* of Oman) are a degree above the *Bahara* in the scale, in that their women do not appear in public. Also only the *Bahara* and slaves fish.

Sulaiman dare not imprison Finkhor, the powerful shaikh of the Qara section involved, though he must parry the affront. A fight at Taqa, in which the government askaris were supported by elements of Al Kathir, produced no casualties on either side—not an unusual state of affairs in Arab warfare with shots exchanged at long range. But it brought a feeling of relief, so that both sides could honourably endure a peace. The place was in favour of Sulaiman, for with the oath of allegiance came the present of a hundred head of cattle.

With insufficient power to rule magnanimously, Sulaiman continued to employ the terrorist methods that better suited his character, and it was not long before the tribe were once more on the war-path. A tribesman had indulged in a time-honoured foray (the fear of raids from the mountains is a daily dread in the plain to this day) and Sulaiman imposed some exemplary punishment. This was disproportionate in the tribal mind, which thereupon flared up, and only a blockade of the mountains[1]—an extremely bold course—brought them to their knees.

The cup of tribal wrath against Sulaiman was full, but did not overflow till he left for Oman on leave, with every apparent reason to be satisfied with the masterful accomplishments of his three years' efforts. He set his two sons 'Ali and Mas'ad to rule in his place, and then the Al Kathir whose support of Sulaiman had made possible his dealing with their old rivals, the Qara, now saw their opportunity in Sulaiman's absence and in the cellars of

[1] The blockade applied only to the transport of sardines. The secret of its success as a weapon lay in the fact that the mountain wealth is chiefly in cattle, and at certain 'dry' seasons of the year, here, as in Oman, sardines are the usual fodder.

[13]

the fort which were full of tithe and customs levies—butter, rice and dates. The instinct of avarice, abnormally developed in the Badu, was astir. A plot was hatched. One party of Kathir would bring a petition against another, and as the case proceeded more Kathiri witnesses would be sent for until the town was possessed by an army of them. And so it happened. Suspicion would have arisen had they come in any other circumstances. As it was the Government troops remained scattered over the plain on their daily duties. This morning, like every other, the two young governors sat at the gateway of the fort holding the morning reception. The coffee cup had gone round the large assembly of Kathir tribesmen present. The moment had come. Consummate treachery! On a signal from the leader the Badawin leapt up and fell upon their hosts, sword in hand. 'Ali and Mas'ad, Sulaiman's sons, with their wretched soldiers were pitilessly murdered, the Badawin rushed down and ransacked the cellars and then razed the new government fort to the ground.

All that was left of Muscat government in Dhufar was one Bakhit bin Nubi and forty soldiers who fled to Murbat to take refuge with some friendly Qara. This Bakhit was a negro and a character withal. He was a slave of Sulaiman, for a slave may own another slave or other chattels, though without the power of bequest, so that on his death his goods revert to his master. Four months must elapse—the south-west monsoon having cut communication with Oman —before news could reach Muscat and reinforcements be sent. Bakhit took upon himself to act, and his actions must have been wise and courageous, for as the days passed and the menace of retribution approached, he induced the rebels to see that to support him was their safest course.

Events in Oman had necessitated the retention there of Sulaiman, so that when later he came to Dhufar it was on a temporary visit to discuss future dispositions. A British man-of-war brought an Ambassador of the Sultan, the erring tribes were punished, and their leaders abased; it was too late for restitution except that the old fort doorway was returned to adorn the bigger and stronger government fort to be built on the site of the old one, where it stands to this day. Bakhit was installed as Governor. His old master Sulaiman (who was himself to die by the hand of an assassin in Oman soon afterwards) left with him this message: 'If I hear that Bait Kathir have chosen a shaikh amongst them and he lives, your head will be cut off.' Bakhit did not falter. During his seven years of office the ten ringleaders of the troubles were one by one quietly despatched by slaves sent for the purpose. True, these shaikhs had been granted a general amnesty by the Envoy from Muscat, but that scarcely affected either party's conscience, for where treachery is a habit of mind, men are actuated by the stern necessities of the moment, not by any principles of morality.

Instability is the chief characteristic of any régime in tribal Arabia. It is inherent in the Arab genius, and springs from the preponderating part played by personalities and the relative unimportance of the machine. Where the strong personality is of the Government or is well disposed to government all will be well. Where stronger men are without, trouble lurks. Thus when in the course of time Bakhit's rule was replaced by that of 'Abdullah bin Sulaiman, a free man of weak character, the prestige of government declined and the tribes ceased to pay their dues. They despised the new Wali for his weakness rather than admired him for his benevolence, so that he died unregretted by good men, leaving to his successor—the present admirable incumbent—whose guest I was for the moment, the task of re-establishing that authority which he had so supinely relinquished.

As I stood on the old battlements reconstituting in my imagination scenes such as these, horses were brought for me to the gateway below from the Court stables—the only specimens of their kind to be found within three hundred miles. They were selected from a dozen or so which the Sultan has brought from time to time, for he was much attached to Dhufar, its gazelle hunting and hawking, and spent more than one summer there during my term of office.

To-day I was riding out to Salala to call on Sa'ad bin 'Abdul 'Aziz, the wealthiest merchant in the place, a man of humble and obscure parentage, as the Arab merchant prince often is. Our way lay past the tiny bazaar, out of the town gateway, and through a deep coco-nut grove (in Dhufar the coco-nut palm takes the place of the date palm found elsewhere in Arabia) on through fields of cotton and indigo and so across the strip of plain that fronts Salala town. Imposing indeed are the lofty many-storeyed houses of dazzling whiteness—the stone hewn from the plain where they stand—the ornamentation[1] giving them a semblance of dignified age which accords ill with the

---

[1] A typical feature of the large houses and the mosques is this roof ornamentation called *tabashir*; it will be found at the corners of the roof and at intervals along the sides. Its stepped design recalls the Nabatean ornament at Petra and Mada'in Salih. I was told that it is met with in Makalla and Sheher and elsewhere in the Hadhramaut, but I have not met with it in Muscat or Oman.

A STREET SCENE IN DHUFAR.

dingy and squalid interiors. Sa'ad's house rose like a palace midway along the front of the town; but even there we found its courtyard hot with flies and heavy with the smell of its stalled cows. The narrowest of steps led thence to the guest-chamber at the top of the house, a large room with a fine central beam of Malabar teak upholding the ceiling and admirably ventilated with many small unglazed windows, for window-panes are unknown.[1] The furnishings were few but luxurious. Every inch of floor space was covered with carpets, pleasant individually, but inharmonious in the mass; a dozen mirrors at least, all life-size and gold-framed, adorned walls as vain as those of any tailor's closet; alcoves were stuffed with silver incense-burners, coffee appurtenances, and gaudy bric-à-brac. We trooped in and sat in line round the four sides of the room, I being motioned to a corner where there were a few extra cushions, tough as medicine balls, but glad to the Oriental eye in their bright scarlet or emerald-coloured trappings. Only our host and his sons and domestic slaves stood to do the honours beside a table arrayed with bottles of almond syrup, coloured sherbets and fancy tumblers. As in all social gatherings in Arab tribal towns, no woman was to be seen or mentioned. Those of any standing at all had, as always, hidden themselves till strange men should have left their house, and any furtive unveiled figure to be seen in the courtyard was surely that of a slave girl.

Next to me sat old Salim al Sail, another merchant, a god-fearing man and a Solomon among his kind. Human frailty made him claim descent from the noble Bait Ghassan,

---

[1] Coco-nut palm is in universal use in Dhufar for window sashes and ceiling rafters, and good and enduring material it is, in contrast to the fibrous and inferior date-palm log of Oman buildings.

while all men whispered that he was a foundling child of low Shahari origin that a mountain torrent had swept down in a summer freshet.[1] Salim's eyes, as became his eighty years, were growing dim, though they were still capable of a twinkle when he begged in secret for an aphrodisiac. At other times, as now, he showed a wider interest in mankind. 'Are any of the nations at war, Sahib?' 'What has happened to the Germans?' And, 'Are the *Italiyaniyin* your friends?'

Dhufar's propinquity to Somaliland and Italian influence in the Yemen may account for the fact that the Italians loom larger in their minds than any other Europeans, and I have never heard aught but good spoken of them and their administration.

And now a mountain shaikh at my side was brightening the conversation.

'Why are you such big men, and we so much smaller?'

'Perhaps on account of our soil and air,' I said.

'But *Allahu 'Alim* (God is the knower) we are much smaller than our forefathers. Look at their graves at Khor Ruri—twenty paces long. They were that great.'

'God is the knower,' I returned, being careful not to offend religious susceptibilities, for one commentator on the Qur'an gives Adam's height as thirty-six feet, and other patriarchs in proportion (a figure modest in comparison with those given by others). 'Is it not God's mercy?'

---

[1] The Four Seasons of the year are called:
Kharif: July to September—the rain months.
Surub: October to December.
Shitta: January to March.
Al Gaidh: April to June.

'How?' said he.

'It is difficult enough,' I replied, 'nowadays with so many men in the world, for all to find nourishment for stomachs this size' (and I held out an imaginary football): 'had we kept so big we should have needed a sack of rice at every meal; think of the cost!'

A general titter went round, and my questioner's silence showed that he was satisfied that the subject was exhausted.

A sailor, one Khamis of Auqad, was brought to my notice as having visited my country. (The native has no idea of the direction of Europe and points to the east, to India, supposing that to be the Englishman's home.) Khamis, a free man, yet was the father of a slave-born child, for he had taken to wife another's slave woman, so by local canons the child belonged to her owner. The three hundred dollars he had paid for the woman was the price of her hand, not of her freedom, and he was now engaged in paying a further five hundred dollars to her master, to buy the freedom of his own offspring.[1]

Fuwala, the light refreshment which is a feature of any visit of courtesy, was brought in by a slave—a large dish-laden tray of fids of beef grilled crisp and black, spaghetti drenched in tomato sauce, and slices of pineapple. Coffee went round after the tit-bits, and lastly the frankincense burner which, however, was not held under the nostrils for a few brief seconds, and handed thus from person to

---

[1] I discovered there was an exception to this rule of a slave wife's progeny belonging exclusively to her owner, but it applies only to the Court. In case of a Court male slave marrying a female slave of a private owner, the progeny, as a Court privilege, must be shared. The result is that a private owner will agree only reluctantly to a Court slave alliance because it is unprofitable for him, and a Court slave finds it correspondingly difficult to find a bride outside the circle of Court negresses.

[19]

person by a slave as in Oman, but left smouldering at my side. And in this land of true frankincense, unexcelled in the world, my host was surpassing himself by using an imported substitute, inferior to my mind, but here more costly. This was *'aud*, a kind of sandal-wood which I understand serves for frankincense in European churches. '*Ba'd al 'aud la tagud*' runs an Arab jingle, which means 'After the incense do not tarry.' The offered incense is indeed a sign not to be mistaken, so after a minute or two of courteous silence one mutters '*tarakhkhus*' (with your permission) and rises to go.

'We hope you are making a long stay,' says my host, partly by way of courtesy, partly to tempt a disclosure of my plans.

'Yes! I am on two months' leave,' I reply. 'Shaikh Hasan has agreed to take me up into his mountains for some shooting next week; he has promised me a panther and an ibex.'

I had barely risen the next morning to wind and record my chronometers when throbbing tom-toms and raucous female voices attracted my notice. Soon through the prison courtyard below came twenty young negresses, dancing a sensuous measure, their heads poised in snake-like detachment balancing full water pitchers. Here was the Bathing Chorus, a recognised institution when the Sultan or I was in residence, and the tank in the bathroom must needs be replenished daily. As they filed past the doorway of my room they ceased to sing; a young one, confident in her youth and greatly daring, risks what may be almost a wink in my direction, for in their world of Dhufar, they were none of them better than they should be. On filing out each halts to turn and make obeisance.

A motherly old negress among them loiters to ask after brothers and husbands in the Muscat Court, and have I brought letters? She soon turns the conversation to the question of customary payment, but with all the black beauties agog in that expectation she is clearly no undisputed representative. Two parties at least are evident, both animated by the single idea of *bakhshish*.

'Have you counted us, O Wazir?' shouts one. 'Four and twenty here, and four downstairs,' says another (this an unblushing lie).

'Count us, O Wazir! Let your servant Muhammad count us!'

I smilingly promise them a basket of dates and some dollars for the morrow, and they gaily respond by lining up in my upper courtyard as for 'Here we come gathering nuts in May,' descending the stairway after a final rollicking ballet, to more drum fingering and chanting. And so I turn complacently to enjoy the bath they have prepared for me while their strains grow fainter and fainter, and at last are no more to be heard.

III: SKULL–MEASURING AND DEVIL DANCING

'FROM what Arabs are you?' Thus has the question been put to me in the desert, by natives conscious that I was of a race different from theirs, for the word Arab is used by them to denote 'people' rather than the particular race we mean.

But is it so certain that the Arabs are themselves racially one? Neither Glaser the scholar nor Burton the traveller thought so. The former held the South Arabian to be Hamitic and not Semitic. The latter declared that he had found proof of three distinct races. Whatever the case, Burton's anticipation that 'physiological differences sufficient to warrant our questioning the common origin of the Arab family would be found' was a sound one. Such differences I discovered in abundance in this central region of South Arabia: not merely physiological, but cultural and linguistic differences that constitute collectively a serious challenge to the conception of a single racial entity for the entire peninsula.

I came indeed prepared with head callipers to make and record skull measurements, for such measurements are vital to anthropologists.[1] Of importance too are visual observations of the foreigner domiciled for some years in Arabia, for his mind becomes unconsciously stamped with the physical characteristics of the natives, and is therefore acutely aware of aberrations from racial types when he meets them. Thus it was that after continuous residence in Arabia from 1915 onwards, serving in capacities that

[1] Sir Arthur Keith has graciously contributed as Appendix I his investigations into these data.

[22]

brought me into close touch with the Arabs of Mesopotamia, Transjordan and the Persian Gulf, I was impressed on meeting the natives of central south Arabia—the Dhufar 'bloc'—with a feeling of some fundamental difference. The Political Resident in Aden, Major-General Maitland, recorded a similar impression in the following terms:

'The people of Arabia belong to two distinct and apparently quite different races. The common idea of the Arab type . . . tall bearded men with clean-cut hawk-like face. The Arabs of South Arabia are smaller, darker, coarser featured and nearly beardless. All authorities agree that the southern Arabs are nearly related by origin to the Abyssinians. Yet strange to say it is the Egypto-African race who are the pure Arabs, while the stately Semite of the north is Musta'rab . . . Arab by adoption and residence rather than by descent.'

Arab scholars themselves have inherited a tradition that their race is derived from two stocks, Qahtan and Adnan, but tribes scattered over the peninsula to-day claiming descent from one or other of these ancestors are of indistinguishable racial types. On the other hand, differences noted by Burton and Maitland and Glaser, and in our own generation by Rathjens, are well marked, and the tribes thus differentiated do not coincide with the Qahtan-Adnan demarcation.

None of these Europeans, moreover, could have been familiar with the group of Dhufar tribes I encountered, which there is very strong anthropological and linguistic evidence for regarding as at most racially peculiar, at least racially different.

Inscriptions and ruined cities in south-west Arabia bear witness to ancient Minaean and Sabaean civilisations that

[23]

decayed before the rise of Islam in the seventh century of our era. We know too of early Abyssinian and Roman invasions and of Greek and Aramæan settlements. Who are these South Arabians? If the answer to the problem rests with anthropologists, as it assuredly does, the collection of relevant data was of never-failing interest to me on my travels.

I had early entertained hopes of unearthing and sending home ancient skulls, but the danger of offending religious susceptibilities in Arabia were great. To disturb a body that has been given Muslim burial is the worst desecration, and has been a fruitful source of trouble as when, for instance, in Mesopotamia during the war, someone un- wittingly drove a car through a derelict Arab cemetery. Hence also the rock tombs faced with loose stones which I had come upon in the Wadi Dhikur in 1927-28 were forbidden ground. On my 1929-1930 journey I had met with better fortune, for at Hasik we passed a cave whose entrance had been forced by a wolf or other wild animal. It was daylight and the presence of my Arab companions imposed restraint, but I contrived to halt near by, and no one knew next morning that a skull found in the cave was in my bedding—though the jawbone was missing and the rest of the skeleton had wholly disappeared. I took it to Muscat and thence to the Royal College of Surgeons in London. But in my house at Muscat where I unpacked the treasure, my servant Mabruk, a manumitted slave, became aware of his master's queer hobby, and announced next day that he had brought a present for me and pro- duced from a bundle a complete human skull. Another Arab servant emerged sniggering from behind the door to explain that Mabruk had been overnight to his father's

A GROUP OF SHAHARA TRIBESMEN.

A GROUP OF YAF'I TRIBESMEN.

A GROUP OF QARA TRIBESMEN.

A GROUP OF RASHID AND MURRA TRIBESMEN.

burial-place, and was presenting me with a once vital part of his revered parent. That night Mabruk, unrewarded and rebuked, restored it to its resting-place. Whether Arab feelings would have been hurt on religious grounds in such a case, it is impossible to tell, certainly slaves do not pray in this part of Arabia, and may not normally be regarded as good Muslims.

To return to Dhufar and head-measuring, it was no easy task to find willing subjects. There is always in the minds of rude people the fear of magic or worse, while the religious among them hate to be pawed by infidel hands. In the desert I would not have dared risk putting callipers over the head of a Badu—an uncouth tribesman might have drawn his dagger, for at times Badawin have turned against me for bringing out a camera at the wrong moment—but here in Dhufar I felt I could safely work upon prisoners, warders and old friends behind closed doors, and with these and some enlightened foreign traders I was able during my stay to make forty-five head-measurements, covering a wide geographical range and to take a hundred 'type' portraits.

The work was enlivened by many amusing episodes, but was physically unpleasant, for the specimens were either Badawin with tousled hair full of sandy and other accumulations or sedentary townsmen whose locks were a mass of grease from applications of coco-nut oil. One morning my clients were to be Somalis, a breed which crosses the Red Sea to set up as petty merchants in the bazaar or as middlemen to contract frankincense orchards. Six of them arrived, and averred in answer to my questions that they were *somal khalis*, *i.e.* Somalis on both sides of the family—a necessary condition, for specimens of mixed parentage are useless anthropologically, but on a closer study their squat noses and receding head axes were so obviously negroid that I dismissed them as unsuitable. 'Are you quite sure you are pure-bred?' I asked a Somali member of the Police who was next. 'I claim to be,' he replied, 'but God is the knower, and then my mother.'

The wit enjoyed his own lewd joke and disappeared laughing down the roof-steps, promising to appear on the morrow with a number of equally uncontaminated fellow-specimens.

Next came the government *askaris*. These mercenary tribesmen of Hadhramaut or of the Aden hinterland who take service with the Sultan of Muscat, like the Nejdis of old, are labelled as *Hadharim* by the local Omanis. There were forty on duty at Dhufar, so I had little difficulty in finding six of undiluted tribal stock. These—of the Ahl Yazid, Yahar, and Ahl Sa'ad sections of the Yafa' confederation, I measured and photographed, but I was soon to discover that they objected to the term *Hadharim* as applied to themselves. '*Hadharim* to us, sahib, are low-caste inhabitants of Shahar and other non-tribesmen: the genuine tribesman will be content only to be regarded as belonging to one of two rival confederations, Yafa' and Hamdan—none other!' they said.

Next day I was measuring a member of another race type, one 'Ali al Dhab'an, a Badawi of the Mashai' that roam the desert on the north side of the Hadhramaut. 'Ali, a very fine shot as Arabs go, had accompanied me on my last year's expedition to Mugshin, and was now my daily companion, and a fount of desert erudition. He knew the southern borderlands well, had shed Rashidi blood and later taken a Rashidi girl to wife to avoid their vengeance.

[26]

From me he wanted a parting present before going into the Qara Mountains to demand four head of sheep from Al Kathir as part payment of blood-money for his son accidentally killed by one of their number the year before.

What he wanted turned out to be a modest fifty rounds of ammunition—the Badu will unblushingly ask for the moon!

'No,' I said, remembering 'Ali's record and propensities. 'Certainly not!' 'Ali was reputed to have taken fifteen lives; the last murder, three years before, immediately followed a visit to my camp at Auhi: he had then shot an 'Amari he met in the wilderness because he coveted the wretch's camel. The camel did not, alas, survive the journey to Dhufar, and 'Ali had nothing to show for his blood-guiltiness, which he ascribed cheerfully to Allah, and himself felt not at all, but he dare not meet a man of that tribe again. 'I will give you three dollars, 'Ali,' I added, 'if you will come on a shooting expedition into the mountains next week: but ammunition, no! You want it for some evil purpose. I will be no party to violence.'

'Then tell me how a man shall live?'

'Till the ground or fish.'

He looked at me incredulously. 'That is not a man's work,' he said.

'Then what is a man's work?'

'The rifle and *janbiya* (dagger).'

'Nonsense,' I returned. 'Fighting is all very well when the time for it comes, but how do you think we English became strong if it was not by work? How do you think we get our ships and our rifles?'

'Money!' he said laconically, and I knew it would be idle to argue. A pause.

[27]

'O 'Ali! if every one lived by his rifle and *janbiya*, whence would we get food? We owe what we eat to the cultivator and the fisherman.'

'But what *qubaili* (tribesman) would stoop so low? Fishing! it is impossible! Tilling! Yes, I will ask Saiyid Taimur (the Sultan) to give me a plot of land. Then I will get a slave to till it for me.'

'But why not till it yourself?'

'Ah! never fear, I'll pay the slave,' said 'Ali, missing the point, but adding ingenuously, 'and I shall live on the produce of the garden.'

How 'Ali was to come by a slave I had every reason to shrink from imagining. Even in Dhufar three hundred dollars would be a moderate price for a slave, and had 'Ali anything like that sum, the desert would call him and he would invest the money in a she-camel. But 'Ali's flight of fancy had carried him into the clouds and he now returned to earth.

'Give me fifty rounds, sahib!' and he slithered the ammunition belt round his body for me to see that it was all but empty. I suppressed a smile at the incongruity of his utter poverty with his opulent optimism.

'*W'allahi!* I would rather ammunition than a camel,' he said. 'The camel dies on her master's hands, but with ammunition! I can repel my enemies when they come after me, and kill an oryx when I am hungry.'

'No, 'Ali! Come to-morrow and you shall have three dollars, but mark you! behave yourself in the mountains, or this is the end of our friendship.'

'Let Saiyid Taimur put me on his pay-roll,' said 'Ali as he went away—he was, maybe, envisaging three dollars a month—'and I will be a brother to all men.'

It was the Acting-Governor's custom to call on me each morning at the fort. Sa'id bin Saif was yellow-faced, with a long scraggy goatee and a miserable physique even for late middle-age. His conversation centred round the poverty of the *Hukuma* (government), the insufficiency of his pay, and the demands of a large family: and in contrast the vast sums of money the English must have, as shown by official salaries. Sa'id lamented his own miserable portion and attributed both extremes to Allah. Work he regarded as undignified, fit for slaves; his hands were pale and delicate as a woman's and his legs never carried him faster than a slow, dignified walk, attended by a squad of soldiers before and behind him. What he did diligently, albeit with extreme deliberation, was to pray five times a day. For the rest, he sat about aimlessly, his sleepy silences broken only with pious ejaculations, '*Al hamdu' l'Illah! al hamdu' l'Illah*'—a most depressing companion.

There were distant sounds of revelry. A soldier rushed to the roof and came back to report it was the slaves. Drums in growing volume confirmed their approach and we now all went to look down on an interesting spectacle.

The occasion of it was merely a slave's death, but when a negro here dies and is buried, instead of two Muslim angels to share his tomb, an evil spirit enters to molest his slumbers, and so the drums and the devil-dance are invoked to drive away the tormentor.

'God forgive them!' murmured the sanctimonious Omani at my side.

'Drums aren't acceptable to you?' I questioned.

'No, nor pipes; but these are slaves and know no better.'

'Yet the Muqabil tribe in Oman have pipes?' I said.

'Yes! but they are Sunnis. We are Ibadhis, and in

[29]

Ibadhi Oman we forbid these instruments of the devil.'

Meanwhile the procession was making its brave way to pay me respects inspired by hope of reward, a basket of dates, perhaps, for death with them, as at an Irish wake, is an occasion for feasting. The banner-carrier and drummers moved slowly forward; the main body of negroes about them, with staves held aloft, were dancing and chanting, and a party of negresses came tripping along in rear. As the fort gates were approached some of the men rushed forward threateningly in a mock attempt at forcing the doorway that was already open.

Within the courtyard a halt was cried and the rhythm changed. With the drums and banners for a centre, the men circled round in single file, hopping now on this foot, now on that and chanting some wild Swahili gibberish while their women moved circumspectly around the outer edge with curious measured step, their mantles lifted suggestively before them. Other negroes detached themselves for a mock fight, one man who presumably impersonated the evil spirit lying on the ground lashing wildly about him, while would-be vanquishers assailed him from all sides.

So many sightseers pressed into the outer gateway that they made the exit of the Omani at my side impossible, and he remained an involuntary spectator. He stood aghast at this exhibition of paganism, which he would have suppressed if he could, while I felt that I was the object of his inward censure for my levity in taking a cine-picture of the proceedings.

In the afternoon I was to witness more elaborate ritual outside in the gardens, for the Sultan had forbidden the rite within city precincts and thereby won the praises of all True Believers.

'Did not these processions on the 'Id of Nayruz (New Year's Day) with loud gibes enter the harlot's house carrying a kitten—her implied offspring? But,' said my pious informant, 'the Sultan's action in suppressing this may have been precipitate for, alas, since then promiscuity has increased.'

The negro community is almost self-contained, and the biggest single element in the population of the Dhufar capital. Awwadh, a Court slave and most exalted above his fellows, was their *ab*, a magistrate to whom negro disputes were usually referred for settlement. Nor was he without an assistant glorying in the high-sounding name of *naqib*, but the rank and file of slaves are *aulad* and *banat*, *i.e.* 'boys' and 'girls,' euphemistic terms when they are applied to wrinkled negroes and aged negresses.

Slaves may have their taboos. One here, for instance, is that they may not touch dead animals other than those properly slaughtered for food. It is the master and not the slave who would remove a dead cat from the house, and where is the Court slave who would willingly consent to drag away the carcass of a horse? For such and other infringements of their code there is punishment (normally ostracism) by communal sentiment, the decision being cried round the town with a conch—the slaves' alarm: while the offender's readmission is celebrated by the slaughter of a sheep in the blood of which he dips his foot.

Negro slaves in my experience are of a contented mind. They have a cheerful demeanour often lacking in their masters, so that they sing and dance apparently unmindful of their political and social disabilities. It is difficult for a

European who has not lived in Muslim countries to form any considered opinion regarding slavery in practice. The lot of the slave must necessarily be compared with that of the freeman in the same environment. Judged by this standard, the life of the slave is not wholly pitiable. The general standard of life is so low—just above the line of bare sufficiency—that the slave-owner, in his own interests, has to feed and clothe the slave nearly as well as himself.

The fundamental difference between them lies in work. In the land of sloth, it is the slave who does the manual labour. He has to produce enough to support both of them, and the freeman sees that he does so. But to suppose that a difference of rewards exists as sharply defined as in the Southern States of the U.S.A. or the West Indian Colonies before the abolition of slavery would be a false assumption. No such difference exists.

Slaves actually enjoy certain fortuitous social advantages. The male, for instance, escapes the perils of the blood-feuds that haunt the 'free' tribesman, and when he is caught in a raid and Arab kills Arab, his life will be spared. It is true he will find himself taken captive and sold to a fresh master, but his lot need not therefore be worsened. As regards females, the slave girl enjoys a social liberty that is in gratifying contrast to the 'free' Arab woman. The latter is probably married at fifteen to a spouse chosen by her father, without being consulted or even seeing him. Thereafter she is destined to close confinement in her house for the rest of her life except for rare excursions out of doors, where she goes closely veiled. The rigidity of the convention increases as her position rises in the social scale, while any sexual lapse—this in contrast to her husband's admitted licence—she will pay for with her life.

[32]

The slave girl, on the other hand, is fancy free, and although her marriage will be likewise arranged by her master with an eye only to his own profit, she will walk abroad unveiled throughout her life, and flirt and fraternise where she will.

A group of desert Badawin were interested spectators of the devil-dancing in the afternoon, and though professing Muslims all, none seemed to have any misgivings of conscience about it, in refreshing contrast to the narrow spirit of the semi-sophisticated Omani official. If the pastoral races of the desert have placed their gods in the skies because they were habitually looking upwards for rain, the giver of life, why should not the agricultural races, with their eyes always on the soil, have their earth-spirits? But with such ideas neither party would have had any sympathy.

It was before Hafa village, picturesque in its setting of coco-nut palms, that the *zenug* rites were customarily performed three days after a death. The sound of well-played drums drew me to the throng. In the midst was a clearing spacious as a riding-school. At one end sat the drummers, a fire before them for the purpose of tuning their drums. Round about them danced the 'drum boys,' a dozen or so stalwart negroes of splendid muscular development. They were naked but for their loin-cloths; about their knees was a rattle of dried mangoes. This *khish khish* swished to the beating of the drums, as the dancers stamped and gyrated.

Across the circle opposite stood the *naqib*. His hands were to his lips as he chanted his incantations—'*Y'Allah ya malengi, y'Allah ya malengi*'—while a chorus of a dozen companions, standing facing him in a row, took up the responses.

[33]

Around the inner edge of the circle Awwadh the *ab*, master of ceremonies, ran hither and thither, slashing with a whip in his hand before the naked feet of spectators, wherever they pressed too closely.

A dozen paces within the ring was the path of the main performers—a stream of young negroes and negresses, who came sweeping round and round the circle in grand parade. Young slave girls, singly or in pairs, sturdy, black as ebony, and high of bosom, selected doubtless for their superior graces in the eyes of men. A black muslin veil shrouded each girl's head and drooped about the shoulders, of so flimsy a material that it did not conceal, but rather accentuated the effect of her flashing eyes, her thick scarlet-painted lips, her nose-ring, ear-rings and necklaces of gold. Her dress, new doubtless for the occasion, was a single mantle of starched indigo that glistened in the sun. One end of its long sweeping train she held up fastidiously between finger and thumb, the arm outstretched level with her shoulder, the other arm lay close to her side with the hand poised a span or so from the hip and palm turned back at almost right angles to the wrist. And thus she moves; her head motionless, her face turning neither to right nor left, her body moving by some subtle shuffle-step that has the sinuous slide of a skater. Before her leaps an eager youth, in his hand a drawn sword that quivers with a flick of the wrist; now on this side, now on that, now turning about to face her—spellbound he seems, like the moth to the candle. Other male slaves, threes and fours in line, rifles held above their heads, stalk round in the more deliberate measure of the horse-dance and looking straight to their front regardless of beauty.

The afternoon wears on. More and more candidates

A SLAVE DANCE.

enter the drum-throbbing ring. The moment for the climax of the rite approaches. The spirit molesting the corpse must be drawn forth and take possession of a 'drum boy' chosen for his powers, who now draws apart from his companions. All eyes are turned upon him. The stamping grows wilder; the spirit-possessed puts forth all the frenzy of which his body is capable. His face is hideously contorted, his eyes wildly stare, he rolls himself on the ground and rubs his head in the dust, he slobbers with his lips as though in a fit. He is clearly overcome by exhaustion, and I, sickened by the sight of the orgy, depart as rifles are discharged into the air, to add to the general tumult.

The muedhdhin's 'Credo' would put an end to the ceremony if the spirit-possessed slave did not, before then, swoon, symbolising the passing of the spirit that otherwise would have given the corpse no rest. But he has fallen and lies motionless; and now the *aulad* and *banat* gather up his limp body and bear it home, thence they joyfully disperse.

IV: IN THE QARA MOUNTAINS—
'AIN AR RIZAT

I HAD already been held up in Dhufar for three weeks with never a sign of the long-awaited camel party from the sands, no word of Sahail, no word of my lately despatched emissaries; only desert news trickled in, disturbing news of wars and rumours of wars.

The curiosity of the market-place concerning my plans[1] was doubtless aroused, and I felt there was no better way to lull it than by an expedition into the Qara Mountains. Here was fresh country, which only Theodore and Mabel Bent had seen forty years before. The land ever surges with tribal unrest, so that only once has the Sultan or his representative, the Governor of Dhufar, seen fit to tour in these mountains, and never at all their predecessors. It was, moreover, the gateway to the great desert. I hoped to make it more than a cloak for my larger plans, for I was eager for the opportunity of living amongst these people, whose heads I had measured; I was curious to discover their customs, their superstitions, their traditions, and for light upon their psychology and way of life. Here would be clues for the anthropologist. Would their languages and culture identify them with the Arabs of the north, or with those of the south-west, or would they

[1] Although my position was that of Wazir to His Highness the Sultan, and I had introduced the copper currency of Muscat into the Province in 1926 (before that time there was only exchange by barter), I had no jurisdiction in Dhufar, nor indeed had the Muscat and Oman Council of State, of which I was a member. The Sultan treated Dhufar as a Royal Domain. His rule through the Wali was personal and untrammelled by any foreign influence; the régime was tribal, which I think to be the best form of government for tribal Arabia.

[36]

challenge any identification to be found within the borders of Arabia?

Another attraction these mountains had for me was the hunting they would afford. I had fondly gone over my new Winchester rifle and ammunition, my butterfly net, collecting-boxes and surgical instruments, jars of formalin, packets of arsenical soap, and cotton wool. Arabia, lying on the borders of three of the great zoological provinces into which the world is divided, presents problems of particular interest, and as the museums of the world had almost no specimens of the fauna of this particular central south region, the joys of hunting would be enhanced.

My gun I deliberately left behind, for if I shot birds to prepare them as specimens would demand too much of my time. My Muscat Arab secretary, 'Ali Muhammad, who had travelled with me on my previous march through these hills in 1929-30 and prepared the birds I shot, had fallen ill in Muscat before we started and had remained behind. As each specimen requires a record of name, locality, altitude, sex and date, besides its preparation, the question I had to solve was how best to divide my waking hours between this and the claims of mapping and note-taking. But experience solved the problem. The preliminary rough skinning of a large mammal—so long as I made the first long incision—could be left to some Badu showing an aptitude, though the finishing touches could not be entrusted to him. The skull, too, could be plunged into hot water and left to clean itself, the snake or other reptile needed only to be gutted before immersion in a jar of formalin; the butterfly and the insect asked for nothing more than loving care; whereas the normal small bird, with a skin as delicate as silk, would make excessive inroads into my time, so I had to neglect the Department at South Kensington of my distinguished friend, Mr. N. B. Kinnear, whose personal interest and encouragement had made me a collector for the Natural History Museum.

We made an afternoon start on 19th October 1930. My companions consisted of two Kathiris and 'Ali al Dhab'an (three companions of my last year's expedition) and five government slaves. A rendezvous had been arranged with my Qara hosts at a point in the foothills.

Our way lay eastward along the beach past Hafa, through the coco-nut grove that separates it from the ancient ruined city of Balid. Thence we entered the plain behind, strewn with other ancient surface ruins[1] now called *hasaila*, yet a civilisation far in advance of that now existing is evidenced by such ruins and monuments as do exist, while old steyned wells, dry water ducts and plough-ridges attest the former industry. The many shallow quarries in the stony plain point to a bygone time when stone was extensively used as building material. Now cultivators may sow a little in them because of favourable sub-surface moisture, and in remoter places they are refuges when leprosy and smallpox periodically ravage the plain.[2]

After a night disturbed by mosquitoes spent in the plain behind Rizat we set out towards Jabal Nashib, the lofty brow of the Qara Mountains. We passed the Sultan's

[1] The most characteristic feature of these ruins is a plain primitive column, with octagonal shaft, square corbelled capital and similar square base, a monolith. It is usually only six feet high, and this and its corbelled cap suggest that it supported arches. A raised plinth, rising in steps to a man's height, supports two columns, or more according to size, and round about lies *débris* of squared stones, black with age.

[2] The infection said to be brought by dhow from the Persian Gulf.

RUINS OF BALID.

experimental garden at Mahmulah and entered the foot-hills beyond. There we halted in a copse, by a babbling brook, in which a herd of cattle slowly waded in single file or stood lazily blinking in the shade of the thick bushes.

This stream of Rizat rises two miles above the tree-garlanded Milwah al 'Aud, and thence is carried in an old aqueduct, green with moss and maidenhair, to skirt by gentle contours of bare red banks until it is diverted across the plain in two man-made courses, one to the shrine of Hamran, the other through Mahmulah to Rizat, whereby it alternates its bounty.

In the morning I took a butterfly net and went down from my camp to the far side of the dry, rocky torrent bed, to investigate some old stones. These proved to be monster graves—giant ovoids of large flat slabs of rock, the monument a dozen paces long such as I had seen at Khor Ruri and Khor Suli. The Arabs regard them as evidence of man's former giant proportions!

Down the valley came a mountain man, afoot. We hailed him, he paused and after acknowledging our summons by raising his rifle above his head, came over to where we stood.

He was a typical man of these mountains, short of stature, dark of skin, with long gollywog curly hair, almost beard-less, with features that distinguished him immediately from the northern Arab, broad brow, very small ears, nose that was not armenoid, small, round black eyes again not armenoid, a pointed receding chin, shallow square jaws under the ears; well-developed and clean legs, but poor body and arms. His dress was a single indigo skirt reaching only to his knees. His black body, purple in places from the stain of indigo, was bare, as also were his legs and feet, and he was bareheaded except for a narrow *mahfif*, a slender thong of plaited leather coiled nine times round his head, and worn like an Arab *aqal*.

'*Het bi Khar?*' said a slave who knew the greeting in the Shahari tongue.

The wild man spoke little, but eyed me wonderingly.

'*Hur! Weled an nas*' (Free—a son of the free) meaning I was not of slave stock.

'That's a *kafir* (infidel), is it not?'

'*Hashak!* he's the Wazir of your Sultan.'

I laughingly asked the man, who said he was of the Qara tribe, whether he would sell me the beans he carried in his *anit*,[1] *i.e.* leather satchel, as he appeared to be on his way to Rizat to sell them.

'How much?'

'A dollar.'

He sniffed, as do all these people, to mean yes, and I took the beans that I did not want, and in so doing distracted attention from religious issues. For the rest of the day he conducted me up the wadi bed to the source of the brook, where I collected a bountiful harvest of dragonflies, butterflies and lizards.

From a cave at the base of a lofty amphitheatre of forested hill-slopes gushed the stream into a wide pool masked by a fringe of reeds, man-high. Under the shadow of some giant overhanging trees I sat down on the edge and watched the tiny fish darting about in shoals, while one of my slaves paddled up and down vainly trying to

---

[1] This is a feature of the mountain dress. A leather bag, with shoulder straps, hangs close under the armpit. The variety used for carrying money and clothes is called *haban*. The *anit* is used only for food, dates and water.

catch them with my butterfly net. My attention was suddenly drawn to millet and other odd fragments of food lying on the bottom. '*Nughush!*' they said. Here men cast bread upon the running waters to propitiate the *subiro* that brood over them. The word, like our familiar equivalent, stands for the spirits of the departed, possessed of powers of good and evil and able to treat man even as they are treated. At night the natives throw morsels of tobacco and food to them, shouting, 'We are your sons, your daughters; do not harm us; be awake so that we are not harmed by evil men or malign spirits.'

This spring of Rizat figured in a famous case of magic in Wali Sulaiman's time. Bait Zaiyan, a section of the Shahara, claimed the exclusive right to practise *nughush* here. The Qara tribe disputed the exclusive right of the Zaiyan, their vassals, and asked for an equal share in the sacrifice and in the ghostly grace accruing. The Wali, with an eye to his government's own share in the plains, decided that both parties had equal rights, but that government itself would provide the litigants with exact quantities of the sacrifice to ensure against cheating, and thus become a partner. But the time came when Sulaiman was fighting these mountain people, and Bait Zaiyan saw their opportunity; they called upon the spirits of their forefathers, who presently made the stream run uphill. Hence the plains dried up and government lost its share; or so runs the legend.

Many other pagan and animistic cults survive and are practised throughout these mountains. All the natives hold them strongly; whereas elsewhere in Muslim Arabia they would be dubbed ungodly at the least. Another local custom is the blood sacrifice carried out in the Jurbaib

[41]

just before the harvest, when a cow is led round the crops and slaughtered, the blood drained into the irrigation ducts and scraps of flesh cast amongst the standing corn.

The wooded hills bright with the tropical sun towered above our pool where we sat in the balmy air and listened to the birds' loud singing in the valley. A herd of cows grazed contentedly on the opposite bank. There, too, was a black and almost naked woman surrounded by her friends, and combing her shaggy locks, her reflection dancing in the water, while another woman lay in her midday sleep under a neighbouring tree.

When asked for milk, an African slave girl tripped across to us with a large bowl full, and received a lewd greeting from my mountain guide. She told us that the other women were her mistresses, the wives of a local Saiyid, who owned the cattle and would himself shortly arrive. From her we also learned that my supposed Qarowi was not of the Qara, as he said, but a Shahari.

Such lying is typical of these mountain folk whom the plainsmen accuse, with reason, of inability to tell the truth. 'If there is a thing they do better than lying, it is stealing,' said the Wali to me. They are expert, incorrigible thieves, brother steals from brother, father from son, and a boy that shows no aptitude is suspect—his manliness is despaired of. For the intended victim to report to government a thief caught in the act would be treachery. If the victim catches the robber then they compact a double requital. Judicial disputes may be brought to government, but never a petty theft; this in contrast with the Badawin, to whom petty larceny is abominable. Yet an open raid upon camels is no reproach, not being sneaking theft, but act of war, by men prepared to deal death and to suffer it.

A SHAHARI AND SNAKE.

This Shahari, however, was to give proof that he too had his qualities. He showed rare courage when he attacked and killed a five-foot four-inch cobra with his two-foot stick. Nor was it a matter of kill where you please. A snake, or any other animal for that matter, must have the head intact to be of use as a scientific specimen, so my rewards were scaled, but a snake with a head intact is usually a live snake, and this Shahari did in fact carry this deadly reptile alive, though with broken back, for many miles on his small stick held out before him. It was dead when laid out on the grass, but for an occasional flick of the tail, with the tip of which the man now anointed his eyelids. He announced that it was medicine for the eyes, but I wondered whether some magical significance originally attached to the end from which life appeared to be ebbing.

And now a large man of the nondescript coastal type, very different from the mountain man, arrived announcing that he was Saiyid Hasan, who owned the women and cows across the stream. Had I enough milk? Let him send for more; and so we fell into a friendly talk about his world, the price of dates in Dhufar and this year's harvest at Basrah and in Oman, which would determine future prices. Now he would tell me of the mountains. Thefts were rife and good men, as well as evil, must lie awake of nights. His rifle was ready loaded. Why was government so weak? Why did not the Sultan cut off an offending hand as aforetime? This system of taking a thief to Muscat and bringing him back whole after a year did no good at all.

But surely, I thought, no tribesman would steal from a Saiyid, else Dhufar is marching with the times. For the

Saiyids and Sharifs[1] of Dhufar are its accepted nobility, ranking above the tribes themselves, being the venerated descendants of the Prophet Muhammad. Whoso holds their hands to his nostrils and takes a few hearty sniffs, as does every local tribesman, will acquire virtue thereby.

The Saiyid had turned to the subject of *afarit*, one of a congeries of evil spirits, but I avowed that as we had none in my country I knew not how to pacify them.

'*W'allahi!* my wife has had seven bellies and she has not delivered one of them,' he said. 'The *afarit* have taken them.'

There are many other evil spirits, *jinns*, *jinniyat* and *zars*. Of these, *zars* are the most accommodating, *jinns* sometimes yield, but *afarit!* they are Allah's worst afflictions.

'Ali al Dhab'an and I had arranged to sit up that night in the hope of shooting a hyena, both hyenas and wolves being common in these foot hills.[2]

We had heard on the previous evening the chatter of hyenas from neighbouring hills; our camp fire seemed to make no difference to them in their caves. To-day while I was away 'Ali had built a *magbin* shelter in the approved manner, a low half-circle of piled stones capable of ac-

---

[1] *Saiyids* are the descendants of Hasan, *Sharifs* of Husain. In reality, of course, they are not the lineal descendants of the Prophet, but of 'Ali, who married the Prophet's daughter, Fatima. The Omanis, whose sect is 'Ibadhism (the ancient Khuwarij) and to whom 'Ali's name is therefore anathema, have the apposite saying, 'Ask a mule what his father was.' His reply will be, 'My mother was a horse.'

[2] I should here mention that the panther is found in the more unfrequented wooded valleys; the Arabian *ibex tar* lives beyond the habitable mountains and in the Jabal Samhan; foxes are found everywhere, and gazelle are numerous in the plains.

commodating us both and hiding us from an approaching animal, as we lay. The loopholes for our rifles were disguised, as was the whole wall, with small tree-branches. For bait, on the first night, he put the entrails of a sheep eight paces from the wall with a fire, lit just after sunset to carry off the scent. On the second night he used a bait of sardines, and again nothing happened. On the third night I withdrew in favour of a Kathiri Badu. The hyena came. Two rapid shots and a pained howl awoke me just before midnight and I ran to the spot. 'Fled and wounded,' they shouted, pointing to a pool of blood. Confident that the wound was mortal, they followed the trail as well as a bright moon would allow, swearing they would find him dead, but on the morrow I woke to hear that the animal had got clean away, probably to die in some cave.

'Had this been in the open desert,' said my two Badus, 'we would have tracked him to his lair, but once he made the rocky wadi, it was his sanctuary.'

V: IN THE QARA MOUNTAINS—
ANCIENT SURVIVALS AND THE
BLOOD SACRIFICE

'Their inward thought is, that their houses shall continue for ever, and their dwelling-places to all generations; they call their lands after their own names.'—Ps. xlix. 11.

THE mountains of the Qara are still locally called after the original masters of the land, the Shahara,[1] who are by universal consent the most ancient tribe in these parts, and by local tradition derive them from Shaddad son of Ad. To-day they are weak, disunited, disrated, none else giving to them in marriage, a dwindling

[1]Shahara Ancestor.	Qara* Section.	Present Regional Name.	Shahari Dialect.
Zuferol	Bait Tabok	Had bi Dhomari	Had bi Dhomari
Gufarim	Bait Kashob	Had bi Dhomari	Had bi Dhomari
Zart	Bait Qutun	Al Khati	At* Khuti
Ainarun	Bait Ma'ashani	Qarha	Ai Qarho
Hizol	Bait Ma'ashani	Faiyah	Ait Fat
	Bait Jabob		
Bil Ziyun	Bait Sa'id	Qibla	Qubulat
Qitun	Bait Umar (Ainr)	Diyan	Adin

The Kathir wedge Zarbiq { Ai Zuftair / Air† Zurbaig / At Ghuzub.

* *at*, *ait*, and *ai* are the Shahari versions of *bait*.
† *ir*, *air*, *bir* are the Shahari versions of *bin*.

[46]

race now numbering scarcely four hundred men who live in groups among their Qara overlords, hewing their wood and drawing their water; yet men say of the ruins of Robat, that here was once Eriyot, their proud city. If this be so, their decline has changed the face of the mountains, for the Qara who are undisputed masters from Dharbat 'Ali to Hadhbaram[1] build neither city nor mosque, but live in the open under forest trees or in caves or houses of hay. Their riches are in camels, and innumerable herds of cattle and groves of frankincense. Yet in mastering the Shahara they seem to have assimilated the Shahara culture, for the language of these mountain folk, their dress and manners are popularly held to have come from their dispossessed liegemen.

When this happened, no one knows. Ibn Battuta, the famous Moorish traveller and theologian, writing in the fourteenth century of our era, after twenty-five years of travel through Egypt, Arabia and Mesopotamia, wrote of Dhufar: 'Another thing is that its people closely resemble the people of north-west Africa in their customs . . . the outlying portion is not Arab, but of a Sudanic type.'

About and beyond these Qara Mountains from long. 51° 10′ to long. 56° 20′ range tribes physically different from the typical Arab of the north, and using non-Arabic mother tongues.[2] These are Qara, Shahara, Mahra, Bara-

[1] Except for the Al Kathir wedge in the central west between Gurzaz and Thifa.

[2] Of the four languages spoken, viz. Shahari, Mahri, Bautahari, Harsusi, I have made vocabularies, each of five hundred words, and deduced a few simple grammatical rules. They belong to the Semitic group, but have closer structural affinities with Ethiopic than with Arabic.

[47]

hama, Bilhaf, Bait ash Shaikh, Bautahara, Harasis, Afar, whom the people of Oman know collectively as Ahl al Hadara, a name possibly identifiable with the Hadoram of Genesis (by the elision of the final 'm' which is a Semitic form of plural and the article in ancient Sabaean) and the Adramitae of Pliny. Hadoram and Hazarmaveth (generally equated with Hadhramaut) come together in Genesis and are called brothers, and Dhufar is contiguous to Hadhramaut.

The Qara Mountains, geographically in the centre of this South Arabian ethnological enclave, seem to have afforded a natural asylum for aborigines or early settlers driven south and east before more virile peoples, or attacked from the sea.

What a glorious place! Mountains three thousand feet high basking above a tropical ocean, their seaward slopes velvety with waving jungle, their roofs fragrant with rolling yellow meadows, beyond which the mountains slope northwards to a red sandstone steppe. Two incongruous aspects, but true at any point throughout the strip above the Jurbaib plain. Great was my delight when in 1928 I suddenly came upon it all from out of the arid

(i) Shahari is spoken by Qara, Shahara, Barahama, Bait ash Shaikh.
(ii) Mahri by Mahra and Bilhaf.
(iii) Bautahari by Bautahara.
(iv) Harsusi (Aforit) by Harasis and Afar.

Shahari is normally unintelligible to users of the other languages, who, however, can understand one another with difficulty.

I was unaware that Mahri and Shahari had been written up by the German philologist Dr. Maximilian Bittner, working on material collected in the Hadhramaut and Socotra by Dr. Müller's Arabian Expedition (1902) and by Count Landberg's Expedition (1898-99).

My Harsusi and Bautahari, which appear to be variants of Mahri, have never before, I think, been recorded.

[48]

IN THE QARA MOUNTAINS: LOOKING DOWN INTO WADI NIHAZ.

wastes of the southern borderlands. The red[1] aspect came first. A white pebbly bed (Wadi Dhikur) led up into a magnificent gorge of red cliffs, three hundred feet high and more, their faces carved by nature into recesses that threw dark fantastic shadows. The scene brought back old Petra to my mind. Thence we crossed the watershed of the Qutun, thick with *tishgaut* jungle, a libaniferous shrub inferior to frankincense, and so on down through wooded valleys to Dahaq, a mighty five-hundred-foot precipice, whither the Bents had come and wondered whether Ptolemy's Abyssapolis was not to be found there. But ere we reached it the hazy rim of the distant sea lifted beyond the mountains rolling down to it. Thence we descended to the brink of the Valley of Darbat, an exquisite picture as we looked down through a tangle of tree-tops to the stream, lined with trembling willows, a wall of tropical jungle rising sheer above us on every side. We made our way towards the plashing waters, the snapping of the undergrowth as we went giving alarm to the herons that lived amid these sylvan scenes.

Rizat's wild life, resentful at our prolonged intrusion, was forsaking its haunts, so I decided to leave on the morrow, 5th November, and move up into the mountains. Shaikh Hasan, to forward my wishes, had arrived with five

---

[1] It is not, I think, impossible that the word Dhufar in origin was susceptible of the division Dhu Afar (the medial Arabic article *al* is not met with in these South Arabian languages), meaning the Red Country. Modifications of the word *Afar* are common, *e.g.*:

Afar = one of the largest frankincense groves.
Afar = a large wadi: is also the name of a tribe.
Afaur = a large wadi.
Aufur = clouds; and the meaning, 'a cloudy country,' would be just as apt as a 'red' country.

[49]

camels, large, fat-humped beasts which favourably impressed me, but when it came to work I was to undergo my usual disillusionment about mountain-bred camels. Unused to any load but sacks of frankincense or sardines, a heavier, more compact load bearing on the wrong part of their backs makes them restive. The habitual bellowing and grumbling when loading was now followed by stamping and wild attempts to shed their burdens, so that after two hours' delay in getting on the move we were held up from hour to hour rescuing or adjusting packs.

For two hours we skirted the foothills, moving west towards the entrance of Wadi Thidot, one of the few great intruding wadis that give access to the mountains.[1] The wadi immediately became wooded as our way led along and up a tortuous path thick with overhanging foliage which brought us to a large pool fed by a tiny stream called Sahalnaut (here, as is commonly the case in these mountains, the water bears a different name from the wadi). We turned out of the right bank to climb more steeply on a general north-westerly bearing. The trees grew thicker as we proceeded, compelling us to dismount, and night fell before we reached our destined halt, so we continued on foot through this dark dense mountain forest. The march was unpleasant, doubly so now from the dread of snakes with which these mountains teem. This was a subject of banter between my companions, whose belief in 'the day' and 'the hour' and a glorious hereafter, makes intolerable positions tolerable for them. I found comfort in the reflection that their jovial attitude and bare legs and feet compared ill with my superior defence, but I was

[1] The large wadis from east to west are Darbat, Ghazot, Ajarthun, Raithot, Arbot, Nihaz, Gurzaz.

QARA MOUNTAINS: ROCK CAVES.

QARA MOUNTAINS: ROCK CAVES.

constantly stumbling over boulders in the path and my long Arab skirt swung awkwardly round my legs.

At last the trees gave place to a grassy upland valley lit by the full moon, and here we halted for the night. The lowing of herds followed by shouts of *Rahalat! Rahalat!*[1] denoted that we had halted just short of the village of Midsaib. Delicious bowls of milk were soon brought along, but I was too tired to deal with a snake that a native had caught and brought to me alive, so it was put in a bottle to await the morning light.

The camp was early astir and I found myself in a glorious grassy valley, with cliffs on either side, here and there revealing natural rock caves fronted with stalactites and stalagmites, suggestive of monster jaws. Trusses of straw or thorn thatch edged the accessible ones which the people in the cold winter and wet summer, when only they require shelter, occupy with their beasts.

A crowd of villagers came along with more milk. This is their staple diet, with honey and beef, the other two luxury items their mountains afford. Another Hasan, an old man suffering from senile decay and almost blind, the father of the village, insisted on leaving his place in the circle to come and sit next to me. I had dates served with the coffee, and he caused mirth by dipping the one into the other. He was clearly unused to these delicacies, if indeed he regarded them as such.

Our Shaikh Hasan excited murmurs of admiration by wearing the new blue indigo mantle that was my gift, and

[1] A name given to a cow with drooping horns. Every cow enjoys a separate name. They are hereditary names (like camel or horse families) deriving through the mother. The herdsman claims to know every head he has, so that if one is stolen, he can identify it a year or two later, even in a strange herd.

[51]

I told the old man that I would like to send him the 'sister of Shaikh Hasan's mantle' as a present.

'*Alaik baidh!*' he cried, a variant of '*Allah baiyidh wijhak*' (God whiten your face), a term of cordiality and gratitude.

'*W'allahi!* I like you, sahib,' he continued. 'I am old and about to die, but if you will say, "There is no God but God, and Muhammad is the Prophet of God," I will give you two girls to wife, and all my property.'

A titter went round and Shaikh Hasan motioned to him to talk less.

My medicine chest had acquired for me a spurious fame and, as ever, afflicted humanity was brought to me. This time it was a young boy, withered apparently by consumption, who spat blood and was subject to fevers.

'Have you any medicine for this, O Wazir?' asked a suppliant father. 'Men say the infidels have drugs for everything.'

My companions stared at the speaker and let him understand that the term *kafir* was distasteful to me, though he really meant no harm, for he used the term to mean merely non-Muslim. 'He is the Sultan's Wazir,' they said.

Loading up was an unpleasant job for the dew had been heavy. Half an hour after starting brought us to a point where we left the wadi by the pass of Sa'arin, to climb five hundred feet into steep stony country. Then followed rolling yellow meadows where hay stood to a man's middle, and occasional clumps of giant fig trees crowned the hills or nestled in the hollows. Behind and below us in the distance was the faint blue sea, and round us undulating down country with the wooded cliffs above Nihaz occasionally edging the western skyline. Here at 1500 feet the bird life so plentiful in the valleys below dwindled to a few sparrow-hawks and many large storks, but butterflies, grasshoppers and locusts were many and various.

And now we looked down upon a pleasant vale that was our immediate destination, Al 'Ain, a Shahari settlement of Had bi Dhomari, where a spring comes bubbling out of the ground in the belly of a wooded trough. Two wild fig trees, as big and shady as good English walnuts, and bursting with apple-like fruit, made inviting bivouacs, and there I halted. A three hours' climb had made me thirsty, but it is impossible to obtain milk during the noonday, and the curds that were brought me arrived belatedly after I had dealt with the milk of a brimming fresh coco-nut.

From over the brow of the hill appeared a party of Qara tribesmen of Shaikh Hasan, in extended order, singing their peculiar *danadon* chant[1] of the mountains. Their fellow-tribesmen of 'Ain mustered to meet them, one drawing his sword to dance in honourable welcome. The approaching party halted in a crowd round their leader while he improvised mock heroics for the occasion, and then lined out again chanting new couplets, and so came facing up to their welcomers whose turn it was to improvise a reply in similar manner. Thus a ding-dong chanting went on for some five minutes on either side.

Of quite a peculiar type are these dark-looking men of the mountains, with their long rough head hair sometimes caught up and tied in a bun on top, but more often left wild and bushy, and practically no growth of hair on the face except a slight chin-tuft, many of them with refined, non-Arab faces. Their dress is the usual indigo mantle, which among the well-to-do is cut to drape half the body,

[1] A list of camel chants and mountain chants recorded as well as European notation would permit is given in Appendix VI.

crossing it diagonally and being brought over one shoulder. A leather girdle, looped as a cartridge belt, encircles the waist. Their heads are uncovered, except for a leather thong to keep their bushy curls in place; their black arms and legs below the knees are bare. Most of them wear a single ear-ring in the right ear and a single bracelet above the right elbow like the Mahra and neighbouring cognate tribes.

The reception of these men of Shaikh Hasan's called for the slaying of a cow on my part, and 'Ali al Dhab'an saw to it that the place of slaughter was within close range of a tree—for to-night's vigil. 'Ali and I were lying in wait expectantly when at about ten p.m. an animal came prowling to where the entrails invitingly lay. It was impossible to see even at a dozen yards what the brute was, and quite out of the question to try to use sights in such darkness. All we could do was to wait for it to come close and take a rough alinement, whence the advantage of our both having rifles. As the sniffing creature came on, we both aimed as we thought best. It could not have been more than seven yards away when 'Ali touched my foot with his, the pre-arranged signal. Two shots rang out and the animal leapt into the air with a snort and fell lifeless in a pool of blood. We both jumped up, 'Ali with his dagger drawn in case of tricks, but the body showed no response as he kicked it, and our further investigations showed that both shots had told, one through the neck, the other through the body. It was a splendid specimen of a full-grown hyena, the first of five I was to get during the next few weeks.

I had hoped for a wolf, and the trumpeting earlier in the night of a donkey—alarmed for her foal—was a sign of the wolf's presence. Our bait was sufficient, for though

QARA MOUNTAINS: THE DAHAQ.

the wolf will attack young domestic animals—goats, lambs and calves—it will also like the hyena prey on carrion. The panther on the other hand scorns a cold carcase, and will, like man, eat only what he kills himself. Here he is held to be a menace to man and camel alike, at least to man who has unsuccessfully attacked him in a tight corner, wherefore the natives of these mountains treat a passing panther at more than a hundred yards' range with respectful inactivity. They would only shoot if coming unexpectedly upon him at close range.

'Panthers?' queried Shaikh Hasan in answer to my importunities, 'they are rare, but a wolf you should get to-night. Send 'Ali to my uncle's. They are slaughtering six cows to-day as the sacrifice to my aunt who died in the middle of last moon. These men of mine are going along for the feast. Surely to-night a wolf must come to the place of slaughter.'

Here was a survival of great interest—the blood sacrifice and the burnt offering. Throughout these mountains it is the inviolable rule that one-half of a man's cows shall be slaughtered as a sacrifice, after his death. Half his wealth must thus be dissipated for the state of his soul—Estate and Legacy Duty with a vengeance, though for a very poor man a single cow or sheep suffices. A limit of twenty cows may be set only for the wealthy men, *i.e.* one possessing upwards of forty head. With them may be slaughtered a camel and some sheep, but the cow's value in sacrifice seems disproportionate to its actual worth.

On the day of burial, normally the day of death, one or two cows will be slaughtered over the grave to the words:
'*Dai bi Huduktos Hadhail ir Hadhail.*'
(See by this gift M. son of N.)

Two nights are allowed to pass and on the third night another cow is sacrificed. This is called *khutum*. A further period elapses, varying according to the means of the deceased's relatives. It may be as little as a fortnight or as much as three months before the big sacrifice takes place, maybe of ten, fifteen or twenty cows, representing half of the deceased man's herds. This is called *yom el nahaira*. Both *khutum* and *nahaira* are performed at the place where the man lived and not upon his grave. More cows will be sacrificed by relatives, and by friends of the deceased whose bereavements he had honoured in like manner during his lifetime. This vast slaughter attracts the whole neighbourhood and the section of the tribe to which the dead man belonged divide up the flesh for themselves, and go away under their handsome burdens. Visitors from other tribes have no such rights, but are invited to partake of the feast, for which one cow will have been roasted.

Then takes place the division of the residue of the estate between the relatives.[1]

Among the southern borderland tribes, such as Bait Kathir, and in the Qara Mountains customary, not Islamic law, prevails. Among the Bait Kathir not more than one-third of a man's estate may go to his creditors. Of the remaining two-thirds, one-fourth goes to the wife that has borne children, one-eighth to the wife that has not borne children and the remainder goes to the children in the

[1] The religious law of Islam prescribes categorically how a man's estate must be divided. The right of bequest is strictly limited, and among tribesmen is almost non-existent. The lawful wives and all children are entitled to a due share of the estate; to a daughter one share, to a son two, and to the wives one-eighth of the estate between them. Where there are no sons, the paternal uncle, or in default of such, the paternal male cousins, receive the son's share.

usual proportion of a double share to each son. Where custom differs from Shara' law is that if there is no son and less than three daughters, the deceased's brother is entitled to only a daughter's share, and if there are three or more daughters, they take the whole, and paternal male relations get nothing.

The laws of inheritance of the Qara Mountains are peculiar. They are bound up with the cult of death sacrifice. Their wealth, as already shown, is generally in cows, and at a man's decease half of his cattle are slaughtered as a blood sacrifice. Creditors are allowed to claim up to one-tenth of the estate, and what remains is divided between wives, sons and daughters. The wives take one-tenth in a small estate and generally five cows when large estates are involved. A peculiar feature of this group of tribes is that if a woman has one daughter, or three daughters and no son, no part of the estate passes to the nearest male relative of the deceased husband's family, who would under Muslim Holy Law normally get the largest share. If she has two daughters it does. There thus seems to be some special significance in the numbers 1 and 3. Another point in which the mountain system differs from the usage of the South Arabian tribes, but accords with Shara', is that all wives get the same share irrespective of whether they have borne children or not.

The wife in these tribes may not betray grief on the death of her husband. Mothers, daughters and sisters may weep and raise their voices, and amongst the Qara they let down their hair, beat their heads, and pour dust upon them; but a public show of pain [for the man's loss would disgrace a wife. She must hide herself.

VI: THE QARA MOUNTAINS—
HYENAS, FAITH CURES AND
CIRCUMCISION

'*Hamr al 'ain! Hamr al 'ain!*' (Red of eye! Red of eye!) Such were the shouts—the usual idiom in praise of manly prowess—that greeted 'Ali as he returned at dawn from the scene of the sacrifice, for with him was a dead wolf straddled across a donkey.

I could not wait to do more than turn and wave greeting, for I had been called to Adaiqaf, the small village of the Shahari headman Juma'an across the meadow from my camp. In one of its miserable hovels a man lay dying. A straw thatch of beehive shape was not more than a man's length in diameter or height and had only a hole as an entrance to crawl through. The floor was strewn with straw, and there was of course no fire hearth. The only furnishings were a plaited reed basin into which they milk, and a few pots for water, butter or honey and the like—both the products of women's industry. Near by were larger and slightly more ambitious buildings having walls of stone, rough, undressed and uncemented. These were for cattle in the temperate seasons, but against the summer rain and winter cold both men and cattle take refuge in caves, which are numerous where, in dips and hollows, the limestone strata obtrude. The winds of the ages have scooped out natural caverns, which only need thatching in front to provide spacious and effective shelter for man and beast.

And so back across the meadow to 'Ali and his hyena. The north wind blew chill at this height of 1600 feet, and the sunlit air, fragrant with the scent of hay, made it feel good to be alive.

[58]

Three snakes had been brought in to me by Badawin, the smallest a rather beautiful black and white barred *shalthum*, which was found to be a new species of colubrid; the second was very much alive and in consequence did not engage my immediate interest; the third was a *dololat*, a hideous monster only nineteen inches long and as squat as a bun with bold V-shaped markings along his back and an enormous flat head—an African puff-adder. Every day one such was brought in, which suggests it must be the commonest snake in the mountains. It is a sluggish mover and deadly poisonous, so those who walk through the undergrowth here do well to move warily, though to pursue a *charaxes* butterfly (those I got were the only known specimens of this African type to have been found in Arabia), head in air, is to forget perils underfoot.

In disembowelling this adder—its body contained seventeen tapeworms which deceived me for a time—I suddenly felt a sharp sting on my finger and had an uncomfortable hour or so afterwards lest, despite my precaution in using tongs, some inward part of the snake were poisonous and I had not been sufficiently careful. No ill effects followed, however, and I decided that a spot of formalin had touched a part of my hand where there must already have been a slight abrasion.

The mountaineers will not eat hyena or fox; and eggs, chicken and all manner of birds are also under a strict taboo[1] like frogs and snails in England. What is or is not permissible to eat throughout the southern borderland of Arabia varies from place to place. Except for the sedentary townsfolk and this central group of tribes with non-Arabic

[1] I am informed that chicken, eggs and fish are not eaten by tribesmen in the Medina area.

languages, the hyena is eaten everywhere from Hadhramaut to Oman; the fox on the other hand is favoured only by the Badawin of Oman and a chance nomad like 'Ali, the mighty hunter; the wolf is eaten by no one. Not only the nature of the meat, but the manner of its killing become a subject of lively debate among the faithful. Like the Hebraic Code, the Islamic Law permits only such animals to be eaten as have been slaughtered by a knife drawn across the throat. It is idle to suggest to the Badu that in days when firearms were unknown, the intention was merely to forbid the eating of animals that had died, perhaps from disease.[1] The illiterate Arab prefers downright guidance and shuns such speculations as *kufr*—heresy. Thus he may not eat of a bird with a hooked beak. The suggestion that a hooked beak implies a carrion eater has for him nothing to do with the religious prohibition. 'Thou shalt not' is the law; its origin, or the underlying reason, is not his concern, nor yours. Thus an Omani townsman askari who delighted in fox flesh stood aghast when I asked him whether hawk was lawful food.

'Never!' said he. 'It has a hooked beak. We will not eat even a partridge,' and he narrowly eyed 'Ali who spent his morning cutting up the hyena into long shreds of meat and hanging them on a tree to dry.

'What's that for, 'Ali?' he asked.

'I'm taking it as medicine for a sick friend in Salala,' he said (a belief in its curative properties for human affliction, for the back—eat of the back, for the right leg—eat of the right leg, and so on, is widespread). Of course every one

---

[1] The origin may well have been to drain away the blood, perhaps to feed the god at the altar; cf. Genesis ix. 4, 'Flesh *with the life thereof, which is the blood thereof*, shall ye not eat.'

knew—even the slave cook who took a malicious joy in circulating the story—that 'Ali, the Hadhramauti, was saving it up for his family.

But the hyena taboo amongst these mountaineers is no ordinary one. Not only will they not eat its flesh, they will not kill it or assist in its destruction. They believe that it is a magic animal; it is the riding-camel of the witch, and those who attack it will incur its mistress's avenging hand. Cows will die or other retribution follow. Thus the Qara were much exercised to find a hyena's head boiling (my way of cleaning the skull) in the pot that was usually used for cooking their rice; Shaikh Hasan, under whose protection I was, counselled caution, possibly, I thought, as a sop to his own conscience, for he was an ardent believer and had vowed to me that he had once come upon a dead hyena actually wearing ear-rings. Doubtless some beldame, its mistress and a caster of spells, had pierced its ears and put them in. The same story was vouched for by the Kathir Shaikh of Dhufar, who called God to witness that he spoke the truth.

'What is there more succulent than hyena flesh?' said 'Ali to me. 'These men are not like us Arabs, for we of the Karab and Sa'ar call it *kabsh an nabi*—the Prophet's ram. The Prophet himself made it lawful for us to eat,' and he proceeded to tell me how it came about.

Once upon a time a hyena claimed the young of a gazelle as its own offspring. Hyena and gazelle appeared before the Prophet, where each pleaded, 'The young gazelle is mine.' The Prophet sent them away and told them to appear before him again the next morning.

And lo! before dawn broke the gazelle came prancing up to the Prophet's tent.

[61]

'How have *you* spent the night, O gazelle?' asked the Prophet.

'I spent the night watch by watch standing like Cassiopæia always in my place.'

Well after sunrise the hyena came leisurely ambling along.

'And how have *you* spent the night, O hyena?' asked the Prophet.

'I spent the night, O Prophet, asleep in the protection of Allah until the rising of his great star, the sun.'

The Prophet (upon him and you be peace) turned to the gazelle. 'Take the kid,' he said, 'it is thine.'

Up leapt the hyena shouting, 'God curse the Prophet and his father!'

Whereupon the Prophet seized the pestle from where it stood in the coffee mortar and struck the hyena as it turned to run away, so that its hindquarters withered to their present miserable proportions, and the hyena became food for man.

Verily the *kabsh an nabi!*

The ape is found in the Hadhramaut, but not in these Qara Mountains. There is a folk story that apes spring from a human being who stole Muhammad's sandals, for which offence the Prophet forbade him to enter the mosque, whereupon he went out into the fields like Nebuchadnezzar and ate grass, and became a *rubah* ape.

My hunting at 'Ain prospered, but I had the greatest difficulty and sometimes failed in persuading my collectors to slaughter in a manner that would not spoil the skin as a scientific specimen. The main difficulty was the religious requirement of a lateral gash across the throat, but 'Ali and I devised a compromise whereby he should first make a longitudinal slit of the skin down the throat (as required

OUR FIRST HYENA: THE SKIN FOR THE MUSEUM, THE FLESH FOR ALI BIN DHAB'AN (ON RIGHT).

for my purposes), fold it back and then perform his ortho-
doxies under the skin.

I had been adamant in refusing any reward for a spoilt
skin, and in the light of our new-found formula, 'Ali now
declared how much he lamented a fox he had killed in the
old way, and was unlawful for eating. I admired such piety
in the acknowledged slayer of fifteen sons of men!

Yet the Omani soldier looked at 'Ali disdainfully as much
as to say, 'That slaughtering is not orthodox—I would not
touch it!'

But to them both, such is custom, a beast could be shot
dead, and all would be well so long as there was a prompt
lateral cutting of the throat made with the pious expression
as the blood gushed forth, '*Bismillah ar rahman ar rahim!*'
(In the name of God the merciful, the compassionate).
But without the lateral gash God would not be pleased.

The scent of cooking food, or was it the hungry sense of
an approaching meal hour, brought natives from all directions about us. And now one of these, an old Mahri who
had not come empty handed, stood by watching me
despatch his chameleon.

'*Wallah!* By God!' he burst out, 'it is treachery. I found
it innocent in a bush and it came along with me trusting,
and this is what I consent to happen to it!'

A dear old man! I thought, you shall have a dollar. He
took his place in the circle of interested onlookers who sat
around.

'Have you any medicine for a barren woman?' he said.

'A strong man,' interjected a youth, and a titter went
round.

'There may be medicine,' I said, 'but I have none with
me. Is she young? Twenty?'

'Older,' he rejoined. 'She has had four husbands and I'm the fifth, and she has never borne a child yet.'

'Then there is no medicine probably,' I said.

'She is as a *bint* [virgin] still!' he returned.

'All the better!' said the youth unhelpfully, amid more tittering.

As the party broke up the old man remained behind, and I saw that he was not despairing.

'I want a writing[1] from you!' he said.

'What for?'

'A woman who is not yielding to her husband.'

'I don't hold with writings for that,' I said, by way of escaping an impossible request.

'But do you understand what I mean?' he returned.

'Yes, perfectly,' and I repeated his story.

'But she is my wife. I would like a letter from the Sultan ordering her to surrender herself.'

'That, I fear, is impossible. Take your case to the Wali.'

He clicked his tongue, which is the mountain negative, then put it into words:

'*Lob! Lob!*' he said. 'It would be shameful for me; promise you will not tell.'

'I promise,' said I, and the old man trudged back, I suppose, to his two unsatisfactory women.

The Qara Shaikh was slaughtering a cow the next day in my honour—let the unwary Arabian traveller be warned that this is the most expensive way of buying one—and a

---

[1] A script worn as a charm is invested with magic virtues. The credulous have no particular concern whether or not it be from Holy Writ, although it is often a verse from the Qur'an, as the scribe knows no other. Venerated Saiyids do very good business, particularly just before the exodus to the mountains, by vending such. A dollar script will protect against the Evil Eye; two dollars for an ailing cow; and more as the price of general immunity.

Shahari vassal of his brought it along. I looked at the Shahari and wondered whether or not it was his 'ewe lamb': it probably was. The neighbourhood came to the feast, which was followed by the usual *haydanadon* chanting, though I gathered that heroic verses are often rendered in the Mahri tongue, as opposed to the love ditties of the mountains which are chanted in Shahari. 'Abdullah, the poet, did the improvising—a friendly garrulous individual from whom I was soon to hear a tale of woes.

'Have you medicine for this?' he asked, calling attention to one of his legs abnormally swollen. It was little good my protesting that I was no doctor, for there was a pitiful predisposition among the sufferers to believe in my powers.

'How long has it been like that?'

'Three years,' said 'Abdullah. 'It does not trouble me when I rest, but when I run it swells and gives pain. And the blood of the sheep has not availed.'

For human sickness these tribes sacrifice a cow or a sheep, and sprinkle its blood over the patient's shoulders and breasts when the sun is high. The animal must be female, a sex distinction not observed at the death sacrifice.

'What is that mark?' and I pointed to a scar over a bunch of the varicose veins from which he clearly suffered.

'The cautery!' he said (the hot iron is a universal medicine throughout these parts), 'but it did no good. Have you no medicine, sahib? *W'allahi!* I have no son, but if I were offered cure of my leg or a son, *W'allahi!* I would choose a whole leg.'

His friends looked at him incredulously.

'I know naught for it but a surgeon's knife, and that means a visit to Aden or Muscat,' I said.

To 'Abdullah, a wild man of the mountains, Aden and

[65]

Muscat were remote as Mars, and a journey thither, entailing an unprecedented absence from his females, about as feasible.

'*Tawakkul al Allah!*' he said resignedly. 'Rely on God,' from whom, such was the implication, affliction and cure alike come.

'Abdullah's geniality was exceptional. The mass of these tribesmen are a dour breed, sly, suspicious, unamiable. They do not invite personal contacts, but the exceptional spirit among them can be cultivated. None thinks it necessary on arrival to bid one the respectful salutation universal throughout Arabia, none says a word of farewell on leaving the circle, but abruptly rises on an impulse, slopes his rifle, and turns silently away. Among themselves they are engaged in constant bickerings and brawlings, and I went among them apprehensive of trouble which might prejudice my own activities. Cow-thieving seemed to be the main cause of the troubles, for adjustment came not by restitution, but by revenge. Shaikh Hasan himself had, he told me, suffered the loss of a hundred head, much of it from the malice of enemies, for the animals were cut down and left where they profited no one. Other men told me that Hasan had despoiled his neighbours of far more, and that much of the repute he now enjoyed derived from the ethically questionable exploits of his youth.

To-day there was an alarm!

'*Ya wulaid! Ya farha! Ya wulaid! Ya farha!*' rang the call throughout the country-side, and all looked at the distant figure on the northern skyline who was raising the *taguwid*—the war alarm! Were the Badawin of the steppe coming, for the Sa'ar have, in times past, raided the Qutun.

Labkhit the Shaikh's son, whom I was on the point of

sending to Dhufar to purchase stores and bring me news, seized his rifle and ran off loading it, with the others, leaving me standing with just a few Shahara who took no action. The Shahara are a spineless people who will meekly consent to be pillaged or allow one of their number to be killed, without raising a finger in defence of themselves.

'*Bahaim taht Allah!*' 'No better than cattle under God,' said Shaikh Hasan, speaking of them afterwards to me. 'They are afraid to shed blood!'

This indeed is the crux of the matter, the dividing line between prestige and discredit, between tribesman and non-tribesman, between Qara, Mahra, Kathir on the one hand, and Shahara, Barahama, Bait ash Shaikh on the other: namely the power and will to fight; it springs from a corporate consciousness on the part of the tribesman by which the acts done by or to any member of his tribe are virtually acts done by or to himself, with all the consequences that that involves.

'The Shahara! they are no better than slaves!' says the tribesman, for whom marriage with a slave would be unthinkable. It is dishonourable; let the nobility—the Saiyids and the merchants of the coast—use their slave girls as concubines at their pleasure!

The treatment of the Shahara by the Qara leaves the traveller in no doubt which is which, though the typical Shahari (who from the interdiction of marriage outside his people, must be racially pure) is distinguishable by having a much broader face than his neighbours or the northern Arab. His weapons help also to distinguish him, for very seldom will you meet him carrying a rifle.

Not only the dress, but the arms of these mountains are unique throughout Arabia—a bare double-bladed sword, a

[67]

buckler (of the circular kind found amongst Hamitic tribes) and also and chiefly an *aget*—a heavy straight stick of *mitain*[1] wood, pointed at both ends and thrown with great skill. This is the regular weapon of the mountains. The well-to-do, chiefly those of the Qara, will carry a rifle, in which case he will not carry the double-bladed sword, but a single-bladed one, and instead of the *aget*, an ordinary stick.

'And whence came these Shahara?' I asked.

'They are the people who killed the Prophet Salih's camel, and are suffering to-day for their wickedness, for they are no longer tribesmen, that is, men of honour,' was the answer.

'And had Salih bin Hut a camel?' I queried, simulating ignorance of their story.

My informant, pitying my ignorance in his branch of learning, continued. 'Not heard of Salih's camel, the most famous was she of all God's creatures ever.' His stick traced the sun's course in heaven as he went on. 'She journeyed from east to west, and from west to east, and she yielded to all peoples honey, milk and wine. That was in the time of Talmud and Ad, but an ignorant man of the Shahara killed the camel and God sent on the Shahara a pestilence of ants, which crawled up their legs and over their bodies and devoured them, so that few have survived to this day!'

The next time I heard this story, an old man told it to me, embellished with a sequel. 'Tempted by a woman this same wicked Shahara pursued the dead camel's calf, hoping to slay that too. But God set a cave in the way, and Nabi

[1] This wood is exceedingly heavy, and sinks in water. It grows only in the mountains of Dhufar.

Salih's camel calf[1] entered into it and the entrance was closed up like a wall of mountain and prevented the man from coming after it any more.' A pause. '*Shuf! Sabhan Allah!*'—'Do you call that nothing?'

'And what of the origin of you Qara?'

'The Arabs call us Qara but we call ourselves Hakalai, and we came here from Hadhramaut, and to Hadhramaut we came from across the sea.'

I had heard this many times, and Shaikh Hasan held that the tribe migrated westwards with the Mahra, and that they had lingered together over Habarut. This seems improbable to me because they, like the Shahara and Barahama, have no camel *wasm*, and for a tribe that was at one time nomadic and still breeds camels not to have had, or to have lost, the camel mark which is the tribal coat of arms, is inconceivable. Its absence suggests that they came in by way of the sea.

'Hakalai was our ancestor, and the Qara sprang from the Guraish. He and the Baliyoz[2] sprang from one race: but we crossed the sea.'

A Saiyid pointed out that this was not the Guraish from which his revered ancestor the Prophet sprang, but from another, only remembered in Qara traditions.

It was interesting to me as implying a consciousness of racial distinction from the typical Arab; it also suggested that the Qara are not improbably a survival—an eddy of that Abyssinian stream of Christian conquerors that invaded and proselytised south-west Arabia before Islam.

[1] I should perhaps use the word 'colt,' following Genesis xxxii. 15: 'Thirty milch camels with their colts.'

[2] This term is used in the Persian Gulf and on the coast of Arabia to denote a British Political Agent. It is said to be derived, by metathesis, from the low Latin *bailus*. Lat. *bajulus*, from Bailo, the title of the representative of the Venetian Republic at the Sublime Porte.

But of this my informants had no knowledge; for them the world is divided into believers and unbelievers, though of the text of the Qur'an they know nothing. Scarcely a man in these mountains can read and write except a few itinerant Saiyids. Writing indeed has a magical significance as the Mahri episode and many like it showed, and whenever applicants for my medicines were about, they were eager that I should look into my book (it was a star-chart) to see the cause of their affliction.

'I have heard men say that the Qara sprang from Himyar,' I continued.

'Do you mean Hamyar or Himyar?' said the learned Saiyid, 'for there are two.'

'*Allahu 'Alim*,' returned the Qarawi. 'I am not the son of yesterday—I was not living then, how should I know.'

It had seemed to me that 'Mahra' and 'Himyar' are not improbably anagrammatic forms of the same word, though here again the word Mahra is used only by the Arabs, but they are called in the language of the mountains Inharo (with a nasal *n*). As between Mahra and Qara there are both physical and linguistic differences, and neither will agree that they had a common origin.

It was their turn. 'And you Inglaiz!' they said.

'Not less honourable than you,' I claimed.

'Then you are *qubaili*?'

This was a poser, for it is difficult within the limits of strict veracity to make plausible an English tribal system in which people do not carry rifles, nor defend their honour with their own right hand; where women are unveiled and men's equals. But I dare not lose caste in the eyes of my companions.

[70]

'We *Nasara*' (it does equally well for English) 'are a very powerful tribe,' I told them.

'And who do you say is your forbear?'

'Adam!' I said, somewhat evasively, 'so that we were all very closely related at first and only fell away afterwards.'

'That's a fact,' they said, looking at one another as much as to say—'he speaks a divine truth.'

'And do you practise cleanliness? (*i.e.* circumcision).'

'It is not compulsory,' I hedged.

'Then there are men and women uncircumcised among you?'

'Yes,' I confessed.

'God forgive you,' he replied.

With these tribes circumcision is a rite of great importance, and is so different from the practices of the rest of Arabia as to suggest an independent origin. The male is circumcised on reaching adolescence; the girl on the day of her birth. This system of adult male and infant female circumcision is the reverse of that found elsewhere in Arabia,[1] notably in Oman where the practice is infant male circumcision (about six years old) and circumcision of the girl when approaching the age of ten. In both regions, with the male the whole of the foreskin is removed, but as regards the female, while the Arabs of Oman merely incise the top of the clitoris, these tribes of the central south perform clitoridectomy. This adult male circumcision conforms to the ancient Egyptian practice, for male mummies dug up at Thebes show that this rite was even then observed. Here in these mountains there are elaborate cere-

[1] I am told that in the Upper Euphrates valley circumcision of males is done at puberty, females never; and puberty is loosely interpreted to mean twelve to eighteen.

monies attending male circumcisions, and batches of youths undergo what is a severe public test of their fortitude on the same day. Large numbers of men and women assemble round a large open space. On a rock in the centre sits the boy of fifteen, a sword in hand. This sword, which has been blunted for the occasion, he throws into the air to catch it again in its descent, his palm clasping the naked blade. Before him sits the circumciser,[1] an old man; behind him stands an unveiled virgin, usually a cousin or a sister, also sword in hand.

She raises and lowers her sword vertically, and at the bottom of the stroke strikes it quiveringly with the palm of her left hand. The stage is now set. The boy sits, his left hand outstretched palm upwards, in suppliant manner, waiting for the actual operation. This done, he has promptly to rise bleeding and run round the assembly raising and lowering his sword as if oblivious of pain, and by his performance his manliness will be judged.[2] The rite is attended by brave songs and drumming and the firing of rifles, the women opening their upper garments as a gesture of baring their breasts. But no such manifestations of joy, indeed no manifestations at all, accompany the clitoridec-tomy of the infant female, which is done in secret.

Hair customs seem to be connected with the sexual life. A conspicuous feature is the central lock worn by boys,

[1] Usually a shaikh or man of good family, whereas in Oman only a gypsy or menial will officiate.

[2] With the Mahra tribe male circumcision at one time was carried out on the eve of a man's marriage. To-day a decent interval is allowed. Men and women foregather round desert fires. Eight or ten of the most presentable females are paraded and the men declare who is the most beautiful of them, while the remaining ladies protest characteristically, 'No! No! No! No!'

[72]

HAIR CUSTOMS (GIRLS).

HAIR CUSTOM (MARRIED WOMAN).

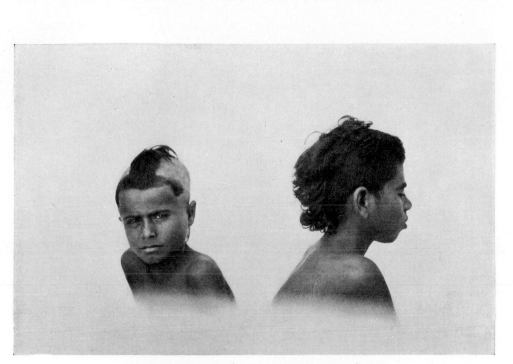

HAIR CUSTOM (UNCIRCUMCISED BOY).

A GROUP OF MOUNTAIN MEN.

connected perhaps with the ancient Egyptian *Horus* lock, giving the effect of a metropolitan policeman's helmet, or recalling a certain Hindu caste. This is cut off only at circumcision, after which time the hair is allowed to grow normally.

Not less strange are the hair customs of the women. The young girl's head is shaven in alternate stripes rather after the manner of a poodle, a brow fringe being left; the back of the head is shaven like a tonsure, except for three or four narrow plaits. When she is betrothed, customarily at the age of thirteen or fourteen, the hair is everywhere allowed to grow freely. Within a month after marriage has taken place, as a sign that she is maiden no longer, a long strip of skin about three-eighths of an inch wide is removed with a razor, like a parting through the centre of the head, so that hair never grows there again[1]—a scalping operation extremely painful and sometimes fatal.

Women paint their faces on ordinary occasions with a curious pattern of striped black markings, on festive occasions with red, black and green paint. The common face paint pattern produces a rather elaborate clownish effect. A continuous black stripe borders the brow hair, cheeks, jaw and chin. Another black line circles the nostrils and runs straight across the cheek on each side to the ear-hole. Straight bars for the eyelashes are at each extremity carried slightly up towards the temple; there are two short vertical lines under the eyes. Broad black stripes encircle the throat. There may be a spot of vermilion in the centre of the forehead, Hindu fashion, and the lips will

---

[1] The presence of pubic and armpit hair in the female is not permissible. She removes it by plucking, using a wax of frankincense.

be painted red. A married woman will have the scalp parting—*munserot*—painted with a central black line. It is a universal practice amongst the women of these tribes to have one tattoo mark on their chins, a stroke between two dots, thus ·|· —a practice noted in Egypt by Lane.

Jewels are elaborate. The edge of her ears, pierced in infancy at equal intervals in six or seven places, are adorned all round with a large light ear-ring, or alternatively a little silver chain. As puberty approaches she will have a nose ring introduced, pointing forward from the left nostril. Her many finger rings have no marital significance; she has elaborate tawdry necklace bands, but wears no anklets, as do the coastal women.

An old Mahra lady, unveiled like all her kin, her face smeared indiscriminately with the greenish yellow *subur* dye (of a local tree) came to see me. The same pigment coated her arms from the elbows downwards, the legs from the knees downwards, and the upper part of the breasts to the neck. Her dress was the normal single loose black garment, low in the neck and reaching to the ground, with a black muslin head-wrap that fell about the shoulders, but her clothes were green and fretted with age—which gave her a monkish look.

She had brought me a present, and on opening the reed basket in which she carried her knick-knacks she exposed other feminine customs. Snuff was there; a most ladylike habit, but not found with men. Men smoke but not women, though both sexes chew—a mixture of tobacco and lime is held between the gum and the cheek; it is said to have a narcotic effect.

The present which the old Mahri now offered me to gladden the heart of some hypothetical European lady was an article of toilet—a small piece of local pottery quite beautifully shaped and recalling a Roman lamp—a nose irrigator, in common use throughout these mountains. It is filled with a kind of clarified butter, and the woman, lying recumbent, applies the spout to her nostril and empties a little of the contents into her head. 'A cure for headaches,' said the donor, 'which will make the eyes bright and the complexion clear.'

A Badu youth who had brought me a badger, a precious specimen because very hard to catch, kissed the old lady a fivefold kiss—left cheek, right cheek, left cheek, right temple and top of head—thereby showing a close relationship.

'This is Halairan bin Mir'ai, my nephew,' she said. 'Don't you know him? He was in Muscat.'

'Yes, *billah*,' laughed the rogue, 'you measured my head in Jalali prison, but I told no one, for they would say, "Why did you let him do it?"'

I enquired the offence that had taken him there. He had squeezed a girl's hand, it seems, and the girl's family petitioned the Governor, and so he was deported for a year: but it had done him no harm, he assured me, for he had found *rizk*—God's bounty—in Muscat, and held up the rifle he had acquired there for me to see.

The salutations among these tribes are peculiar. Hand touching, universal among Arabs, is reserved for meeting the woman, and becomes only a smart tap of the fingers, the lady withdrawing her hand sharply. For a man to squeeze a girl's hand, or clasp it as in a European handshake, is to make an improper overture, for which the girl's relations may take blood. Men salute on meeting with a reciprocal kiss on the left cheek, the right arm of each resting on the

[75]

other's left shoulder, but they are so uncouth that if one party is sitting he often does not bother to get up—unthinkable boorishness judged by any Arabian standard; for a shaikh or old man the cheek kiss is sometimes followed by kissing his brow; if shaikhs or persons of quality meet they will kiss, then withdraw and stand facing one another for a few seconds in dignified silence, before sitting.

I now rewarded the two Mahris who deserved well at my hands, and they withdrew with the usual remarks of the satisfied, 'God whiten your face,' and 'God preserve you.'

Sounds of girls' voices came floating up from the spring in the valley where a party of Qarawiya had gone off with their water-pitchers. Their song was said to be one of joy, but the love-fraught lyrics needed a bilingual native to turn them into Arabic for me, and none was present, so I must be content to record in our musical notation the curious wail of its melody. Where else in tribal Arabia would an honourable woman dare sing in public, if indeed at all? In puritanical Oman she would be beaten for a hussy, but here in these mountains and valleys I often heard the distant chanting of girls, and very pleasing it was to my ears.

VII: THE QARA MOUNTAINS—
EXORCISING THE EVIL EYE, AND
ORDEAL BY FIRE

A IN. The second week of November. A big moon sailed in and out of low-driving clouds, and I remembered the last full moon that had shone on my unobtrusive departure from Muscat harbour, but how different the scenes I had then envisaged for this moon, and their realities. Yet, though the sands seemed unattainable, and therefore in prospect very sweet, there was solace in these mountains.

Against the night the twisted branches of the fig tree that was my roof made an exquisite picture; loud and continuous were the hissings of crickets, and eerie the darting of large black bats from tree to tree; a rush of air betrayed the vulture that glided swiftly overhead; white and brown storks gathered in their accustomed tree-tops for the night, but took to flight at early dawn, for they seemed to resent our intrusion, and no longer gladdened the sunlit fields of 'Ain with their grotesque but decorative presence.

The dawn was heralded by the curious *glissando* note of a bee-eater calling to his mate. A joyous dawn? No, for the baby coney we had caught two nights before and had kept alive with cow's milk, was found rolled up in a cold stiff ball. It needed us no more, and Sa'id, a young *askari* whose practice it was to come and fondle it, could not bring himself to watch it skinned, but walked away with bowed head—a display of sentiment unusual in these barbarous places!

We were leaving to-day for another camp four miles to the westward. My old camels that brought us here I had dismissed at the instance of their owners, who considered that they would be safer in their own district, and because I found that I could raise local ones. The problem when carrying precious specimens is to avoid having them dashed to the earth and ruined by restive pack animals, consequently the selection of new beasts demanded infinite care.

Our route climbed westwards from the basin of 'Ain through rolling stony meadows; it was nowhere so steep as to make us dismount, yet here and there it crossed high ground commanding magnificent views of the whole mountain chain. To the northward spacious downs, gentle and undulating, rose to the skyline. Behind us they swept downwards till they merged into the forested ridges and valleys that tumbled to the plain of Jurbaib. I halted to take bearings on known points on the coast seventeen miles below, while one of my party raced down the grassy slope to a clump of trees that marked the spring of Isam, famous for its wild-growing, bitter limes, soon to return with his skirt full of them. Thence we reached the brink of a wooded vale, one of the upper sources of the Wadi Arbot, and moved down to camp in it at 1650 feet.

There I was soon to grow familiar with the cry of herdsmen—*whop—whop—whop r-r-r-r-r*, and the swish of moving cattle herds, for the pool of Khiyunt was only a little way up the valley, and the hills about my camp swarmed each morning, at intervals of half an hour or so, with droves on their way to or from watering.

The cattle wealth of these mountains must be prodigious by Arabian standards. Every man and woman possesses some head of kine. A few individuals of the Qara and Shahara may have upwards of a hundred, though the line

[78]

BELOW KHIYUNT—TYPICAL MEADOWS.

of prosperity starts at about twenty, and the owner of forty is passing rich. Only the cow calf is reared—for her milk and butter. One or two bulls will suffice a herd, so that the bull calf is slaughtered and eaten. His stuffed skin is placed before the mother at milking time that she may lick it and yield more freely—a universal Arabian practice recalling the camel *bau* of Oman.

The camel is bred in the wooded valleys below on a fairly extensive scale, but by limited groups, for its rewards to man are less and its care makes greater demands; even the sexual act necessitates man's assistance.[1]

Milch camels normally never know a saddle, and miserable mounts they make, as I know by costly experience. Their breeding is only for the production of he-camels, the stronger sex, to serve the transport needs of the province, and carry frankincense from the mountains to the coast, and to return with sardines to the mountains for cattle fodder.

Flocks are raised to a small extent on the Qutun, the grassy roof of these mountains, and also in the plain of Jurbaib, very largely also in the Zaulaul below Jabal Samhan. The flocks are of goats, not sheep, for mountain men think ill of mutton, and refuse to eat of it when they find themselves at a feast in Ehufar. Yet to be served with it is not a personal affront, as eggs or chicken would be. There are no dogs in these mountains and few donkeys. The latter are bred by Shahara and kept by them and Al Kathir.

As for cultivation, the Qara may sow a few beans in the western mountains or elsewhere, where there are no meadows to yield grass; eastward in Jabal Samhan under the same conditions they collect frankincense, or get the Mahra

[1] See page 214.

to harvest their groves for them. But the predominant means of life is cattle raising; for these mountaineers are essentially a race of non-nomadic herdsmen. Only males may milk cattle. No woman dares to touch the udders of cow, camel or sheep. It would be the greatest offence.[1]

Illness, such as failure of milk in their animals, is readily ascribed to the Evil Eye—*'Ain Balis*—which in consequence has terrors for them. Exorcism is by a frankincense rite, performed usually at sunrise or sunset, of which I was on more than one occasion an interested witness. The practitioner, the cow owner, brought an incense burner containing smouldering wood. He broke a fragment of incense into three pieces, and spitting upon them three times introduced them into the burner. The animal was held by two other tribesmen, one seizing it by the lower jaw, the other making it doubly secure by twisting its tail and lifting its near hind-leg off the ground.

And now the first tribesman circled the burning incense over the animal's head, chanting a rhymed sacrificial chant in the Shahari tongue.

'Look at this your sacrifice: frankincense and fire: from eye of the evil spirit: of mankind: from afar: of kindred: near by: and from afar: be redeemed if from me: be redeemed if from another: from the evil spirit: from mankind: I am a man: bringing expiation: for the Evil Eye: of man: of woman: look at this your sacrifice: frankincense and fire.'

[1] This is the contrary, as regards cows, of the rule observed by the Arabs of Oman, where a man would lose caste by milking. The Mahra and Al Kathir of these mountains allow their women to milk sheep, but not cows or camels.

EXORCISM OF THE EVIL EYE.

His companions now released their hold and the animal bounded off, swishing its tail merrily and doubtless no worse for the experience,[1] to join its kindred that had passed on up the valley.

'But you Badawin have no such practices?' I said, turning to a Bait Kathiri of the steppes.

'*Tawakkul al Allah*,' uttered with upturned eyes, was the pious response of this man—'but after cauterising a camel for lameness we sometimes break a twig to throw after her and say, "*Kesert 'aud: wa sher ma'aud*"—a twig [incense?] is broken: evil return not.'

Next morning I went over to witness the practice of *nafakh* or vaginal blowing, which is universal amongst these tribes, as a stimulant to milk production. The animal stood, its hind legs firmly bound, while a boy coaxed it with food to be still. The owner took a deep breath, and holding the cow's tail to the side, applied his lips to the vagina and emptied his lungs: he drew back for a moment, holding her with his other hand, so as to prevent the escape of air, then took another deep breath and repeated the performance, running his hand along the udder at the same time to see whether she was responding to his action. This practice is said sometimes to be undertaken by the practitioner with his mouth full of salt, but I have not seen this done, though I have often witnessed *nafakh* operations.

The Qara at Khiyunt seemed in a bad temper. At first I fancied I might be the cause of their dispute, and wondered if they meant to hold me to ransom—a thing never yet done, to my knowledge, in Arabia. There was a real risk of bloodshed, however, and of my being unluckily

---

[1] After cattle are stalled at night, women will sometimes go among them carrying burning incense.

[81]

involved. The disputants would settle by my tree, a ring of gollywog mountaineers, half-kneeling, with one hand resting on the muzzles of their upright rifles. They would begin peaceably enough, though with no sign of laughter, and with a running babble of voices, unlike the typical Arab gathering, with its major intervals of silence. Suddenly the tone would change, one man rising in his place and gesticulating wildly, to be met by another who would get up and harangue his adversary with an intensity that surely presaged trouble. Everybody now seemed to start shouting and nobody to listen. On this occasion a small boy tugged at his father, one of the most excited disputants, to come away. The others shouted gibes at the man as he went. Suddenly he turned round and walked back towards them.

'*Zir-r-r-r-r-r-r-han alaik*,' he snarled, drawing his forefinger across his teeth, a challenge to someone to come and fight it out, presumably with sticks or rifles, and the challenged one jumped up excitedly and fingered the bolt of his rifle, but wiser counsels among those present prevailed, and the parties were separated.

As in most tribal societies in Arabia, *hukm al hauz* or system of precedents and ancient sanctions is the law.[1]

This varies regionally, but is generally based upon the eye-for-eye principle, that the punishment may fit the crime. A recent example was told me by the Governor of Dhufar. A certain man was going on a journey and took

[1] The Shara' or Islamic code is distasteful to them, and runs only in the coastal townships where the government imposes it by force. It may be resorted to, elsewhere, in matrimonial cause, but civil disputes and crimes are the province of the *hauz*, who is the tribal law-man, holding office not infrequently by inheritance. He may, or may not, be the tribal shaikh.

THE SPRING OF KHIYUNT.

a *rabia*[1] from another tribe into whose country he was going. On arriving there the sacred law of protection was transgressed and the traveller found himself wounded with a bullet through the fleshy part of his thigh. A *hauz* heard the case and decided that he who had furnished the *rabia*, an innocent party but a member of the offending tribe, must submit to the infliction of a wound similar to that which the traveller had sustained. For this purpose a piece of stick was brought and sharpened skewer-fashion. This was thrust into the defendant's leg and a bullet was threaded and drawn in its path. By local canons the plaintiff's grievance was removed.

In Oman abuse of the *rabia* would be followed by war between the two tribes unless the offended party agreed to the ruling of the *hauz*, when he would receive from the offenders, *laum-al-wijh* (blame of the face), which is usually assessed at four hundred dollars. Murder, which in Arab tribal societies is almost invariably settled by blood-money varying between four hundred and a thousand dollars (or the equivalent in kind) in these Qara mountains is assessed prodigiously high, in theory something like five thousand dollars, which may take a lifetime to pay off, but settlement is usually complicated by a vendetta. The murdered man may be poor, so that his close relatives will in any case be impoverished, but collections are made from all members of the tribe who, as a point of honour or from immemorial custom, must bear the burden. A Shahari or a slave may be murdered almost with impunity, for he is not a tribesman, that is, an equal, and has no clan to avenge him.

The tribes of the central south have a poor reputation as

---

[1] A *rabia* is a representative of a tribe whose presence ensures protection from that particular tribe.

[83]

regards the *radud-as-salam*[1]—response to salutations. In other parts of Arabia it is commonly accepted that when two men meet, between whose tribes there is 'blood,' and one says to the other, 'Peace be upon you' and the other replies, 'And upon you be peace,' they have put aside their enmity for the nonce. For one now to take advantage of the other and slay him in his sleep, for instance, would be the deepest treachery, and would be punished by expulsion from the tribe with name besmirched. Not so amongst this lawless brood of the central south, who also neglect to observe the *thamn-al-batn* or 'stomach price.' This seems to be an extension of the law of three days' hospitality. If a South Arabian Badu has 'eaten the salt' of a man, that man and his goods are safe for a period of four days and four nights, the time for the last vestige of food to have passed from the Badu's body. Should the latter's tribe unwittingly raid the man during these four days they must and will return the loot. This *thamn-al-batn* is sacred with the other tribes of the southern fringe, but not with the mountain group.

Another peculiarity of these tribes is their addiction to oaths upon shrines (many of pre-Islamic origin) and the ordeal by fire. In cases of offences against their code, the oath or the ordeal will be adjudged necessary by the *hauz*.

Swearing on the Qur'an or in the name of God, as practised throughout Arabia, is nothing to them. They will do it and lie cheerfully. Sometimes, indeed, the accuser will not accept such an oath, but insist on the accused swearing by a sacred shrine. Powers of vengeance in varying degree

[1] Only within comparatively recent times would the Bautahara recognise a *rabia* at all.

are attributed to these shrines.[1] The foremost of the hierarchy appears as ferocious to local minds as Hazrat 'Abbas the hothead is to the Shi'ahs of Kerbela. The petitioner in a dispute will often demand an oath on one of the higher order, while the defendant will be prepared only to swear on a lower one. Public opinion in the tribe, which is formed from the degree of suspicion attaching to the accused, will then usually decide which shrine it must be. Oftentimes the accused will confess rather than face the consequences of false swearing.

'Ali, a well-known Kathiri of Dhufar, once stole a camel and killed and ate it. He was suspected and accused, and thought he would take the risk of swearing a denial on the shrine of Bin Othman. He swore; that night he was stung by a snake in the foot and his foot withered. He promptly betook himself to the man he had robbed, confessed his guilt and paid him the price of his camel, lest worse befall. 'Ali lives to this day, and if asked what caused his foot to wither will reply, 'Bin Othman.'

[1] The complete list of local shrines in the order of their avenging powers is as follows:

Name.	Place.
Salih bin Hud	(Between Hasik and Ras Nus).
Bir 'Ali	Murbat.
Bir 'Arabiya	Risut.
Shaikh 'Ali 'Afif	Taqa.
Shaikh 'Isa	Khor Taqa.
Zahair	Murbat.
Nabi 'Umran	Hafa.

There is in Hadhramaut the famous Qabr al Nabi Hud, the prophet sent to 'Aj, according to the Qur'an, and therefore a personage of the first rank, but perhaps the most famous anywhere is Bin Juwahir in Mahri country. It is so potent that murder will be tried by it. Two lesser local ones are Bin Othman at Rakhiyot and Nabi 'Aiyub, the only one to be found in the Qara Mountains.

But swearing on a shrine is not always sufficient. A suspected murderer may be called upon to undergo the ordeal by fire—*tamrit* or *besh'a*, and my Qara host, Shaikh Hasan, had as a young man been sent to the Hadhramaut to undergo the ordeal before the *mabesh'a*, had emerged vindicated, and lived, as he assured me, to believe in its efficacy.

Not every man, however endowed with these powers and with the requisite learning, will dare to practise for fear of the assassin's dagger, for so suffered Baihan, a blacksmith of the Yaham tribe, a famous *mabesh'a* or master of ordeals in Wadi Irma. 'But,' said my informant, 'who is there who will not accept the decisions of 'Ali bin 'Abdullah bin 'Abdul Wadud, whether he be *dheheb* or *hadid*, gold or iron, innocent or guilty.'

The ceremony takes place between the dawn and noon prayers. The parties assemble before the fire. The inquisitor inserts a knife blade into the fire, and after some time has elapsed the accused opens his mouth and puts his tongue out. The inquisitor then takes the tip of the accused man's tongue in his kerchief between finger and thumb with one hand; with the other he withdraws the red-hot blade, holds it to his own lips in benediction and then gives two smart raps, first with one flat side, then the other, laterally across the outstretched tongue. The accused should be able to spit at once if the portents are propitious, but two hours are allowed to elapse before the tongue is examined. If there are signs of swelling or undue burning, or gland affection in the neck, he is declared guilty and must pay with his life or as his accusers may require, but if there be none of these symptoms, he is adjudged innocent.

'But what of its justice?' I asked.

'It is true *wallahi*, by God, the fire is powerless to harm the innocent,' Sa'id replied, and I thought of Nebuchad-nezzar and his burning fiery furnace, and 'the furnace of affliction' of Isaiah. Sa'id's sophistication dated from journeys to the pearl fisheries of Oman and was increased by his being able to read a little. 'Does not the *mabesh'a*,' he continued, 'invoke God to witness by kissing the blade and saying:

   ' "In the name of God, the Compassionate, the Merciful,
   O fire, O fire, be cold and at peace,
   As it was to the Prophet Abraham (upon him be prayer
      and peace!)." '

'What, O Sa'id, is this you say concerning the Prophet Abraham?'

'Surely you have an account in the Old Testament?' he asked.

'No,' I returned.

'Don't you know,' he said, 'that the *Nasara*— Nazarenes —Christians, your forefathers, wishing to kill the Prophet Abraham, hurled him into a burning wadi, and God sent the Angel Gabriel and quenched the fire's appetite so that it did no hurt to the Prophet, and he was delivered?"[1]

I have already dwelt at length upon their pagan cults, but the account would be incomplete without a word about witchcraft, in which there is widespread belief. Old men are particularly liable to suspicion, and are sometimes killed on the grounds that they could never have attained so ripe an age except by communion with supernatural powers.

[1] The story is in the Qur'an, but not, of course, with Christians as the tormentors.

[87]

Death is often attributed to the spell of some suspected witch, who is forthwith persecuted. A tribesman of Bait ash Shaikh, who incidentally fired on us when we approached his camels in Wadi Afar, had as a young man killed his widowed cousin for a witch—an act which received public approbation, if indeed it was not actuated by public opinion; and a case occurred within a month of my arrival, where an alleged witch had been done to death by unknown hands. It appeared that she had long been accused, but had proclaimed her innocence and had submitted herself to the ordeal of fire. She emerged from the test vindicated, but even this failed to convince her tribe. It was a case of lynch-law in its most elementary form.

Murder in these mountains is, however, a common occurrence. Life appears to have a low value. Blood feuds actually divide the Qara one from another, and exist between sections of them and sections of Al Kathir and Al Mahra. None of these tribes acknowledge one paramount shaikh, and their relations one with the other vary from time to time. They seem to regard government as a superior tribal section.

At my camel side one day ran a Qara tribesman. The quality of his rifle and full bandolier, to say nothing of his self-complacency, showed him to be a man of standing, a *qubaili*. Salim was his name.

As I was riding on ahead of my party he took my camel rope from time to time to lead me along the path in the jungle least obstructed with overhanging branches, that I might not have to dismount.

'Are all infidels like you?' he presently asked. 'Big red men, with red beards and blue eyes?'

'Yes,' I told him.

[88]

'And how many cows have you got?'

'None, alas!'

He eyed me critically, wondering where my dollars could have come from.

'And is it true you *kuffar* find your money in the rocks of mountains?'

'Quite true.'

'God pardon you,' he returned, as though to ask forgiveness for the possessors of this black magic.

'Is there money in our mountains here?'

'I don't know, Salim.'

'Then why do you come here?'

'Because I like to travel, and meet the sons of men, and study all God's creatures.'

'But do you get money for it?'

'No, it costs me money,' I said. 'These specimens that I pay you a dollar each for, nobody in my tribe will give me a dollar for the whole lot.'

He looked at me strangely. 'And these mountains, are not you afraid to come into them?'

'No! Why should I be?'

'*Ya hamr al 'ain*'—*i.e.* O red of eye—he said flatteringly, 'Taimur the Sultan has been here only once.'

'But I love your country, Salim. It reminds me of my own,' I added.

Murder was the subject which seemed to obsess my questioner, however, for he kept returning to it. Did I know, he went on, that a man of his tribe had recently killed a government *askari*?

'Why did he do it?' I asked.

'Well, don't you know that in Wali Sulaiman's time government had murdered a Qarowi?'

'But that was fifty years ago,' I said, 'and this *askari* lately murdered wasn't born then.'

'True,' said Salim, 'but he came and mocked a Qarowi who was the nephew of the man Sulaiman had murdered. *Wallahi!* he cursed the memory of the man's uncle, so that the man was blinded by fury and shot the government slave.'

'Well, Salim!' I said, 'in our country we have one remedy and a good remedy it is. If one man kills another, we kill the murderer. His tribe dare not protect him, and government will not accept any requital but the life of the culprit.'

'Indeed,' said Salim, 'but with us, a life from the man's tribe will do; and did not government privily send out another slave who killed one of our men last year, so that now we are on level terms? But why did they kill Hamdan ibn Jasim (a stalwart of the tribe)? *Wallahi!* he was a good man, and I had rather that they had murdered thirty others and spared him. But *ham katib*—it is written.'

I enquired for Salim the next day as I had taken a liking to the man, and thought of taking him to Dhufar and giving him a small present. But there was no sign of him. He had fled, and for good reason, for I discovered afterwards that he was the actual murderer of the government *askari* and conceived himself as having a blood feud with the Sultan's government, which had indeed at the time of the soldier's murder wished to take Salim's life.

I thought of our hour together through the lonely forest yesterday, and breathed a sigh of relief.

VIII: THE QARA MOUNTAINS— FAREWELL

Dawn brought with it the hour of prayer. The figures of my companions sleeping everywhere on the grass now began to show signs of life. Individuals, Qara and Shahara, roused themselves to pray where they stood, using dry earth for the prescribed ablutions, and I wondered how their Shafi' tenets permitted this laxness; while my three Omanis of the more punctilious Ibadhi sect went off with their rifles—in these mountains no one would move a yard without rifle in hand—up the valley to the pool for the ablutions without which their prayers would be null and void.

The Muslim prayer duly offered five times a day by these wild men seemed more like an incantation in magic than any stirring of the spirit. Even with the orthodox, more importance attaches to correct ablution, the exact hour and posture than to the very words, or so it would seem to a disinterested onlooker; while these mountain men just gabble the lines aloud with impious haste, looking irreverently this way and that throughout.

As to women and prayer, about half the mountain women are said to pray; probably a liberal estimate, for I have never seen one in the act of prayer in public view, and here as elsewhere in Arabia it would be as unthinkable for men and women together to pray in public as to eat. Yet if report be true everybody, man and woman alike, observes the Fast of Ramadhan which again would seem of less spiritual than ritual significance—something that if neglected might bring down God's wrath.

Later came along five travelling Badawin of the steppe,

easily distinguishable, for environment and calling have left their mark. Legs not required to climb mountains are less muscular, and tend to bandiness with much riding; while feet that turn inwards are an unmistakable sign, when accentuated, of the man of the desert steppe. Their dress was typical too, *musur* and long-sleeved *dish-dasheh* reaching below the knees. Their names added confirmation, Bir[1] Annekid, Bir 'Uwaiga, Bir Annegim, on the pattern of son of Kate, son of Jane, etc., for the nomad practice is that a man as often as not is named after his mother instead of his father, a custom nowhere to be found among town dwellers, or these mountain tribes. These five Mahra had come by ship to Sudh, a frankincense port under Ras Nus, to collect dues of debtors (their slaves?) who were 'serving the frankincense' this season, and now they were returning to their place, the mighty Wadi Rama (sometimes Arma).

Next came another Mahri, but obviously a native of these mountains, bringing a snake which he held by the back of the neck between finger and thumb, while it coiled itself menacingly about his wrist. 'It has stung me,' he said, and holding up his other hand showed a pin-point of blood on his second finger, which was much swollen from being tied tightly round the bottom to prevent the poison from spreading. He now put the snake on the ground and it showed itself still full of life. As I edged away I saw him dart his hand out to secure it once more, but it was too quick for him, so that he caught only the tail. The monster immediately veered round and, with a sharp strike, stung his hand again, and I turned away sickened, for the bystanders declared it to be poisonous. Holding it out by the tail at

---

[1] *bin* (Ar.), *bint* (Ar.),=son of, daughter of, become in these languages *bir* and *birt*. Sometimes the *b* is elided, whence *ir* and *irt*.

arm's length, so that its head hung earthwards, he slid the other hand gently from the tail downwards to its middle, and then with a lightning movement grasped it again by the back of the head, and so squeezed out its life. I handed him over the customary dollar, but without the customary joke, for I was much exercised lest the man should die and the tragedy put an end to further hunting in these mountains, and even prejudice my larger schemes.

Yet another party of local Mahra, Bait Shaitana—the Devil's Family—suitably named, for they are of evil repute, headed by their crippled Shaikh Labkhit, came to see me. One of them wanted a drug against shortness of breath dating from a bullet wound received in a raid. He showed me where the bullet had entered and left his body, clearly to the hurt of both lungs.

'Then have you any medicine for a useless leg? The man isn't here, he can't walk.'

'Since when?' I asked.

'Since getting a bullet through the head.'

'There isn't any remedy in the world that will help,' I said, scenting paralysis.

'*Al hamdu lillah rabb al alimin,*' (Glory to God, Lord of the Two Worlds), said one, in a spirit of resignation, and the four men looked disconsolately at one another, but I felt myself being judged. Either I was too niggardly to help them, or I lacked the magic or skill which they had believed me to possess. I gave them some dates and sent them away with promises of reward if they could bring me a badger, most difficult of all specimens to collect.

After dark the shaikh and his four sons came over to my tree and entertained me with their mountain songs in Shahari, while the carcase of a coney I had shot that day was left out where I hoped its scent would attract a wolf or a fox. The big red Arabian fox—the local ones seem to have an abnormally dark ventral surface—is very common in these mountains, and whenever I swept a torch round my camp bed, I could be certain of lighting up a pair of bright and brazen eyes. My Arabs were supposed to keep watch by turns, but to-night I walked across to their tree to find them all fast asleep, the Kathiri whose watch it was having first hauled the coney up into the branches, so that there should be no gnawed remains in the morning to show his lapse. I touched him with my foot, whereupon he leapt up with a startled shout and grasped his rifle, as every Arab in such circumstances does, for there is no tribe without its hereditary blood-feud that makes each man of it fair game for some enemy. Sa'id now kept his vigil and was rewarded almost immediately by a fox that prowled in his way, but this scarcely made up for a panther which had been shot at and missed in the Wadi Nihaz.

These mountain tribes, being sedentary, have a sense of proprietary right not found in the Badawin. While in theory trees and grazing belong to no man, sections of tribes hold squatters' rights. Caves, too, are privately owned. They pass from father to son, but are not entailed, so that a present owner could at any time dispose of his, within the limits of his tribal section.

'But what of your caves bordering the steppe?' I asked a Bait Kathiri.

'As free as the air and the desert,' he said. 'To-day I occupy one and move on, to-morrow it is occupied by another. They belong to no man, but are of God's creation.'

In the villages of the coastal plain, where man makes a house to shelter himself, the first thing he does on staking it out is to hammer four long nails into the corners to keep out the Evil Eye. When the house is completed he slaughters a lamb on the threshold as a sacrifice to his walls enduring—a ceremony such as we perform in a degenerate fashion when ships are launched with a bottle of wine. In some parts of Oman when a new house is finished the prospective occupant will first slay a sheep, dabble his hand in the pool of blood, and smear the door-posts. A similar custom is also observed in the plain of Dhufar, but during building operations. The meat is eaten by the builders themselves and the blood is smeared indiscriminately over the walls. On the completion of the house the incomer dashes two hen's eggs on the threshold, two on the stair-way, and two on the upstairs doorway.

Fifteen is the customary age for both sexes to marry, but a boy is sometimes married before that age to prevent his acquiring bad habits. A girl too may be given in marriage before attaining puberty if her father is alive and gives his consent. If one party is of age, immaturity in the other is not held to be a hindrance to sexual relationship.

'But are these marriages common? What of your own?' I asked Shaikh Hasan.

'I was grown up, sixteen, perhaps,' he said, 'when my father found me a woman, but Labkhit here,' and he pointed to his eldest son, who appeared to be on the brink of manhood, 'I married him to his *bint 'am* (paternal cousin) two years ago. Now he has grown up he loves another, and when you dismiss him at Dhufar, he will, of your bounty, return and marry her.'

'And what of his cousin wife?'

'*Wallahi*, she is the fairest girl in the mountains, and has property as well, but he does not love her, but the other.'

'Is she young?'

'No, old!'

'Twenty,' I suggested.

'God forbid,' he replied, 'eighteen perhaps. He will divorce her and she also will marry another.'

It is scarcely surprising that marriage in these mountains is embarked upon in a spirit of levity. The bride is a marketable chattel. The most expensive costs about twenty cows (four hundred dollars), the cheapest one cow or even ten dollars—this marriage price is termed *gailap*. The bridegroom and bride's male representative, generally father or brother, descend to the plain where a *Qadhi* legalises the marriage, and on returning, the womenfolk of the tribe, preceded by men of her locality, conduct her to the cave of her spouse, where the only furniture will be a small carpet bought for the occasion. The man will have slaughtered a cow or perhaps two, if he is well off, as a feast, but beyond the *rabot* chanting of the men[1] there is no wild dancing and merry-making such as mark the rite of male circumcision.

Divorce is supremely easy for the man, as throughout all Arabia. He has only to tire of his wife and say so in the usual formula and she must go home to her father, with a parting gift of half a cow. Divorce by the woman is also easy, though financially more onerous, for she must return to him half the marriage price, which may amount to ten cows. Both are immediately free to marry again. Divorce does not require a Qadhi's sanction, so marriages and divorces are frequent. A man may by religious law have four wives at any one time, but the general rule is one, or at most two. If a woman has borne her husband children

[1] See Appendix VI.

[96]

LOOKING DOWN INTO WADI ARBOT FROM FUZAH.

he is usually unwilling to divorce her, but when he marries again, inevitably a young girl, it is customary for him to pacify the older woman with a gift equivalent to the new bride's marriage price. Thus women acquire wealth; indeed the independent possession of property by man and wife is regarded in a favourable light.

'How many children have you got, Instahail?' I asked of one of my Qara escort.

'Three,' he said, 'a girl and two boys.'

'From the same wife?'

'No, the girl is old and is the woman of Fadhlallah here. Her mother I divorced.'

'Why?' I said.

'She bore me nothing (that is, no sons). But it was she who asked for the divorce.'

'And did you claim half your *gailap* back?'

'More. I gave six cows for her, and demanded and got eight for her divorce.'

'And what *gailap* did you get for your daughter's marriage?'

'Four cows. She was worth more, but Fadhlallah is her cousin, and could afford no more, so I let him have her.'

'So you were six cows to the good. Two from your wife, and four from your daughter?'

He laughed. '*Wallahi!* I was a fool, for she married Bir Zaidi and bore him four sons.'

'And your second wife?' I enquired.

'She bore me three sons and six daughters, but only two of my sons live.'

'And supposing you meet the first wife who is the wife of another, what are your relations?'

'I may not salute her cheek or hand, but only ask "*het*

bi khar"—Are you well?'—(the usual greeting of the mountains).

A woman works under two extraordinary interdictions. She may not milk the animals; she may not cook the food. These are men's prerogatives. Her occupations will be grazing and tending cattle, collecting firewood and water, making pottery, cutting hay for the bed. But her main object in life is to bear children, preferably males. Contraception is unknown, and the idea abhorrent. Child-bearing is easy to her. She works up to one day before the birth and bears under a tree in the open or in a cave, in the standing position of a quadruped, with the assistance possibly but not always of one other tribal woman, who may be her mother or sister. She is fit for work the next day.

Illegitimacy is almost unknown throughout these mountains, despite the greater freedom enjoyed by women. This is due to easy marriage, divorce, and re-marriage, not to drastic penal measures such as are resorted to elsewhere in the peninsula. In Oman, for instance, a girl, unmarried or married, who had willingly transgressed and was with child, would be killed by her father, brother or paternal cousin, but not by her husband. Here she would be turned out of the tribe and permitted to go off to the coast to fend for herself. In Oman the man who had seduced her would, if the act was by her consent, escape penalty and be free to come and go. In the Qara Mountains he would be pursued by her male relations. If they could wound him with a sword so much the better, but if he fled, they would hunt his wife, or sister, or mother, and make the punishment fit the crime.

The girl of the mountains having been affianced while she is yet unfledged in body and mind is safe from irregular overtures. For a girl's first marriage it is the inviolable rule

[98]

for her father to provide a husband without consulting her. This rule in Ibadhi Oman is so rigorous among the elect that it would be shameful for a father to consult the wishes of his daughter or tell her of his visit to the Qadhi concerning the nuptials, so that she knows very little until the night she is conducted to her new home.

Here, on the other hand, the boy's father may speak to the betrothed girl herself, and will certainly speak to her mother, praising the qualities of his son. Once the mountain girl has been divorced and is considered a woman, her wishes concerning a future husband will be consulted, and cases occur of her marrying the man of her choice if he have the approval of her father. The right of *bin 'am,* the paternal cousin, elsewhere in Arabia universally accepted,[1] is not insisted upon in these mountains, except by the Mahra, where the sole right of disposal vests in the father.

We left Khiyunt. Our way climbed by a wooded bank out of the valley on its south-west side to a point 1850 feet above sea-level, where I was able to check my position by compass bearings on known coastal points. Thence we proceeded for the rest of the day on a course a little to the east of south, through rolling meadows of wild oats. The country became very stony and wooded and the valleys deeper as we went; so I dismounted and proceeded on foot with a butterfly net and killing bottle, sending the camels by an easier but longer way round.

I was thus separated from the rest of my party when a Kathiri Badu came running up behind, shouting in alarm.

'Stop, Sahib, stop! You have no *rabia* with you, and Bait Qutun have held up our camels.'

[1] The Prophet himself was the issue, not of cousins german, but very distantly related.

Bait Qutun, a section of the Qara, were in evil odour with Government at Dhufar; one of their headmen I had left in prison at Salala; they had refused to pay the year's taxes and were raiding.

However, I was in no mood for halting.

'*Wallahi!*' he shouted excitedly. 'Bait Qutun are capable of any evil. Did they not kill a government *askari* last year?'

I had no Qarawi at hand and in fact could do no good if I went back; so I decided to press on with the single slave that was with me in the hope that we would meet no evil in our way. The road of Hamirir led along a ridge that sloped on either hand into thickly wooded wadis, Arbot on our left hand, Nihaz, of Bait Qutun, on our right. And thus early in the afternoon, after a three hours' unprotected tramp, we arrived weary and footsore at the water-hole of Fuzah, overlooking the Arbot; my aneroid read 1350 feet.

For our camp at Fuzah I chose a tree at the top of a field of waving grass that looked out across a scene of much grandeur. The yawning valley of Arbot below us went sweeping round to where it debouches in the Jurbaib, the plain on its far side framed with a ribbon of silver sea. Here edging the plain the seaward slopes of the mountains stretched away in diminishing perspective to hog-backed Nashib, the great wadi entrances marked by spurs were discernible at this distance only by the shadow that each cast upon its neighbour.

Here at Fuzah was no lurking enemy, but only a young shepherdess passing, and from her I bought a goat to take down into the wadi that night and tie up over the water as decoy for a possible panther.

Two hours later my delayed camels arrived, the Qara being reluctant to talk of what untoward events had

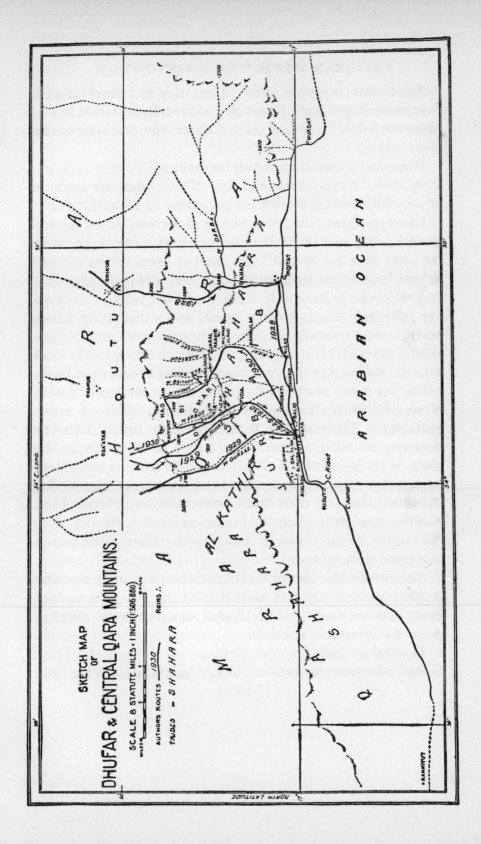

SKETCH MAP
OF
DHUFAR & CENTRAL QARA MOUNTAINS.

SCALE 8 STATUTE MILES. 1 INCH (1:506880)

AUTHOR'S ROUTES 1930 .... RUINS :.
TRIBES = SHAHARA

ARABIAN OCEAN

NORTH LATITUDE

befallen them upon the road. Their day had been exhausting, nevertheless they cheerfully took their water-skins and descended to the Arbot to bring water from the pool of 'In, Fuzah being merely a dirty trickle.

Magnificent climbers are these men, with clean muscular legs, and the eight hundred feet of steep descent followed by a climb with full water-skins across their backs was as nothing to them, nor did they find terrors in the undergrowth after nightfall, though it proved to be a veritable snakepit and I collected four snakes (two of them puff-adders) within the first twenty-four hours of arriving.

Two nights had passed. I lay awake at 3.30 a.m., a dark, raw, damp night, under low clouds and a dwindling moon, when suddenly a distant rifle shot rang out, and a little later came the faint sound of men chanting. My first impulse was to rejoice at the thought that my panther party sitting up over a sheep in the valley below were celebrating a kill. But it was a kill of a different kind.

A young Qara shaikh tripped against my bed in the darkness, startling me, for I had heard no footsteps; off he went in the direction of the chanting to investigate it, and on a hill but two miles away found the corpse of a Mahri tribesman, hot still with lately ebbed life, and bloody from a shot wound in the heart.

Early in the morning he and Shaikh Hasan came to me to suggest that we could not safely remain longer. We must move, and in this the Kathiris, a lazy pair, agreed. The memory of their own blood-feud with the Mahra rendered them unusually alert. They feared that the deed was that of some hothead of their tribe, so that their own lives would be exposed to peril.

'And who do you suppose did it, Shaikh Hasan?' I asked.

'God knows. Bait Jabob (a Qara section), I fear. Did you not hear a fusillade after the chanting? That came from their direction and sounded to me like a tribal celebration of the murder,' which indeed it proved to be. 'The Mahra killed a Jabobi last year in a raid. Bait Jabob have now had their revenge.'

'But the Mahri must have known. Why did he travel in Qara country? Was there not a truce between them?' I said.

'Yes, the Sultan made a truce for one year. That expired two months ago, and the two tribes between them then made another truce for another year.'

'So this was treachery?'

'*Ham katib*,' said the shaikh. 'It is written.'

A truce had indeed been signed. The signatory of that truce was none other than the murderer himself. He had sworn that his whole tribe would avoid shedding Mahri blood for a year. After two months he had himself dogged a Mahri's footsteps and slain him while he slept.

I knew the murdered man, Sahail. He was one of those four of the Bait Shaitana who had come to see me at Khiyunt but three days before, and had told me a folk story. A young man and a splendid specimen of his kind. That indeed is the way of the blood-feud. It is not always the murderer who is pursued; some outstanding man in the tribe, particularly if he be the culprit's cousin, is usually marked down and ambushed, as on this occasion.

'But why, O Hasan, did it take place here close to my camp? Whose territory is it? Bait Jabob's?'

'No, my own!' replied Shaikh Hasan, 'but by our sanctions I am not to blame, for he had no *rabia* from me. If a *rabia* had been with him, then would our faces have been blackened by an abominable crime. If Bakhit (pointing to his son) were *rabia* to anyone killed by the Qara, we could not rest until it were revenged. I would rather Bakhit were killed than that the man under my protection should die and my son live.'

The speech was according to the book, but I thought how much more suitably it would have come from a noble Arab tribe.

Shaikh Hasan and the perpetrators of last night's murder were sworn enemies, for the Qara are much divided among themselves, yet one detected in his faint damning a certain gratification that a Qara life had been avenged.

I turned to the Kathiri. 'You must be relieved it was by no Kathiri's hand.'

'God pardon them, we Badus respect a truce, but in these mountains there is treachery. The Qara and Mahra think naught of outraging conditions to which they have called God to witness. *Wallahi!* even the *rabia* is not sacred with them. Do you know—but you will not believe it—Sahail who was murdered last night drank the milk of his murderer overnight. God forgive them!'

I decided to descend to Dhufar on the following morning and bring to an end my sojourn in these mountains. The hyenas, at least, would not regret my going. But, in spite of recent sinister events the thought of going was an unhappy one, for I was leaving what surely must be a unique land in all Arabia, a land of perpetual feasts for the artist, of endless surprises for the anthropologist, a naturalist's paradise, and to me, the wayfarer, a source of much interest and delight. On this last journey my party did not retire with the sun as was their wont, and the camp was alive until far into the night with brisk noises as they went

IN THE BED OF WADI ARBOT.

about roping up my trophies[1] and preparing packs against an early start.

I slept fitfully, and awoke to look down in farewell upon the valley of Arbot, softly alluring as it came to life from its still slumbers. The crickets seemed to be silenced by the false dawn. From the top of the hill where my Arabs were worshipping, came an indistinct drone, like a mumbled prayer heard distantly in some vast cathedral. The stars grew dim in a slaty sky that already turned amber over the sea whence a great golden disc came blazing up.

The long grass rustled, stirred by morning airs, and in the trees birds twittered with the joy of a new-found warmth. The hill crests lit up while the soft valley between them still lay hushed under a purple mantle.

But now the sun is risen, radiant, all-pervading. Only mighty Jabal Nashib with its back to him dare still resist, its dark mass gaunt beside the shimmering sea. The passing minutes paint the scene in brighter colours—the clouds like a mass of thistle-down have changed from green to salmon pink, and the sky is an intenser blue, the deep valley has at last awakened, and thence the bare-bosomed foothills beyond are delicately tinted pinks and mauves, and above them, meadows edging the sky bask in a golden light.

---

[1] My collection from these mountains was composed of the following:

Hyenas	5	Tree rats	2	Lizards	28
Foxes	3	Tree bats	2	Snakes	21
Wolf	1	Scorpions	16	Butterflies	96
Conies	2	Centipedes	4	Dragonflies	61
Badger	1	Various Insects*	112	Locusts	50
Identifications are given in Appendix II.				Frog	1

* Praying mantis, spiders, hornets, etc.

IX: DHUFAR—THE ELEVENTH HOUR

DHUFAR fort. It was 6th December. I was recovering from an attack of dysentery that had kept me to my bed for three days since I returned from the mountains.

Two months had passed since I had set out from Muscat; six weeks and more since my emissaries had disappeared into the sands. But those sands seemed to me to be even more pitiless than their own evil repute and I despaired of receiving news. Perhaps my envoys had been intercepted by their enemies and put to death, wasting all my years of preparation and the largess I had so carefully designed and cunningly dispensed.

To-morrow the Muscat State gunboat *Al Sa'idi* was arriving. I must return in her. Surely there would be official instructions brought by the Commander's hand to do so. Some situation might have arisen in Oman, a war perhaps, a riot, or even lesser mischief to require my presence. In any event, I was due back.

A messenger ran through the streets below the fort keep. The crowd kept barring his way to hear his news, for he had galloped from Murbat after hearing a ship's salute, and seeing the red flag of Muscat flying at her forepeak, and to be first into the market-place with these wares always brought rewards. From the housetops around rang out a fusillade to spread the good news, while within the fort I sat ruminating upon the failure of my designs. Last year a caravan had taken me some two hundred miles northward to the very edge of the sands—to be driven back, it is true —but this year I had not even gazed beyond the Qara Range.

[106]

Half an hour may have passed in such gloomy reflections and the sun was near to setting when my servant Muhammad came bounding up the steps.

'News! Sahib! Two Badus have just arrived in the bazaar from the desert, and they say they are an advance party of some forty others with camels, and of them are Ma'yuf and Khuwaitim whom you sent. To-night they halt over the water-hole of Forum; to-morrow, *insha'llah*, they will be coming down to the Jurbaib.'

Joyous news indeed if true; but the gunboat would also arrive for me to-morrow. Had my desert party—if such it was—come a day too late? Was I to be cheated at the eleventh hour?

I looked down into the fort courtyard upon forty dainty riding camels and as many ragged Badawin, that had come two hundred miles at my secret bidding out of the sands of Rub' al Khali. I looked out seawards where *Al Sa'idi* rode at anchor. And now her gallant commander, Captain Salih al Mandhari, came ashore cheerful as always, and expecting to take me back to Muscat. I eagerly ran through the sheaf of letters that he brought. The first bore the Sultan's crest. It was dated from India and was in that intimate and friendly hand I knew so well. I read it a second time, a third time, and in the strength of the confidence which marked our relations for six years, I made a decision. I would send the gunboat back without me to Muscat. I would attempt the return by another way. I would join fortune with those attractive ruffians below, strangers all, and take the plunge with them into the uncharted wilderness.

Khuwaitim and Ma'yuf brought Shaikh Salih to see me, and all were at pains to enlarge upon the difficulties they had had in getting the party together, and persuading it to come, the dangers of encountering their enemies, the hunger of the road (to which the condition of their camels bore witness), and lastly and inevitably the rich reward they expected at my hands.

I took an immediate liking to Shaikh Salih. He bore the magic name of Bin Kalut—Kalut, the most famous lady in all the sands, daughter of a famous warrior, and mother of three warrior sons, for to have kindred who destroy their enemies (and cleave to their friends) is of the very essence of nobility in this environment. Salih was a short man, big of bone, with a rather large head, bald—unusual for a Badu, even of Salih's sixty years, and a heavy jowl. His brow was big, perhaps from his baldness, and his eyes large, his countenance open and frank, his voice slow and measured; he inspired confidence.

I swore him to secrecy and unfolded my plans. I wanted no less than to cross the desert from sea to sea.

'But at what place do you want to come out?'

'Wherever it is possible,' I said. 'Riyadh, Bahrain, Abu Dhabi.'

'Impossible, Sahib!' he said emphatically.

'What is possible then?'

'We can take you into our country, the Rashidi *dira* of the southern sands, and bring you back, and God deliver us from the Sa'ar, but we cannot take you into the grazing grounds of another tribe.'

I was adamant. Either I must cross the desert or never start at all. It would profit me nothing to do as he suggested.

'But,' returned Salih, 'the Fast of Ramadhan falls a month hence. Who will travel at such a time, when he should be fasting in the bosom of his family?'

SHAIKH SALIH BIN KALUT.

Naturally Salih was in no mood to travel in Ramadhan or to undertake a longer journey than was necessary. But a Badu cannot be browbeaten. An inflammable person himself, he will not stand bullying, but he understands resolution, though it is well to give him a day or two to accommodate his mind to any idea that at first is unpalatable to him.

The next day Salih came to see me again, and I once more set forth my irreducible requirements, for which I was prepared to pay generously. I importuned him, lest I be driven to embark in the gunboat for Abu Dhabi and enlist 'Awamir help for my designs from that side. I hoped he would come with me in that event; this with my tongue in my cheek. Salih was impressed by this hint that I had the means of achieving my ends without Rashidi assistance (though I had not, despite the 'Awamir being old friends), and he became more amenable.

'But, Sahib, you don't understand. What you are asking is not in my power to do. Within Rashidi country I can and will take you as you wish, God sparing us from the enemy, but where you want to go is Murra territory. I am no *rabia* for the Murra, and dare not enter their marches myself without their consent and protection. I do not know whether they will have you in their place. I cannot give you the undertaking you want.'

It was a fortunate occurrence that *Al Sa'idi* was here. If the Badawin were in earnest about the difficulties, then it would be idle to start on a journey with them; their resistance would harden as we went along, an experience that befell me the previous year when I started without a clear understanding. To start and fail meant returning to Dhufar a month hence defeated in my major aim and proceeding thence to Muscat by dhow, a forbidding prospect. So I must for the moment keep *Al Sa'idi* standing by.

A third day passed and the Badawin from the desert were reported to be getting restless, for they had expected money and I had given them only food and camel rations.

Salih came again protesting that he was in an awkward position, with myself and his men equally unreasonable. There were murmurs about my objectives, and the most improbable motive would be accepted by these simple and gullible folk. It was essential to win their confidence and to disabuse their minds of ulterior motives, such, for instance, as spying out the number of their camels for the ear of Bin Sa'ud or the Sultan Taimur or some other hypothetical collector of dues, so I deemed it wise to dissociate myself from any external authority, and avow, what was indeed the truth, that I made my journeys first because I liked travelling, and secondly to serve the cause of *'ilm* (science), which my tribe considered honourable.

'Well, Shaikh Salih, and what is the position now?'

'As I told you, Sahib, I want to help you, but cannot promise what you want.'

I was indeed aware of the genuineness of Salih's argument, but it would never have done to accept the position that it implied. Obviously Salih was not in a position to guarantee the protection of another tribe, especially for a foreigner and an avowed non-Muslim.

'But you know well, Shaikh Salih, that the Murra are your friends; if I pay them well and they see that I have your goodwill they will make a way.'

'I believe they will, Sahib, if there is pasture and water, but only they know the way into their sands.'

This was my real object; to obtain the sworn support of

Salih that he himself would come the whole way with me, and work to ensure Murra co-operation, and their marching through the fasting month of Ramadhan. If he did these things he should have at my hands a camel, a rifle and a robe. In our bargainings I induced Saiyid Sa'ud the Wali, who had just returned, to arbitrate between us, for he was a man of good standing and much respected, and I was deeply grateful for his kindness. As a pious Muslim too he bore witness to Salih's oath to me that I would be under his protection, and that no treachery should befall me subject to two provisos, which were beyond his control—the *gom*, *i.e.* enemy raiding party—and the will of God.

I felt, knowing Salih's fatalistic standards, that the latter proviso would render the oath nugatory, but I was careful not to press for a precise definition, lest it raise a delicate religious issue, which would have been most inopportune. It was the spirit and not the word that I valued.

So I had Salih's sworn promise that he would co-operate in my design in good faith: 'But none of these Badawin with me must know,' he added. 'They have come expecting you to visit Dakaka, our present camp, as you arranged with Sahail the Rashidi last year. They heard of your bounty to him, and that is what has brought them to you—*toma!*— greed. Avarice. That is the Badu's burning passion. But it is well. When we come to the water of Dhahiya their camels will be exhausted. You shall dismiss them while I ride ahead and arrange that others come there to carry us on.'

'But what of the way, Shaikh Salih?'

'War, Sahib, war, the Ghafariya of the Ma'arab[1] there

---

[1] There are two hostile political factions, Hinawi and Ghafari, to one or other of which every tribe in South-east Arabia owes allegiance. Superficially the terms Hinawi and Ghafari would appear to date from a dynas-

is blood betwixt them and us; they are strong. We shall not, *insha'llah*, meet them upon the road. But the Murra, them you must meet else you cannot go on.'

We had to compute our precise number and rations most carefully. It was clear that with one set of camels or even two, I could not possibly carry loads across these hungry sands in the quick marches I desired; the beasts would lose condition. 'Four relays,' said Shaikh Salih, 'do not count on less than four relays.' He thought that their numbers could be reduced as we went along, but in the first march across the steppe, exposed to the Sa'ar, it would not be safe to move with less than forty. For financial reasons I would have preferred a smaller party, but my counsellor was right. Indeed, forty might be inadequate, remembering that raiding parties of two hundred and three hundred are not unknown in these southern borderlands where the shedding of blood, and the robbing of camels and rifles are among the normal activities of life.

'And if we meet a party larger than ourselves, Salih?'

'There is no might and no power except in God the Almighty.'

tic squabble over succession in Oman in the early eighteenth century, but, as I have observed elsewhere, they are of much deeper significance, for, generally speaking, the Hinawi label coincides with the tribes of avowed Qahtani descent and the Ghafari label with those of Ma'adic or Nizari origin, and all other non-Yemeni stock. Within limits, therefore, the division is in origin racial. These labels apply as far west as the Sa'ar tribe, who are regarded as Ghafari, whereas Al Kathir, of which Ar Rashid are a section, are Hinawi. So also is the central *bloc* labelled Ghafari, though in South Arabia as distinct from Oman, there is no factional solidarity, and these labels have no political significance.

Ma'arab and Mishgas are used in South Arabia as regional terms for westwards and eastwards of Dhufar respectively. Thus the Sa'ar and all other western tribes are Ahl al Ma'arab.

Rations were to consist of butter, rice, dates and flour. The quantities would determine the numbers of pack animals required to carry them on each successive stage of the journey. Too much food would be a great source of expense, not so much on account of its value, as because of camel hire, for these desert camels are small and light, and cannot carry a big load; too few rations would effectively destroy all chance of fulfilling my aims. I must budget for four separate relays of men: forty, thirty, twenty, fifteen. The first party would have their rations issued to them individually before starting; the pack animals would be carrying rations of the next three parties. The process would be repeated at each stage. By this progressive reduction I estimated I should require fifteen pack camels at the outset.

Accurate and careful organisation was essential to success, but could not itself ensure it. We might meet a larger party of Sa'ar upon the road (news of the three thousand silver dollars I carried would bring upon me a thousand raiders), while we would reach the desert only to face three more incalculable factors, the first being the Murra attitude towards my passage through their country, the second whether the pastures and water-holes were good enough this year, and the third the possibility of finding Arabs prepared to risk their camels and themselves and travel during the fasting month of Ramadhan. The Murra attitude was at present indeterminable. No stranger had ever been into this territory, certainly no white man and Christian. Would they co-operate? Shaikh Salih thought the chances were even. It was in this uncertain mood, after being held up for two months, that I marched from Dhufar on 10th December 1930.

X: OVER THE HILLS AND FAR AWAY!

A STREAM of camels issued from the town gate of the Husn quarter, where an interested crowd of black gollywog humanity had assembled to see our departure and to commit us *fi aman Illah*—to God's protection.

The departure of the Badu is ever sluggish; his thoughts are with his camel under its strange and heavy load; then he himself has forgotten something he wanted from the bazaar which he sees but once in many moons, and he hands his camel over to a neighbour's charge and goes back to dally there for an hour or more.

Khuwaitim came riding up with three giant iron nails in his hand. 'Did you remember these?' he says as he hands them up to my servant. 'You will require them for a hob in the sands, where you will find no stones for your fire.' So we halted at Salala while the blacksmith was made to produce a dollar's worth, to complete the deficiencies of the entire party.

'Drink, Sahib!' and two Badus handed me up a bowl of water drawn from the mosque well, and after I had had my fill, themselves squatted down, for it is *'aib*—shameful—for a son of the desert to drink standing, and drank after me— a display of tolerance gratifying to me after residence in 'Iraq, where close contact with the priesthood of the Holy Places of the Shi'ah persuasion has had its effect on tribal custom in such matters.

We had scarcely gone five miles, my party straggling out across the plain in aimless formation, when as we approached some camel thorn, shouts came from the rear, 'Let the camels eat,' 'Let the camels eat,' and the tribesmen, upon overtaking us, counselled our dismounting, their excuse being that Shaikh Salih was still behind. No sooner had I dismounted than they off-saddled; the animals were knee-hobbled by the two forelegs, and so sent off to feed at the bushes near by. We were there for the night. The rations were heaped up into a single pile, as precaution against arch-thieves of the district, for whom the sight of such plenty must have been a sore temptation. Shaikh Salih knew their kind too, for when he came along a little later he stood amidst the baggage, loudly exhorting his party.

'*Ya Juma'a! Ya Gom*'—O Assembly! O braves!

'*Zad al Wazir*'—The stores of the Wazir!

'*Fi aman Illah*'—are in God's keeping.

'*Wa fi amankum*'—and in your keeping.

'*Tam tam*' came an acquiescent chorus from my Badawin, distributed and busied upon a multitude of activities. Some were cutting riding-canes from thickets; some oiling their water-skins to make them tight against the long marches ahead; the owners of pack animals sat sewing up sacks of hay as improvised pack saddles, for the ready-to-wear article does not exist in this remote corner of Arabia, and I had to buy a supply of sacks at Dhufar; others were looking over their bazaar purchases, including a large aluminium kettle, while one fine youth romantically fondled a golden coloured mirror, probably destined to call a sparkle to the wondering eyes of some frail and cherished being in the sands. 'Come and see *ahfat an naga*,' shouted Shaikh Salih, who sat on the ground with a large sail-maker's needle in his hand, bending over a camel that was held down on her side by a few Arabs in the customary way; one held the head turned back along the body; another had a twitch on her upper lip, a third held one leg stretched out behind. The operation was to sew a small leather patch on the side of the foot over an abrasion which had been caused by the unaccustomed stony tracks of the mountains; it would be a protection on the morrow's journey.

No sooner did the Badawin come to the end of their tasks than they fell to arguing, as they inevitably do, about the inequality of the loads, each Badu being jealous for a light task for his own camels: as a result the loads were reshuffled and I found myself a sufferer thereby, for the mount I had ridden was taken from me on the pretext that she was not good enough, and on the morrow I found myself riding an animal much less to my liking. A day never passed without some such wrangling about loads, for the camel is her master's dearest dear, and he will cease fighting her battles only with his latest breath.

Two parties lined up for sunset prayer, one led by Shaikh Salih, the other by my Karabi *rabia*. According to my servant, their performance was in pleasing contrast to that of my Bait Kathir party of the previous year, men who prayed not in a line but individually, and though they declaimed aloud were woefully ignorant of the words which to instructed ears became a sorry jumble.

We were mounted by seven next morning, and after two hours' ride across the plain towards Wadi Nihaz made Ghaur Fazl, a hole in the grassy foothills. So far as I could ascertain from local enquiries, this is the only place answering to Bent's description of a natural phenomenon he identified with Ptolemy's Diana Oraculum. I confess to a sense of disappointment. It was unusually large, certainly some twenty feet across, and round its top is a circular mound which may conceivably conceal a wall as described by Bent, but appears to contain excavated material as well.

[116]

The sides of the gaping hole are of bright red clay and show signs of having, at one time, been bricked or stone-lined. A pebble dropped into it took approximately two seconds to reach the dry bottom. It may therefore be assumed to be a hundred feet deep. The Qara attributed it to Minguwi, most famous of their mediæval rulers, as they do every old relic, and to me also, Ghaur Fazl was the work of man's hands. Scattered around it, indeed throughout these foot-hills, were beehive-shaped mounds the height of a camel. They are not archæological remains, as Bent suggests, but ant-heaps[1]—in the language of the mountains, *izdirit*.

A mile beyond, within the entrance to the Nihaz valley and on the west side of it, was the famous cave of Sahaur, a black, gaping hole two hundred and fifty feet above, amidst a dense forest of trees. Thither I had climbed with Sahail, a Bait Qutuni, and grandson of that Sahail with whom the Bents came to see this cave, though they did not enter. Its mouth proved to be a yawning alcove a hundred feet wide and some forty feet to its roof of stumpy weathered stalactites whence rock pigeons fluttered at our approach. Legend has it that *jinns* share a dark existence here with snakes and scorpions, but when I pointed to a tiny low hole on the left side of the caverned mouth which alone gave entrance to the interior and asked for volunteers, my party of five men, *jinn*-believers to a man, said that they were ready. So we cheerfully said *tawakkul al Allah* and one by one slithered feet foremost into the dark sloping hole. It was so small that we could enter only lying flat, but a wriggle of ten feet brought us into a large inner chamber of irregular shape with comfortable head room, and utterly dark. My torch showed its formation to be a

[1] Ant-hills are *sidr* in Shahari, the ants themselves *izdirit*.

[117]

pure dazzling white crystalline rock. There was a slow but continuous drip of water from innumerable stalactites of slightly darker hue, and small stalagmites sprang up in places from the floor. A giant pillar had a basin-like annexe some three feet in diameter on an almost perfect hollow hemisphere of the same formation. This chamber led to others, their entrances often very narrow, the one we explored being only accessible on all fours. The natives say (though few, if any, have dared its hazards) that the cave continues as a series of connected chambers for miles back into the mountains, and at one point is so spacious that a stone thrown by a man will not reach its roof. It was so stiflingly hot and sweaty inside that I stayed only for half an hour to collect some geological specimens and a bat (one chamber proved to be a veritable cage of bats) before leading the way out with my torch. One by one we emerged into the refreshing air and light of day.

We now climbed the Aqabet al Hamra on the opposite side of the valley through thickly wooded slopes, reaching the top an hour and a half later, where just short of our old camp of Fuzah my aneroid read 1300 feet. Thence onward through undulating meadow country on a northerly course to halt at half-past two at Lehez (2370 feet), just below the Qutun.

Khuwaitim came to me. 'The water of Aduwiz,' he said, 'lies a mile to the west. It is like honey. To-morrow we Badawin will water our camels and fill our own water-skins at Hanun, but the water of Hanun is not like the water of Aduwiz. It is better that we halt here for your water-skin to be filled with this sweet water.'

'Why, oh why dissemble, Ya Khuwaitim,' I thought, for the real reason, and a very good one too, was that here were some *ghaf* acacias, a most unusual tree in these latitudes at this height, and incomparable food for our camels. I readily commended the halt, for the best way to win esteem was to show not indifference but solicitude for the camels' welfare.

The party straggled uphill into camp and turned to replacing the old straw stuffing of their pack-saddles with the new standing hay. Shaikh Salih, like Shaikh Hasan on my mountain expedition, was the most active of all his tribesmen in collecting firewood, for tribal shaikhs lead their followers in war and work alike.

The inescapable crowd of natives surged round our camp-fires, and my Badawin showed their previous anxiety for our rations and kit, gathering them into a heap upon which some of them slept while the others lay round it, for they ascribe to the mountain men almost supernatural powers of thieving.

'There is only one medicine. Would you like to see a "cure," Sahib; an old patient is in the camp,' and they brought along a man of the Qara. After some persuasion he allowed his indigo mantle[1] to be drawn back, and there appeared a withered arm. The offending hand had been cut off in accordance with the 'Law of God'—Shara' law—by order of the Sultan when on his first visit to Dhufar. The man had been caught red-handed thieving, and the appointed slave at the fort had made a good job of it with one fall of the axe. Good people saw in it a religious act, but as a deterrent its effect was short-lived.

The southerly wind veered round to the south-west and blew cold at this altitude. The sky was veiled with low dark clouds, and the heavy dew vexed me, for I was carrying no tent with me into the sands. Previous journeys made me fear that the Murra or other Badawin would so resent the camels having to bear the intolerable burden of my tent as

[1] *subaigha.*

[119]

to prejudice them against the trip. So I left it behind, and regretted it during these two December nights in the hills. The wet and dry bulb thermometers registered almost alike, my upper blanket was wringing wet and the pillow so damp that it had to be turned over during the night. I wore my Arab head-dress as a shawl to sleep in, but woke up with eyes sticky from external moisture.

The camels couched around the fires sat all night contentedly chewing the cud. They were astir with their masters' dawn prayer, and stood like so many statuesque sentinels, waiting till a little more light and warmth should sharpen their appetites. Then their masters came to drive them off to crop the nearest thickets until we set out on the day's march.

Our north-westerly course led up into the Qutun, the roof of the Qara Mountains, and I turned in my saddle to take a last glimpse of the Indian Ocean three thousand feet below. Here the meadows ceased and gave place to stretches of *gudelat*, a large gum-yielding shrub. Children, in the hope of *bakhshish*, ran at my side to hand up plants that they hoped would excite my favour, now *halgum*, a tomato-like fruit used to clean hides, now *subur*, a cactus whose bitter sap is medicine for the belly and balm for the eye, whilst the skin yields a greenish-yellow dye beloved of local ladies. Bare bleak hills about us, with rough going, drew out the party into single file. The divide passed, we began to descend the far side of the Qara Mountains by the torrent beds of Qabliya (2500 feet). Our route lay at the bottom of its bleak gorge, sculped on both sides with deep cavities—one of these Reddit, a shelter for flocks—while the boulders lying in the valley were speckled with a white efflorescence.

'*Rahman ar Rahim*,' muttered Shaikh Salih, riding immediately behind me, as we passed some graves.

'We bare our heads in the presence of a corpse,' I said.

'And how do you bury your dead? Is it true the *kuffar* burn them?'

To burn a body destined for physical resurrection would be sacrilege indeed, and I deemed it wise to pass over the growing practice of cremation.

'We take our dead into the masjid,' I said, 'and pray over them to Allah, and then we wrap them in a white shroud (this very important!) and so bury them in the ground.'

'*Wallahi Muslimin!*' said one of the Rashidis approvingly.

But later in the day I found my view of religion not so widely shared. A Bait Kathiri youth ran at the side of my camel and seemed very friendly disposed. By and by he dropped a little behind and I heard myself being discussed.

'They are a truthful people,' said Shaikh Salih.

'You don't say so,' said the youth.

'And success is theirs in this world!'

'*Rubi y'hassabhum*.' 'My Lord will hold them to reckoning (in the next),' came the youthful response.

'*Istaghfirullah*.' 'May God forgive them,' said the shaikh, as if apologising for acting as my guardian.

The aneroid fell gradually as we moved along the gorge and after four miles we came to the soft sand of the wadi bed of Sa'atan. Before us was a panorama of pale sandstone hills, characteristic in their conical and pyramidal shapes. Amongst those that bore names the most conspicuous were the Horn of Fahad, which lay due west, and soon before us, bearing north-west, the Horn of Shaiba, below which we proposed to camp for the night. Beyond these nearer hills we could see a vast waste of red rolling country, its ruddy wastes in pointed contrast to the hills and their wooded meadows behind us.

Hidden in these desolate wadi beds, which drain north across the steppe, flourishes the wild *mughur*, frankincense tree. In appearance it is a young sapling, having almost no central trunk, but from near the ground there spring out a clump of branches which grow to a camel's height and more, with ash-coloured bark and tiny crumpled leaves. One of my men leapt off his camel to bring a specimen of the sap in the raw condition on his dagger blade for me to see; it resembled green transparent lard and was very fragrant. The tree begins to bear in its third or fourth year. The collectors, women as well as men, come to make slight incisions here and there in the low and stout branches with a special knife. A gum exudes at these points and hardens into large lozenge-shaped tears of resinous substance which is known as frankincense (*liban*). After ten days the drops are large enough for collection, and the tree will continue to yield from these old incisions deepened as necessary at intervals of ten days for a further period of five months. After this the tree dries up and is left to recover, the period varying from six months to two years according to its condition. Collection of the *liban* is made chiefly during the summer months. It is stored in the mountain caves till the winter, when it is sent down to the ports for export, for no country craft put to sea during the gales of the summer south-west monsoon. This delay enables the product to dry well, though normally it is ready for export in from ten to twenty days after collection.

From Bombay it finds its way to the Temples of the East, a little being kept in Dhufar where the good housewife may put an incense-burner under the bed at sunset to keep

A FRANKINCENSE TREE.

away evil. Frankincense has from the earliest times been a precious spice and the most acceptable of offerings. It was used by the Egyptians to preserve the bodies they held sacred, Pharaohs and others of royal blood, and crocodiles; it was burned before the tabernacle of the Israelites in the days of Moses, the hill of frankincense is mentioned in the Song of Solomon, and it was brought as a gift, with gold and myrrh, to our Infant Lord.

It is found growing, as a commercial crop, only in Central South Arabia between two thousand and two thousand five hundred feet in a region[1] which happens to be identical with the territorial limits of the Qara tribe, from long. 53°00 E. to long. 55°21′. Its occurrence on the edge of the unique summer rain belt of Dhufar suggests that climatic conditions favourable to its growth exist nowhere else in the peninsula. If so, this region is not improbably the famous frankincense region of historic Arabia. In any case, the famed groves of the Yemen and Hadhramaut have become insignificant; the tribes of Dhufar remember them not.

For an hour we passed through a grove of young frankincense trees scarred with the marks of recent milking. Its Qara owners, herdsmen and not pickers, are content to rent it to Kathiri and Mashaiyikh for half the produce.

---

[1] Groves are graded by size into, (1) *manzila*, of great extent, of which the most famous are Afaur, Asug, Afar, Gizilaut, Zuwa, Ata, Tanshit, Qaim and Amaut; (2) *hawil*, of a size workable by five collectors or fewer.

There are three varieties of frankincense: *negedi* (*nejdi*), *shazari* and *sha'abi*, their quality descending in the same order. *Negedi*, the silver variety, is the product of the intramontane uplands of the Samhan and Qara mountains; *shazari* is the product of the mountain region of that name at the junction of the Qamar and Qara ranges; and *sha'abi* is a poor quality of the plain around Risut. The frankincense ports from west to east are Jadhib, Rakhiyut, Risut, 'Auqad, Salala, Hafa, Taqa, Murbat, Sudh and Hadhbaram.

This point, but a bare twenty miles from the sea, marks the northward limit of the settled tribes—the Qara, Shahara, and mountain elements of Al Kathir and Mahra; it also roughly approximates to a geological division. Behind us were the limestone mountains, Upper Cretaceous to Eocene; before us was a great wilderness of sandstone steppe sloping down a six days' march to the edge of the sands, the scene of a sparse and sporadic nomad life of Bait Kathir, Mahra and Bait ash Shaikh Badawin.

It was a joy to be in the saddle again, and a joy to have left the busy humdrum world of Dhufar behind for these wide clean spaces. My companions were as yet songless on the march, as indeed were the other South Arabians of my last journey, and I missed the rousing camel chanties of the march in Oman; only Sahail[1] occasionally broke into song. Still, they were merry enough conversationalists, even if their subjects were limited to camels, rifles and women. The conspiracy of silence of European convention is completely absent; with it the element of conscious indecency. It was like schoolboys ridiculing a bad bowler, or deriding one of their number who persistently failed to 'convert' a 'try,' for they see no shame in joking about each other's impotence with women, and Sahail, the most persistent of them, wondered whether in my medicine box of magic I carried no aphrodisiac. But one thing was even more important, Could I divine water?

Qarn Shaiba, under which we halted for the night, is a conical hill lying on the north side of the shallow wadi bed of Sa'atan.

Salih and I being mounted were with a few other favoured spirits first into the jungle of *samr* acacia where we

---

[1] Sahail = Canopus, a name common among Badawin.

were to camp, while the rest of the party, afoot and leading
their unused camels down the rough mountain gorge behind
us, came trickling in, and soon a dozen camp fires sprang
up along the valley. Shisur lay four days ahead, and there
was no water, except the neighbouring water-hole of
Hanun, until we reached it, so we must water camels here
to-morrow and leave with full water-skins for ourselves.

Dawn prayers over, the Badawin scattered in all directions
to round up their camels, and soon they came riding in bare-
backed, and so off to Hanun. Two hours due east, in and
out amongst desolate hills surfaced in places with black flint,
brought us to the high conical hill of Qarn Hanun on the one
hand and a triple-horned system called Ardaf on the other.

Just beyond the earth suddenly opened to form a V-
shaped fissure of crystalline rock, which descended in
terraces of sparkling whiteness to a green wadi floor one
hundred and fifty feet below. The uppermost stratum was
often overhanging; the lowest also had been eroded here
and there into long shallow caves. This was Ghabartan, a
tiny winding wadi which joins the Rakibit within view, and
is thus a source of the Katibit, a big trunk wadi running
north to the sands. Here at its tapering source we looked
down upon the green pond of Hanun in its bed. The
water-hole occasioned the usual disillusionment when I
recalled the Badu stories in its praise—intelligible enough
in a very thirsty land.

Sweet, the Badawin of the sands called it, but I found it
intolerably brackish, and wondered what the water of the
sands they called brackish would be like, for they held
no water so sweet as Hanun. But all such terms are relative,
and to the contented mind the water available is sweet
enough. Hanun was doubtless sweet to the Arab who called

it so, and I recalled a parched and pallid spot in Ghudun which had been described to me as the gem of all camping grounds, a ludicrous but doubtless, to my informant, an honest view. I recalled the Arab proverb, 'One's own ass is preferable to the horse of another.'

The little wadi leading down into Ghabartan is called Ba Musgaiyif, 'the place of tombstones,' and I was anxious to explore it as its name promised more archæological remains of a kind I had discovered throughout this frankincense belt, and for some miles eastward of it. This was a crude ground monument sometimes bearing pre-Arabic, possibly early Ethiopic inscriptions, thereby suggesting that the central south tribes speaking tongues having Ethiopic affinities may be of considerable local antiquity. Ba Musgaiyif proved a disappointment in that there was no inscribed material among the numerous but badly weathered monuments.

The more elaborate kind I had met with elsewhere consisted of a system of triliths, three elongated blocks of undressed stone (or sometimes round boulders with a naturally smooth surface), about eighteen inches high, standing on end and leaning inwards with their tops touching to ensure stability. These triliths were set up in series along one alinement, each pile standing at about one and a half paces from its neighbour. Sometimes the trilith had a fourth and smaller capping boulder, and occasionally a series of triliths was enclosed by an elliptical line of small pebbles. The series varied in number. I found them of five, seven, nine, fourteen and fifteen triliths. Running parallel to each series at about three paces distant was a smaller series of large conical rubble heaps, such as I have seen elsewhere used for *mashuwa* cooking, a method of grilling

TRILITH MONUMENTS.

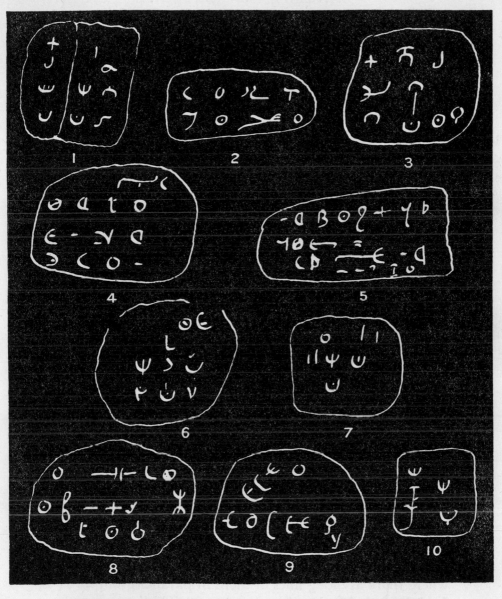

INSCRIPTIONS ON LARGE ROUNDED BLOCKS OF STONE OF TRILITH
MONUMENTS

NOS. 1-3. IN WADI ANDHAUR. 4. IN WADI DHAGHAUB. 5-10. IN WADI DHIKUR. (NO. 5 IS BROKEN
AT BOTH ENDS, AND PROBABLY FORMS PART OF A LONGER INSCRIPTION)

flesh on heated stones. These, I suggest, had some sacrificial significance. Some of the smaller series of triliths, *e.g.* the runs of five, were without them; the longer lines had a stone pile to three or four triliths. Between triliths and sacrificial piles were sometimes small square boulders which might have been used as seats.

These monuments had no common orientation; wherever I found them they lay in wadi beds and were in line with their courses. Most of them lacked inscriptions, which may in part be accounted for by weathering of the soft local limestone. Inscribed boulders were first met lying near the monuments in Wadi Andhaur, but in Wadi Dhikur I found them as the headstone of one of the terminal triliths. The inscriptions were generally separate characters an inch and a half high, rudely done, and having a dotted superficial impression which suggested that the implement used was a pointed flint. On account of the weathering of the stone many of the inscriptions were so blurred as to be unrecognisable, except for a character here and there. For the same reason the squeeze and the photographs I took were unsatisfactory, but I copied the better preserved inscriptions in full. Transport limitations prevented my bringing back more than one specimen of this work. It appeared to represent a camel; this I presented to the British Museum.

I found the monuments in the following wadi beds: Sarab, Ainain, Banat ar Raghaif, Haradha, Andhaur (below Khungari Pass), Dhaghaub, Dhikur, Ba Musgaiyif, and near Aiyun water-hole. The majority (and most of the inscriptions) occur in Wadi Dhaghaub and Wadi Dhikur where there are long lines of them in parallel groups. It is, I think, probable that they are graves. This is suggested not merely by their appearance, but by their abundance in Wadi Dhikur, which preserves a continuous burial tradition, having a large recent Muslim cemetery, as well as two other cemeteries of pre-Islamic or at least non-oriented types of grave, namely, rock burial and the mammoth grave, while its name could be taken to mean 'Vale of Remembrance.'

The natives were unaware that the scrollings were 'writing,' nor had they any precise knowledge of the origin of the monument, though they vaguely associated it with the Prophet's daughter (Salih bin Hud. Hud's camel?).

In Bait Kathir country to the west they call the monuments Bit Aba Ghassan, which name would appear to preserve the Ghassanitae of Ptolemy. There was, of course, a post-Islamic Ghassanid dynasty of Dhufar, but the distribution of triliths is beyond Dhufar limits, and the monuments themselves, judging from their pre-Arabic inscriptions, where inscribed, their non-Islamic orientation, and local tradition, belong to 'The Days of Ignorance.' The religion of ancient south-west Arabia was the star worship of the Sabaeans, and it is not impossible that the triliths were in origin symbolic of the ancient South Arabian Trinity of Sun God, Moon God and Zahra, the Venus of the Arabs.

The sun was getting high, and I was anxious to be on the move, so as I returned past Hanun where my men were watering, I called to them urging haste, and they cheerfully shouted back 'Yes'; but I knew well as I rode on that it would not make them hurry. Their love of dallying over a water-hole, especially if the next one be remote, I knew from long experience to be an incurable tendency to which I must resign myself. Shaikh Salih was not watering here; he and one other were leaving me to-day to go ahead for shared their conversation and food till after dark. I would then retire for the night, and my servant allowed it to be known that no one who wished to see me after that would be welcome. My three chronometers, two aneroid barometers and a wet and dry bulb thermometer were set out on the table by routine on arrival in camp and were packed again in the morning just before leaving. It was necessary after each day's march to compare and record the time of all the chronometers and this was done again the first thing in the morning to ascertain the performance of each, and deduce daily rates and Greenwich Mean Time. Height readings and temperatures as registered by the other instruments were recorded at intervals as time afforded, at sunset and sunrise always, and probably twice or thrice during the night as well. Some of my companions had never seen a watch. All of them were greatly excited when allowed to place their ears against the face of the biggest chronometer to hear the ticking. As they heard the marvel, their faces would light up with a smile and one would look at the other in wonderment before suddenly bursting out, '*La Illah il' Allah*'—'There is no god, but God.'

Sa'a, that is, a watch, became the generic name for each and every instrument. It did for my prismatic compass which I must hold to my eye every ten minutes of the march for recording our direction against the time (wrist watch), and cross-bearings on topographical points—necessary data for a route traverse of my journey. But the 'tick tick' was unquestionably *the* watch. Once when we halted to change camels, I found one Arab who had travelled with me holding a thermometer to the ear of a friend that he had brought as a recruit. He was showing off, but his friend was not impressed, so he set the aneroid to his own ear and was chagrined; somewhere, he felt, there had been cheating.

Our march the next day only lasted for three hours. The Badawin straggled out from the first and spoke of companions in the rear who had not caught up with us from yesterday. The reason was obvious. Here we were back in the Istah where there was good pasture while the way before us to Shisur—and a bare palm was held before me to indicate its barrenness—was hungry going. Impatient to get on to the sands, I had hoped to make a good day's march, but that suggestion found small favour. The traveller in the great desert soon discovers that the welfare of the camel is the supreme consideration. Starts and halts are normally determined by the quality of the grazing. Fodder is almost more important than water, for the camel can carry a load for a week and more without water, but food is a daily want. The European accustomed to a programme, a time to start, a time to halt, a time to eat and an expectation of a certain average daily mileage, gets a rude shock. The son of these barren marches subordinates everything to the efficiency of his transport—the health of his camel. Camp over good pasture with water at hand and he will not leave it; come upon a few verdant bushes at noonday, and, though the hot sun is striking down, he will dally for an hour; arrive at sunset after a gruelling day in the saddle and if the pasture does not please him he will insist on riding on, indifferent to fatigue.

And so, to-day, it was with a sad heart I had to couch my camel at a miserable seven or eight miles from last night's camping ground. I went off at once with my rifle into the wadi jungle. There were traces of a wolf, and marks of fox, hare and gazelle, but the afternoon proved barren.

THE VIRTUES OF THE ANTELOPE

In Wadi Ghudun, a few miles to the west at 1200 feet, where *samr* acacias gave place to the willowy tamarisk, I had got my first antelope, *Oryx leucoryx*, a full-sized cow. I took great precautions to secure her skin whole as a scientific specimen, for the Badu normally esteems her face skin as a trophy, like a fox-hunter the brush, and makes from it a rifle-butt cover. Indeed there was scarcely a man in my party whose rifle-butt was not adorned with the face skin of an antelope or a gazelle: scarcely less solicitous were they for the paunch, the gastric juices of which they carefully drained and drank with relish before administering the solid contents in handfuls to their bellowing, protesting camels. The benefit to the stomachs alike of man and mount is said to be equalled by nothing else in the desert. These are but two of the antelope's seven virtues.[1]

Out of the antelope's horn is made a pipe upon which the girls of South Arabia play. There is no drum, no stringed instrument or other manner of music to be found throughout these marches, but only the antelope horn, and if the shepherdess may not sing to her flock she may soothe them with the pipe and find consolation in it for herself. There may be here some remote connection with our mediæval legend of the maiden and the unicorn, for it is commonly supposed that the antelope is the prototype of that mythical beast. Certain it is that he runs with his head down so that his sloping horns appear almost vertical, and in profile seem

---

[1] The antelope's other virtues are its skin for leather; its blood for snake bite; its flesh for exorcism (*hamara*, to be described later); its soup for joint pains; its flesh for meat. They rate it better food than any other beast, a view I could not subscribe to. Perhaps they reckon by the after-effects of gluttony upon an empty stomach, for though their diet is usually frugal, moderation on such an occasion is an unknown virtue, and my medicine chest was always in requisition after a night orgy following a 'kill.'

to be one, whence the one-horned oryx of Aristotle, and in the Hebrew text of Deuteronomy xxxiii. 17: 'His horns are like the horns of unicorns.'[1] The unicorn of tradition was a symbol of strength and a guardian of chastity, a terror to men, whom he devoured at sight, but according to mediæval legend a ready victim to a pure young virgin. On seeing her his ferocity abated, and he would meekly come and lay his head in her lap, and submit to the caresses that made him her willing captive.

We made an early start, and left the last slight ridges behind to move across an utterly flat and featureless plain, now a hard sandy floor where in places we came upon nests of fossilised oysters, lying on the surface as they might have on an ocean bed barely covered by the fine sand, now fields of flint or rubble and at rare intervals an outcrop of laminated red sandstone. There was no animal life and all I collected was a beetle, a snake (*colubrid*) and a lizard, the last named, however, of great interest to the Natural History Museum, for it was new to science—*abu qursh*, 'the father of the dollar,' the Badawin called it, on account of its round tail. And so a dreary ride for seven hours, when I judged we had made twenty-one and a half miles. The next two days, which brought us to Shisur, were alike—a vast expanse of featureless wilderness. The only movement came from sand devils, which raised their spinning columns, bringing with them a refreshing gust of wind. Not a vestige of vegetation, and our camels seemed to know that here it was they must step out. We pressed on towards a white expanse of shimmering mirage that obscured the skyline and practised its habitual deceit as it receded before our thirsty column.

[1] The Hebrew word used is *rim.*

[135]

XI: NEJD—LIFE IN THE SOUTHERN STEPPE

SHISUR to-morrow. No wonder it looms so large in the Arab mind, for it is the first water-hole we meet for five days, and after leaving it there will be none for a further seven or eight. To-day a long anxious march across the barren plain, sun-baked and filmy with mirage, brought us just before nightfall to a copse where it bears due east. Approach to a water-hole is made with much caution, for if an enemy is already in possession, there is a choice between hasty retreat tormented by thirst and fear of pursuit, or a fight for possession. As always we arrived with empty water-skins. The Badawin no sooner off-saddled and hobbled their camels than they wandered off on all sides with their eyes to the earth for sign of an enemy, or fresh tracks of a raiding party, while three chosen men went in a wide cast round the water-hole to see if all were safe to dig it out for to-morrow's watering. Shisur's loneliness makes it an inevitable place of call for raiders, and it is a proper practice to fill in a water-hole when leaving to delay possible pursuers. Here Nature does the work, sand filtering in and filling it up after a day or two.

Next day we went off there by relays of six to eight camels, for the thirsty brutes take hours to water out of the small leathern buckets and the spring is a mere trickle. The way lies across a spacious stoneless plain (an excellent landing ground) to a rocky eminence crowned by conspicuous ruins of a rude fort. Undercutting the knoll lies a cave some fifty feet deep, and in the base of its sloping floor is a fissure which barely admits a human arm to the water beneath. According to legend, one Badr bin Tuwairij was

[136]

A GROUP OF MOUNTAIN MEN.

the builder of the fort of Shisur in some distant past, and I have heard that in the surrounding desert plain are still to be seen shadowed furrowings as though once it had known the plough; astonishing if true, for so limited is the water of Shisur and so arid the place that a fair-sized raiding party could not last out there for more than a week. 'The sword of God has been upon the *dira*,' said one Badu to me in allusion to the drought of recent years.[1]

Beyond to the eastwards in the otherwise naked plain lay Hailat ash Shisur, another tiny copse, the scene only three years before of a bloody affray between rival raiders, amongst whom were members of my escorting Arabs. Their story was of particular interest to me because I had myself barely escaped colliding with one of these parties a hundred miles to the eastwards. It comprised twenty-five men of the Sa'ar and Karab tribes who had come by this way to fall upon a small Mahra encampment at the water-hole of Andhaur. There they killed seven men for the loss of one, but he a shaikh, and departed with booty of forty camels. Four or five days later my exhausted little party reached Andhaur from the east after a six hundred miles' march to hear of the disaster from a terror-stricken member of the Bait ash Shaikh; and I remember well taking part in a discussion upon the unhealthiness of camp-fires by night; we discontinued them forthwith in spite of bitter cold.

Now I heard that this particular raiding party, which had

[1] On every journey I have made during the past six years, in Oman, and in south-east and central south Arabia, I have heard the same story. The natives avow that there has been a falling off of rains, scant though they ever were, within their lifetime. The date crop of interior Oman is but a half of what it was a generation ago, and many plantations have perished of drought.

been a nightmare to me in that winter of 1927-28, was intercepted by a chance raiding party of forty Mahra and Kathir, amongst whom were two of my present escort. Nukhaiyir took me over the ground and reconstructed the attack. 'This is where we came up with them; this is where I lay. We had followed their tracks all day and judged them to be returning raiders who must halt here at Shisur, for westwards there is no water until Sanau. There under that skyline we halted and waited till after the sunset prayers. Leaving our camels with a few men we crept on, under cover of darkness, towards their camp-fires. It was nearly midnight and they had mostly fallen asleep, for we could see their sprawling bodies in the dying glow. We crept till within fifty paces and then suddenly opened fire. They leapt up wildly in the darkness shouting, but in utter confusion, and we drawing our daggers fell upon them and God gave us the victory. Praise God from whom all blessings flow. Four of them fell, and all the booty that they had taken at Andhaur was restored to our hands, and we took five of their own camels, too, so that many of those that escaped in the darkness must have left riding two to a camel.'

A Badu at Nukhaiyir's side now interjected, 'Next day as I was grazing my camels in Wadi Ghudun one of those Sa'ar who had been in hiding all night emerged, and coming up to me implored sanctuary, and I call God to witness that he had no arms and I spared his life.'

'Then supposing they had made no fight for it,' I asked, 'and all had thrown down their rifles, would you have shown them mercy?'

'No,' said Nukhaiyir, 'in time of declared war between tribes, it is shameful, amongst Arabs.'

[138]

A SON OF THE STEPPE: A BAIT IMANI.

Shisur lay ninety miles from the south coast, 935 feet above sea-level, near the foot of the steppe where it verges on the sands—from which indeed we were now only a day's march.

We had crossed the Nejd, this wide southern borderland of steppe between ocean escarpments and sands, that stretches west-south-westwards to the confines of Najran and east-north-eastwards to merge into the Jaddat Harasis. Last year I had explored the sand border in the latter direction for a distance of one hundred miles to the famous oasis of Mugshin.[1] This year I was turning westwards and would explore its southern edge. But before continuing the narrative of my journey it may be well to turn aside to consider briefly the geography of the southern steppe that lay behind me.

Reference to my map will show between longitudes 51° 40' and 54° 40' a continuous coastal mountain chain that is known sectionally from west to east by the names Fatk-Shaghuwat, Jabal Qamr, Jabal Qara and Jabal Samhan. From its intra-montane side falls away a series of dry old torrent courses which form a large single wadi system, and must have constituted from remote times the drainage of the great steppe. This system consists of seven main tributary wadis running in more or less parallel courses northwards from the coastal range to the verge of

[1] Wadi Mugshin, surely the Prince of Wadis in all south-east Arabia, for nowhere have I met its like, consists of a belt of giant acacia (*ghaf*) jungle thirty miles long (east and west axis) on the south-eastern edge of Ar Rimal. At its eastern extremity (altitude about 400 feet) drinkable water comes to the surface at 'Ain or 'Ainain. A considerable date grove growing wild and unattended lines the banks of a marshy bed, and to the eastward is a trough-like pond a few hundred yards long and some fifteen wide.

the sands where they join a trunk wadi, and the trunk wadi marches with the sands in a general north-easterly direction to a point where it turns and is lost in them in lat. 19° 35′, long. 54° 50′, a point marked by the bountiful oasis of Mugshin. The seven wadis all rise in the neighbourhood of the divide, averaging three thousand feet at a two days' march from the coast, so that their sources are the region of the frankincense groves. From east to west they are called Katibit, Dauka, Ghudun, Aidam, Hagulun, Shihin and Hat,[1] and their lengths, diminishing, broadly speaking, in the same order, vary from an eight days' march in Katibit to a four days' march in Hat. The main trunk wadi has six sectional names, Hat, Shihin, Atina, Umm al Hait, Al 'Aradh and Mugshin, in its course from south-west to north-east, but the whole system may conveniently be termed by the generic name Umm al Hait (mother of life), which name has also the sectional connotation referred to.

To the northward and westward of the trunk wadi, the Great Sands stretch continuously westward to the confines of Dawasir and Najran. Actually the southern edge of the

---

[1] The tributary wadis are systems in themselves. Thus Wadi Katibit has affluents Andhaur, Dhahibun, Ingudan, Ghazal and Rakibit draining the eastern part of the Qara Mountains and the western part of Samhan. The eastern limit of the system in Andhaur which rises approximately north of Murbat Peak (whose alternative name shown on the chart as Jabal Du'an is unknown to the inhabitants, by whom it is known as Zairutun). Wadi Dauka rises in the longitude of Salala and receives Al Hauf, Dha'arfit and Ista. Wadi Ghudun rises slightly to the west of Dauka and receives Hila, Dhuhair and Haluf on its right bank and Ghara on its left. Wadi Aidan rises in the longitude of Rakhiyut and with its two large tributaries Difin and Habarut, rising respectively north of Jadhib and Damkut, drains the whole of the Qamr range. Wadi Shihin and Wadi Hat are shorter systems rising at the respective eastern and western extremities of Fatk-Shaghuwat.

THE WILD DATE-GROVE OF MUGSHIN.

desolate and hence these borderlands are capable of supporting only nomad Badawin. The summer drought drives them back into the mountain courses around the perennial water-holes—Andhaur, Hanun, Shuwairima, Aiyun and Habarut (these in Umm al Hait longitudes). But immediately after rain they sally out again and in winter they may remain for a month or two in favoured localities, their movements often being guided by their pillar of fire, the direction of lightning. It is a hungry and thirsty life and those whose habitat is the hinterland of Dhufar are drawn back to the settled comfort of the frankincense orchard, especially during the summer, when its comparatively rich rewards are the means of acquiring rifle, ammunition, clothes, coffee, and sometimes rice. But the true Badawin despise any but their spartan existence. They live mainly on camels' milk and hold life cheap. Raiding to them is the spice of life, and there was never a man in any of my escorts who had not raided into the Hadhramaut, nor one who had not been raided in his own grazing grounds, and some bore honourable scars of bullet or dagger wounds. Arms and ammunition and the health of the camel are thus the primary necessities of life; where hereditary blood-feuds divide the tribes, might is right, and man ever walks in fear for his life and possessions.

The tribes of importance occupying these southern borderlands are, from east to west, Bait Kathir, Mahra, Manahil, 'Awamir, Sa'ar, Nahad and Karab.[1] The Mahra

[1] Tribal distribution is as follows: the Umm al Hait system is the habitat mainly of two tribes, Mahra and Bait Kathir; they also extend to the west. Nominally the lower wadi reaches of Dauka, Ghudun, Aidam and Hat belong to Bait Kathir, though the Mahra use them freely; the upper sources of the wadis (except Ghudun) are largely in Mahra hands, particularly Habarut, Ghazal, Ingudan and Dhahibun, as well as the indi-

AN UPPER WADI COURSE.

A MIDDLE WADI COURSE.

are the largest, and number many thousands; the Nahad and Karab, the smallest tribes, only a hundred or two each.

The life of the steppe is primitive in the extreme. I have already observed that drought and the fear of raiders drive these tribes back on to their water in the mountains. But at heart they are wedded to their nomadic existence, and whenever rain comes they launch out with their flocks and herds into the desert, where every little rock hollow capable of holding rain-water has a name and a memory. Here they remain for a space till once more drought threatens and hunger drives. There is not sufficient water to support the horse or the dog. Tents or houses are unknown. In the steppe their place is taken by the shade of an acacia, and in the mountains by a cave. The people are wholly illiterate.

vidual wadis immediately to the west. Scattered about amidst the Mahra and Bait Kathir are a number of small Hadara tribes, non-Arab survivals. Thus to the westward of Hat in its lower courses is found the Bilhaf, a rather nondescript tribe owing allegiance to no faction, but Mahri in speech. A distinguishing feature of their dress is that they carry a knife, not a dagger, in their belts. They neither raid nor are raided, and like the Salub of Nejd are accepted as a *rabia* by all. They are also servants of the Shrine of Jauhari (Umm al Tabbakh) where the Mahra pay pilgrimages and make sacrifices. At the eastern extremity of the Umm al Hait system Wadi Andhaur is nominally a possession of the Bautahara (Bit Bohor) though the Mahra tribesmen are usually in evidence there. The Bautahara, a now dwindling and *déclassé* tribe, most of whom are fishermen, with an exclusive language, were once the reputed possessors of the whole eastern steppe from Wadi Ghudun (of the Kathir) to Wadi Qadun (?) (of the Harasis), while the western steppe is reputed to have belonged to the now legendary Bin Dhurbut. Elements of another small tribe 'Afar live in Habarut with the Mahra and the equally obscure Bait ash Shaikh (Bit Istait or sometimes Insakht), and thought to be collateral with the Shahara, occupy Wadi Ingudan near the water-hole of Hanun. To the westwards of the Umm al Hait system the Mahra tribe extends to Wadi Rama, thence Manahil to Wadi al Jauf: 'Awamir succeed as far as Wadi Khadhra, whence commences the Sa'ar habitat.

[143]

Few know anything of the Qur'an, though they pray zealously. They have a reverence for shrines, and are of the Shafi' rite. Alcohol is unknown, but tobacco much esteemed.

The usual Arab practices of polygamous marriage and facile divorce obtain, but it is rare for a Badu to have more than one wife or at most two, at any one time, though a quiver full of sons is a much-desired blessing. The woman looks after the flocks,[1] which she is here allowed to milk.

Disputes within the tribe are settled, as is general in tribal Arabia, by the *hukm al hauz*, a code of local sanctions, not the holy or Shara' law. Petty theft is rare and looked on as immoral: but robbery with violence a manly act, and the raid, with murder and looting, as unquestionably honourable as military prowess in Europe.

Bodily illness is dealt with by certain herbs (see Appendix IV), by the branding iron, by exorcism, by the gastric juices of animals slaughtered in the chase, and by the urine of the young cow camel. The cautery comes first, and few, if any, are the dwellers of these steppe lands who do not bear scars of the hot iron. One process I met with seemed

[1] With the Harasis and Mahra a curious custom obtains—that of never milking their sheep into a cold receptacle. A hot stone, heated in a fire, must first be introduced. The explanation it suggests, that the warmth thus applied to the udders encourages a facile milking, is not wholly satisfactory, because the practice is observed only in respect of sheep, not of camels.

A shepherdess of the Bait ash Shaikh tribe, from whom I purchased a sheep in Wadi Dhikur, would not agree to its being slaughtered in sunlight because of the fear that it would bring misfortune to her family, and this also was a common belief. A Harsusi of my escort informed me that in no very distant times past the Harasis would not only not slaughter, but not milk their flocks in sunlight, and to this day there are two breeds of sheep, *banat al murtal* and *banat al muqtuf*, which no tribesman of whatsoever tribe would dare slaughter until after dark.

[144]

to me to have some magical significance. My party was held up by the sickness of one of its number; he had been suffering for several days from stoppage of the bowels, which had not responded to all my explosive medicines. His companions now resorted to a measure they called *ghuwaira*. A rifle-bolt striker was introduced into the fire, and when it became red-hot was applied to seven prescribed places on the man's body: left heel, right heel, behind right ear, behind left ear, centre of forehead—where it joins the hair—top of the head, and immediately above the navel. The cure was instantaneous, and we moved the next morning.

For the Evil Eye, I have often witnessed a rite of exorcism called *hamra ra'aba*,[1] which is held equally efficacious for the recurrent three days' fever from which they suffer, and for snake-bite. The patient is laid amidst the circle of his sitting friends and the affected part of his body laid bare. They then commence bowing low over it and chanting one of two formulae; slow at first, the imprecations growing quicker and louder and the body bowing more energetically as the rite proceeds. A leader chants the lines in a vigorous voice and the rest of the party excitedly shout their responses, often just '*hamra ra'aba*.' Now and again one bowing head lingers, with lips to the patient's abdomen in the region of his liver, to draw up a mouthful of flesh and let it flick back as he raises his head; others from time to time bark, and spit upon the body. And so a climax is reached. A rifle is sometimes fired at the termination of proceedings, but that bravery is only used for the 'Evil Eye.'

I once observed a different rite after *hamra ra'aba* had

[1] The Kathiri tribesmen use a formula in the Shahari dialect of the mountains. This I have recorded but not yet translated.

failed to achieve results. It is a kind of divination and propitiation called *habil*, *i.e.* the rope, and perhaps may not be unconnected with the Quranic reference to 'blowing on knots.' The practitioner, rope in hand, sat about three paces from his patient. A third party was called to hold the end of the rope. Taking an arbitrary length of it with the thumb and forefinger of one hand, the practitioner measured the outstretched length of it with his disengaged arm by means of forearm's length, hand span and finger breadth. The operation he repeated three times, each occasion preceded by a pause to bend his head low over the rope and shake his head, making a curious burbling noise with his lips, and to take a handful of sand which he sprinkled up and down the rope. In conclusion he looked up at his patient and gave him the following remedy: 'At sunset take so many dates and so much butter and go and cast it away upon the sands.'

So much for man and his ways.

The animal life of the southern steppe is limited. A point of interest is that from the nature of their almost rainless environment animals here must be able to do without water and to content themselves with the moisture contained in herbage, or collected in rocks from dews. Zoologically they belong to the Palæarctic group.

Among the mammals that I shot were the antelope (*oryx Leucoryx*)—a comparatively rare kind, gazelle, and fox. I saw marks of wolf, wild cat and badger, but did not get the steppe varieties of these. The *rim* or pure white gazelle is said to be almost extinct, though I picked up a pair of its horns, lyre-shaped, and with a characteristic tuft of white hair still attaching to it; in reality this animal, unlike the red gazelle, belongs to the sands rather than the steppe. Two hedgehogs which I caught were of a sandy colour and small in comparison with the larger black type of Oman. Here they are said to attack and kill snakes, but to go in craven fear of the vulture, on whose approach they weakly unbend and, abandoning their natural protection, become ready victims.

Of birds, I saw no vulture in the steppe, though I had expected to meet it, but came upon the lifeless body of a large black eagle. The presence of either vulture or eagle in the sky is regarded as a sign that an encampment may be near. The black raven was common, and I shot an interesting example with a neck ringed with white feathers. A Badu asked for the heart of another pure black specimen which he proposed to eat raw because of some virtue it possessed: its bile is also used by them for the eyes in the same way as *kohl* (antimony) by the sedentary Arab. A bird which I did not see but heard night after night at Mugshin was the owl. Ostriches had been shot in this steppe by members of my escort in past years, but they are now extinct (except for a few in the Sa'ar habitat to the west), though I picked up many fragments of petrified ostrich shell. The extinction of the ostrich in the southern steppe dates from its pursuit by Badawin armed with modern rifles. Of the smaller birds I shot, a finch lark was the rarest and most interesting scientific specimen; the bulbul, Senegal sandgrouse, and a brown babbler were indigenous creatures one expected to find, and a Kashmir redstart, white wagtail and Tibetan desert chat were all migrants either passing to winter in Africa, or possibly cold weather visitors to the Hadhramaut. I also collected butterflies, wasps, ants and spiders, a list of which are given in Appendix II.

My Badus toyed bare-handed with a large scorpion,

[147]

picking it up, scatheless, by the tail just below its sting. Of reptiles there were three different snakes—the inevitable horned viper amongst them—very few compared with lizards, of which I met ten different kinds. These included three new species and also the three largest edible varieties— regarded by the Arabs as a most succulent dish, and more nourishing even than the larger mammals of the chase. One of these gave us an exciting hunt. I saw it disappear down its hole, and soon had three Badawin in chase prodding the roof with their sticks. Suddenly the tip of a tail appeared and one of the diggers was just able to get hold of it between finger and thumb, and although cautioned by his companions to beware lest it should be a snake, he held on while they continued digging. Able in time to get a better grip of its tail, he now, as he knelt over the hole, pulled it out with a vigorous tug and held it in the air head downwards, its eyes rolling wildly and its jaws gaping menacingly. The Badu now slipped his other hand down its back and catching hold behind the head held it the other way up, but the creature finding its tail free lashed back with it and caught another Badu on the knee, drawing blood. This man later came to me for *duwa* for his knee, and I for once diagnosing correctly the complaint gave him a dollar and he went away cured.

Another interesting reptile, an inedible lizard, was the *shuwaira ash shams*, so called because it delights to sit on the most glaring eminences in the face of the tropical sun towards which it nods its head—a large creature with a tail red and smooth and ratlike, and a heavy pouch of royal blue under the chin which changes at death to silver. This creature alone of all the steppe life that I met scorns refuge from the sun.

[148]

XII: MARCHING ALONG THE SOUTHERN FRINGE OF THE SANDS

WE bade farewell to the little copse of Mutugtaig in the bed of the Ghudun, where two days had been spent resting and grazing our camels and watering them at neighbouring Shisur. Under an eastern sky crayoned with crimson and gold we turned our backs upon it this cold December morning and marched out into the plain—a wilderness that recalled to me the Land of the Two Rivers. Scarcely had we been on the move an hour when my companions started shouting excitedly, '*ar raml! ar raml!*' sweeping their canes as they did so along our right front, where in the far distance a sunlit yellow ribbon now edged the skyline; and I gazed eagerly towards this southern bulwark of the sands of my desire.

Between the sands and us stretched a dreary plain unrelieved except by low whitish outcrops, forming low, rocky ridges—Dhim Himla, Thuwairib, Lahaga, Qarun Kelba—places honourably known to the Arabs, for here water collects after rain.

Before us stretched a hundred miles of perilous incalculable marches. The open state of war existing between the tribe I travelled with and their powerful neighbours made this stage of my journey very dangerous. Many had been (and will be) the bloody conflicts upon this road along the southern borderlands, for waterless no-man's-lands as they are, yet they are the fairway between water-holes which are used only and inevitably by raiders on murder and plunder bent. Any party we met would be a potential enemy. The stronger or warier party would announce itself with a volley of rifle fire, prelude to fight or, alternatively, to

[149]

flight. My party betrayed by word, look and act that they were on tenterhooks, and whenever my camel bore me ahead of them or lagged behind, someone was soon beside me to remind me that we were in dangerous country; yet on making camp never were there dispositions made so far as I could see for meeting an attack or escaping from one. The desert holds a philosophy of the inevitability of events. 'Reliance is in God,' 'What is written must come to pass,' 'God be praised, the Lord of the Worlds'—these expressions are always on Badawin lips, to meet death or adversity or the expectation of them. In the acceptance of destiny is comfort; the doctrine of Free Will a disturbing heresy. Unless the beast became his by the will of God, a man could not enjoy killing the master and riding away upon her. War would become wicked, blood-feuds impious, and the practice of religion impossible.

Before us the conspicuous large white dune of Bin Juli marked where Umm al Hait, the great trunk drainage system of the steppe, changes its name to Atina. To the northwards the great sands reappeared in the distance as a pale wall backed by ridges of rosier hue. Before them ran the verdant line of Umm al Hait. When nearer we found the sands of the valley gathered in hummocks like the roofs of multitudinous mosques with their thousand cupolas. The thick tamarisk looked inviting to our fasting camels, and the poor brutes that had shuffled sluggishly across the plain trotted eagerly up to the scanty diet before them.

Umm al Hait is a precious name to the steppe dweller, though if no rain falls for two or three years together, as sometimes happens, the wadi becomes hungry, bleak and deserted. The meagrest winter rain will, however, quicken it into fertility and life—though the blessedness actually

A FRINGE OF THE SOUTHERN SANDS.

before us was the result of the unusually heavy rains I had experienced in the eastern marches last year.

How well I remembered members of my party pointing out to my unaccustomed eyes the evidences of some shower, here the pitted surface of sandy elephant masks[1] about some tree-roots, there the swept path of some tiny freshet! How joyously they talked of rain! That night low heavy clouds raced northwards and forked lightning lit up the black heavens, while we and our beasts sought refuge from a howling sand-blast behind the solid hummocks that grew about the *selem* bushes. But no one was unhappy. Rain was about and rain to the Badu is as gold to the prospector; the morning was welcomed with rousing chanties on the march. The low, rumbling thunder was like music to our ears. A drenching would have been glorious. As we went on the sky grew dark, the lightning nearer, and the thunder-claps more violent; our camels shared the excitement, sniffing with their monstrous noses in the air, to the delight of their masters. We split up into three parties and spread fan-wise to scout the plain for rain-pools, rather against my judgment, for I felt they would be insufficient, and I would have preferred to press on towards the certainty of our next water-hole. Some twenty minutes later a rifle shot rang out. Ordinarily it would have been interpreted as an alarm or as a promise of gazelle flesh for dinner. 'Water!' exclaimed Nukhaiyir excitedly. 'The Arabs' (Badawin in conversation always thus refer to themselves in the third person) 'have found water.'

'True,' said another jubilantly; we wheeled about and proceeded in that direction. For some time I had felt my

[1] The configuration of the accretions of sand curiously resembles the front of an elephant's head.

own camel edging that way, never imagining that she smelt water, but supposing that she fretted after a particular companion in one of the other parties, for camels that have been reared together, whether or not of the same sex, find separation irksome.

'Are you quite sure it is water?' I had said a little testily, for we had already been six hours in the saddle and our halting place was said to be three hours ahead.

'*Isqut*,' replied Nukhaiyir, which in other parts of Arabia is an imperative order to 'shut up,' but here has the idiomatic meaning of 'without doubt.' We soon breasted a rise in the plain to see our party beneath us upon a stony outcrop with the camels' long necks stretched down, and themselves frantically scooping handfuls of water into their water-skins. My thirst soon had me on my hands and knees beside them, with my parched lips in the saucers of the rocky floor; and very sweet the collected rain-drops tasted, after the water of our march, which had been sand-coloured or pestiferously green to begin with, and had acquired the taste of rank meat from its churning day after day in goat skins 'cured' in crude Badawin fashion. There were times when I elected to go thirsty, though the stuff was wholesome enough, and I have never suffered any serious ill-effects from drinking it, despite my never having taken measures to doctor my water on any desert journey; there is neither time nor opportunity for such refinements.

And now Tha'ailib, a Bait Kathiri, in a high, reedy voice raised again the lyric that had cheered the morning's march while his companions showed they knew and loved it by joining in, either one by one, in a duet, or together, making some last phrase of a line into a chorus.

I translated it at the time to run:

A HALT TO GRAZE IN THE HUNGRY SOUTHERN BORDERLANDS.

'Behold lightning in the far distance,
May its bounty fall in Umm al Hait,
Continuous and flowing rain
Flowing along between sand and stream course
Until it pass from Bu Warid onwards,
Thence shall a beautiful woman live and enjoy,
She, who standing up unveiled,
Her lover falleth at her feet
And is healed of the wounds of his heart-veins.'

Our march that day was cut short abruptly by the over-mastering need to rejoice. These few spots of falling rain were reason enough for my vanguard to halt and graze their camels.

Sahail, a Rashidi, announced that he would smoke, and a circle soon squatted about him, for a pipe in the desert invites all to share. His hand disappeared down the opening of his shirt front (Badu clothes have no pockets) towards the region of his dagger belt, and drew forth his smoking outfit—the typical tobacco pouch of cowhide, flapped over and roughly sewn, carrying a leather thong with wooden toggle. It was one of Sahail's few possessions, but clearly had a sentimental value of its own. As ever, it must be lovingly unrolled with all eyes upon it. It had two partitions, one for tobacco, the other for pipe, flint and steel striker, for matches in the desert if not quite unknown are a rare luxury, and fires invariably lighted with a flint. The pipe, also typical, was an empty ·303 cartridge case, the mouthpiece being the flat-rimmed end with the cap removed. He proceeded to fill it with the green local leaf of Oman or Dhufar, holding the end well up to avoid spilling the precious stuff. A scrap of rag which probably

belonged to his last shirt was next ignited by a spark from
the flint, then placed on the ground, and a little dry camel
dung sprinkled over and blown upon to make it smoulder;
to this little fire a twig was added, till it charred red. The
glowing cinder was then placed over the mouth of his pipe,
as for a *narghileh* or hubble-bubble. It was filling the pipe
that took up the time so pleasantly; smoking was to be a
matter of a few crowded seconds. Sahail took six or eight
quick, deep inhalations, holding on to the last one until
his eyes rolled and his body swayed; meanwhile he had
passed the pipe to his neighbour, who similarly intoxicated
himself and so it went round the circle. This pipe was
smoked clarinet fashion, others of the same type I have
seen smoked flute-wise. The experience did not tempt me,
so I refrained from asking my almost speechless company
which was the better mode; nor could I find heart to mock
Sahail, whose pipe was one of his rare indulgences.

We camped in Umm al Hait at a point where Nukhdat
Waraiga, a distributary, takes off on a north-easterly bearing.
A twin Nukhdat Hishman lying to the north-west has a
more northerly course, both penetrating into these southern
sands for a distance of a day and a half's march to embrace
a region called Umm Dharta.

The temperature fell to 47° F. that night, and we felt
the cold bitterly as we were sleeping in the open after a hot
day in the saddle, and on waking my hands were too
numbed with cold to do much note-taking. For the next
six nights the temperature fell about as low. My two
blankets made it endurable for me, wearing all my clothes
as well, but for my companions it meant wretchedness.
The Badawin sleep on the sands, which are very hot by
day and very cold by night; they have no other clothes

than the cotton rags they wear by day; no bedding, which would be a nuisance, anyhow, and be thought effeminate. They collect a night's store of brushwood for the camp-fire, and curl up before it, naked but for a loin-cloth, for their other garment, a shirt, is doffed and used as a sheet. So also the women folk, though they have 'tents of hair' in the sands for a shelter, and a rug to sleep upon, wear only their trousers by night, their outer garment—except in case of the well-to-do—serving again as sheet. By day nearly all go barefoot; but if the sands are very hot, both sexes may use a roughly knitted sock. Excessive indulgence is, however, deprecated.

Our course for the next five days skirted this southern fringe of the great sands, first west-north-west, then gradually veering to west. The altitude remained fairly constant at about 950 feet, though the fall of wadi courses made me think that higher ground lay to the west. The afternoon march was unpleasant, as we were marching into the sun's eye. I had experienced this in former journeys, when long marches into the sun turned my face first lobster colour, then blistering raw; but now I had learnt the secret of swathing my head in the full wraps of an Arab head-dress and so saved all but my nose and lips. A more lasting disadvantage of a westerly course was that map-making became a difficult task, as I was equipped only with chronometers as a means of obtaining Greenwich Mean Time. I could obtain latitudes with fair accuracy and thus check daily my dead-reckoning by watch and compass when marches were from south to north (and fortunately nearly the whole of my journey lay in this direction); but longitudes which check traverses east and west are untrustworthy when obtained with chronometers carried on camel back, even with three chronometers checked one against another and recorded before and after every march. A wireless set would have given perfect accuracy, but I feared to excite the suspicions of my company with such an apparatus, whose bulk and weight would in any case have been too much for my limited transport.

Three and a half hours through hummocky sand after leaving Hishman brought us to the bordering plain, which we crossed at a good pace, scarcely checked by groups of small white sand-drifts that ran out at intervals of a mile and a half or so. Beyond Umm al Ru'us these grew to be transverse ridges so that we were slowed down, losing a half-hour in crossing the first one, into a long corridor flanked on our left hand by a single sand ridge at about a mile's distance, and on the right by the Great Sands. *Kharaiyim*, as the skirting corridor is called, became the characteristic feature of the next few days' marches. Hungry marches they were, for the only verdure was sparse willowy *abala* or *markh* on the sides of the dunes. These formed part of a system which lay athwart our path, and ran south into the plain on the flank of a wadi, shrinking steadily to disappear, it was said, at no great distance.

Such were our halting-places. The camp in Nukhdat Fasad—a distributary of the Atina that gives its name to the local sands—lay below three mighty dunes of Umm al Jau, Umm al Laisa and Umm al Dhalua (mother of ribs). So wretched was the grazing that we were obliged to split up into three parties and distribute our animals over an area of a mile or more. The party with which I found myself consisted of Karab, 'Awamir and Bait Kathir *rabias*, and they immediately clambered up into the tall spiky bushes of *markh*, to snap off the youngest and most succulent

[156]

A SON OF THE SANDS.

fodder for their particular mounts, so that my own beast and the baggage animals came off second-best. This greed for their camels aroused my interest because of its strange conflict with the generosity of their personal relationships. Where water or food was short, no one of them would think of not sharing it equally with his companions, and if any one was away, perhaps tending his camels, all would wait his return, to eat together. But over camel fodder or camel loads each Badu will take any unscrupulous advantage to best his fellows in his camel's interests; her welfare he seems to set above every other consideration.

On the march no halt was cried for the midday prayer; the five daily observances are reduced to three when men are marching, midday and afternoon prayers being said together, so also the sunset and evening prayers. This is an orthodox expedient and does not reflect upon desert piety. The assertion sometimes made by prejudiced townsmen, that the Badawin neither pray nor fast, is not borne out by my experience. My companions always prayed diligently; ever mindful of the many perils through which they have to go, they call upon God morning, noon and night. Hunger and thirst are never far distant phantoms, the hosts of Midian are ever prowling around; the knowledge of such present dangers has implanted in them, as in our soldiers and sailors of a past generation, a combination of resignation and of trust in the supernatural that is childlike in its simplicity. Nor is simplicity its only virtue; it is a rule of life that is pragmatically justified by the fact that it forms a working basis for daily life in a harsh environment. It is an attitude of mind which is closely paralleled in its essentials by the accepted conventions of the West.

'In the name of God the Compassionate, the Merciful,'

was shouted as we moved off each morning. Suddenly at my side after long silences a Badu would burst out like our Puritan forefathers with, 'Deliver me from mine enemies, O God,' 'Deliver me, O Lord, from evil.' The last note of the Credo calling them to prayer at dawn would be greeted with long-drawn-out supplications to Allah, as the shivering wretches struggled to their feet to worship as their first act of the day. Even a devout Christian travelling in their company, his mind obsessed with worldly affairs, might well learn something from their complete acceptance of and trust in the Unseen but Ever Present God. As we sat in circle the silence would be broken by a mumbled, 'There is no god but God,' while twice a hysterical Murri exploded with, 'Hide not your faith, O Muslimin!' Yet these outbursts I knew affected not their relations with me at all, and I felt among these wild men a tolerance rare amongst townsmen, whose smattering of the Qur'an gives them an intolerable religious conceit, because they feel themselves in exclusive possession of divine truth.

In contrast let me recall my encounter with Shaikh Salih at the outset of this journey.

'Bear witness!' one of his men had begun, inviting me to repeat the Islamic creed, in affirmation of my avowed belief in God, and prayer, and fasting. So I took hold of my beard—which I had let grow, as must any European who would travel here; for by his beard a man must swear. I said in Arabic after him, 'God is great.'

'There is no god but God,' said he, and I repeated it.

'And Muhummad is the Prophet of God,' came his third and last tenet.

'Let me explain,' said I. 'He is your prophet, a great and good man of your race of Arabs; but we are of another race, also creatures of God, and we say and believe that Jesus is our prophet.'

'Jesus, son of whom?' they asked, for they are universally illiterate, and have no acquaintance with the Qur'an, which records that Jesus was the Spirit of God.

'True,' intervened Shaikh Salih to close the breach, 'to every people their prophet. But, God be praised, this man is no unbeliever, but a confessor of Allah, the One and Indivisible.'

My companions were at pains to discover whether we burned our dead, whether our marriages were 'knotted' (sacred from free-love), whether we fasted and prayed. My replies assured them and corrected another illusion which I had met with on my earlier journeys and is, indeed, widespread throughout the Muslim East; they pointed to the skies, saying that unbelievers hide their faces from God. This I suspect originated in the sun helmet of modern use,[1] which for obvious reasons comes well down over the eyes. It is interesting to note too in this connection that prayer according to Islamic practice necessitates the brow touching the earth. Clearly a hat with a brim will not allow of this, and therefore the outcry amongst conservative men of religion in Persia, Iraq, Afghanistan and other Muslim countries against the adoption by their armies of a head-dress based on European models.

On my journeys I wore the Arab kerchief, and hidden beneath it a shallow flying helmet with the brim removed, an antiquity inscribed 'Southey, Royal Air Force.' My dress and beard and food and talk must be as like those of my

[1] The notion must be modern, for the sun helmet has not been in use among Europeans in the East for more than a century; it is unknown in the Americas, and not, I believe, worn in Australia or South Africa.

insular companions as possible to soften the differences between us. For the same reason I did not wear glare glasses or other obtrusive sun-protection, as the suspicions of my desert friends to sun helmets showed that these might have hindered the successful prosecution of my plans, nor have I ever found them necessary.

Beyond Fasad the edging plain which yesterday had been stoneless, to-day became stony and undulating. Gravelly outcrops (*hazm*) some twenty feet high were followed by others of putty colour, red-veined and highly glazed. Through my telescope the bases of the distant sand dunes here also appeared from a distance, similar solid rock. On the surface I found oyster and other fossils, *Ostrea, Lucina* and *Rostallaria*, all much weathered but with sufficient ornament to date them geologically.

Mitan was another hungry camp, and our poor camels standing silent, idle and hobbled were more than ready for the onward move. Unlovely beast the camel may be, but what patience in adversity she shows! All her delight is in fodder, and if she find it in sufficiency you may put upon her a heavy daily load, permit her to drink but once a week, and manacle her at every halt, lest she stray.

Our morning start from Mitan was sluggish. We straggled because of the cold and the hunger and the many transverse sand ridges, and straggling camels mean a slow caravan. An hour's march brought us to a wide depression, whose high western bank, Tof Mitan, marked the miserable end of the wadi of that name, so mighty and fruitful at its source in Shaghuwat, six days' march south. Beyond it was the hard steppe again and better going. Suddenly the Arabs, who were always childishly anxious to draw attention to anything they thought would interest me, pointed to the ground. 'Look, Sahib,' they cried. 'There is the road to Ubar.'

'Ubar?' I wondered.

'It was a great city, our fathers have told us, that existed of old; a city rich in treasure, with date gardens and a fort of red silver. [Gold?] It now lies buried beneath the sands in the Ramlat Shu'ait, some few days to the north.'

Other Arabs on my previous journeys had told me of Ubar,[1] the Atlantis of the sands, but none could say where it lay. All thought of it had been banished from my mind when my companions cried their news and pointed to the well-worn tracks, about a hundred yards in cross section, graven in the plain. They bore 325°, approximately lat. 18° 45' N., long. 52° 30' E. on the verge of the sands.

Some days later Ma'yuf, the most intelligent Rashidi in my party, volunteered the information that as a boy while

[1] I am indebted to Mr. Philby for drawing my attention to the similarity of Ubar with the form Wabar. None of the 'serious' Arab geographers mention the place, but Yaqut gives a copious selection of local tradition, all to the same purpose. The place is generally defined as lying in the sands 'between Shihir and Sana'.' It was a great city in a fertile oasis belonging to the tribe of Ad, and its inhabitants were punished for their sins by being turned into *nasnas*—a kind of monkey with only half a body, one eye, one arm, one leg and so on. Since then it has been inhabited by *jinn* who endeavour to prevent approach to it and destroy those who reach it. The Mahra camels are descended from the offspring of the camels of these *jinn*. In some stories the people of Shihir are represented as hunting the *nasnas* and even eating them. The South Arabian archæologist Nashwan bin Sa'id d/573 AH/1117 A.D., says only: 'Wabar is the name of the land which belonged to 'Ad in the eastern parts of Yemen; to-day it is an untrodden desert owing to the drying up of its water. There are to be found in it great buildings which the wind has smothered in sand. It is said also that it belonged to the people of Ar Ras.'

It is possibly more than a coincidence that ARISHA (the land of the Ruler Zenaiti of the desert folklore) is the Shahari equivalent of RAS (Arabic).

grazing his father's herds after rain, between Mitan and Fasad (he had long ago forgotten the precise site, but thought it within two days' march of the sand border) he had come upon a complete earthenware pot, with broken potsherds of red and yellow, a part of a grindstone, two coffee pestles (?) of black polished stone, and two large white rounded blocks of stone, notched at the edge and both alike, but each so big as to require two men to lift it (drums of a column?): he had turned the sand over to look for more, only to come upon black ashes. But these humble things he had never associated with a mighty city; though it had surprised him to find pottery in the sands, for no true nomad of the desert carries earthenware pots on his camels, but only vessels of woven reeds and an occasional iron one.

It would have been suicidal for me (even if I could have carried my companions—an unlikely event in their present nervous temper) to have turned aside into that arid pastureless waste: moreover our water was scarcely sufficient to carry us along to the next water-hole. According to Badawin report, the tracks are lost in the plain to the southwards. This is probably due partly to wind erosion in the soft sandy floors there, and partly to the fact that the ancient road must have followed a pebbly wadi course, the natural avenue of approach to the mountains, where there never would have been tracks. That the sands are encroaching southwards is in accordance with Arab tradition and supported by the prevailing northerly winds all along these southern borderlands which account for the orientation of the sand-drifts' steep and gentle slopes. These deep tracks in the steppe are explicable if climatic conditions have changed within historic times. Just to the south lay the ancient and famous frankincense groves, which were probably connected by an overland route with Gerrha, the old port of the Persian Gulf, or with Petra of the Nabataeans, and Ubar may well have lain upon it. Can there be any connection between the words Ophir and Ubar by the change—a philological commonplace—of *f* for *b?*

This tradition of ancient trade routes across what is now an almost prohibitive barrier of sands should not be lightly dismissed as impossible. South Arabia is held never to have had an Ice Age, so that when the higher latitudes of the northern hemisphere lay beneath an ice cap, Arabia was enjoying a pluvial period, from which epoch date the great gorges draining the coastal mountains, and the limestone fossils washed down to the edge of the sands. This very different climate may have long persisted in modified form and made possible a very early civilisation in this region.

Another interesting link in the chain of evidence has been established by zoologists from the distribution of animal life in South Arabia. The animals I collected in the Qara Mountains have proved to be mainly African or Ethiopic in affinity; they form an enclave there, for those I collected to north, east and west have been found to be exclusively Palæarctic. This enclave may well be a relic of the former animal population of the entire southern part of the peninsula when India, South Arabia and Africa had a common climate and fauna. Later, desiccation may have confined this primitive fauna to the Dhufar province, which alone in Arabia has continued to enjoy a tropical rainfall and flora, thanks to an adventitious south-west monsoon, while the denuded spaces round about have come to be re-populated by another group of animals from the north.

XIII: ACROSS THE MOUNTAINOUS SANDS OF URUQ ADH DHAHIYA

THE bordering sands of Shu'ait now veered to south of west and our course lay facing them. Here and there we seemed to have bid adieu to steppe only once more to emerge upon it, now it was obscured by a single high ridge, now reported to have receded to half a day's march to the south. The light colour that distinguished the southern aspect of the bordering fringe gave place to red interior ridges that as we proceeded grew into vast squat hills mounting up in billowing masses. Gentle valleys and saddles marked our way except when we saw scant herbage upon some slope, which we climbed, there to stop and graze.

My attention was suddenly arrested by the phenomenon of silver patches in the low troughs, looking from a distance like sheets of ice or the salt residues of dried-up lakes. Such *ghadhera*—they proved to be gypsum—appeared with growing frequency throughout these dunes of Yibaila and Yadila[1] and two days later in the sand mountains of Uruq adh Dhahiya.

Hungry marches of nine and ten hours a day had told in varying degree on our camels, so that we had been obliged to make a redistribution of loads. The two sixty-pound baskets of dates that had been a normal camel load were now found excessive; each basket was halved and spread among such camels as were in better fettle for the rugged way before us. Their masters grumbled and I must needs

[1] In the Rashidi dialect of the southern sands, as distinct from the northern dialect of the Murra, J is pronounced Y, thus Jaub = Yaub, and Jiban = Yiban. It is possible that the Y in Yin Miniyor, Yadila and Yibaila is a J.

requisition animals of unattached Badawin with us at added expense. At last we agreed that the riding camels of my party would carry a small load every second or third day, though it meant much argument and the promise of reward, and there were moments of apparent deadlock when I sorely felt the absence of Shaikh Salih.

Rougher marching and tired camels stretched out the column interminably at times, so that parts of it were lost to sight in the folds and turnings of the sands. This was by no means satisfactory in the face of possible ambush, for we were daily growing more exhausted and less mobile, and must be easy prey for a larger raiding party, operating light and fresh from one of the three water-holes now within a two days' radius. As we neared each high hill one of my Arabs whose turn that day it was to be free of a load, went ahead, as our custom was, and clambered to the top, there to spy out the country before us for sign of raiders, keeping his head below the ridge to avoid detection, and there he lay motionless but ever watchful while we came pounding along to pass beneath. An hour later another would repeat the performance, and so a look-out was kept during the long day while we below scanned the ridges of distant hills for any sign of similar activity on the part of an enemy.

The straggling meant a long-drawn-out arrival, and made the daily choice of a halting-place increasingly difficult. The spot must be determined according to what pasture availed in this barren country, having regard to the time it took for the last animals to make camp in daylight. The procedure was for two or three leading men to scout ahead some two hours before sunset and for us to follow to the best of any pastures that were reported. An unusually happy find on one occasion was signalled from afar by the scout waving his head-dress and shouting madly from the highest ridge, so drunk with the sight of good grazing as to forget the possibility of any enemies.

The camels dribbled in to be couched, off-loaded, knee-hobbled and driven off to the nearest scrub. But in a hungry camp the Badawin would scour the neighbouring hills for armfuls of fodder with which to feed their couched animals by hand, as a mother her child. After the camels had been provided for, the party lined up for evening prayer before they broke their own fast. Stacks of kindling rose by the side of the four or five camp-fires against the cold of the night. Round these the little self-chosen parties habitually ranged themselves and it was my daily custom to go and sit with one or other in turn.

This night I was interested in their manner of making unleavened bread. Ma'yuf, who was the cook of our particular party, squatted amid the circle of hungry and expectant watchers, while he filled his cooking-pot with flour, poured water upon it, punched and kneaded it into an excessively soft and slimy dough. He divided it into fistful shares, one for each of those present, rolling the lumps into balls to prove their size. He balanced them in his hands in the manner of scales, one eye upon the dough and the other upon his neighbours. Then any ball that had had an unfair start in life grew at the expense of another, until all were equal and laid out at his feet. Next he took up the first ball, sprinkled more water on it, flattened it with his palm into a bun some four inches in diameter and an inch thick, and laid it sagging across the glowing embers. A scorching smell was the signal that it needed turning, and so both sides came to be baked. Afterwards he made a hole in the hot sands under the fire, tumbled it into this and

[166]

covered it again, and so with the rest of the batch. After a term of burial deemed meet, the loaves were one by one disinterred, and the caked sand partly brushed off by hand, partly blown away with a deep breath, but most of it left on to give the customary flavour. My companions favoured this delicacy piping hot; a little sufficed me—it was very heavy, perhaps two or three times the weight of English bread, and though baked to a cinder on the outside was doughy within. This may be one of its attractions, and yet be the main source of the stomach trouble which they all complained of. They were unused to solid food, so that the rations I provided of dates every day and bread and rice on alternate days were luxuries such as may have come their way once a year, for the Feast of Ramadhan perhaps: Ma'yuf, however, had a side-dish to-night: a hare pulled out of its two-foot hole as we came along was simmering in the pot. But the amateur cook of the sands is a stranger to the use of butter, camel's milk being so poor in fat content that it will make neither butter nor cheese (though the hump of a young camel on the rare occasions of slaughter affords excellent fat), so that I found hare boiled in brackish water unattractive fare and, with little virtue, left my share to my companions.

Did I prefer the flesh of the gazelle? The question led on to the tale of the gazelle and the hare—one of those animal stories beloved of Badawin, which are indeed attractive as told in the simple rhythm of their vigorous dialect, for Badu narrative speech tends to fall into the measure of blank verse.

A gazelle came grazing to a juicy tuft of *thamama*, not noticing that beneath it lay a hare asleep. The hare startled, leapt up and fled, the gazelle jumping back at the same time, even more frightened, so that it forgot itself.

[167]

But now, coming to its senses, and feeling annoyed, it shouted in mock heroics after the hare:

> '*Hubi!* whose flesh is of small account,
> Whose skin gives no pleasure
> O joy-giver but to children,
> O vexer of neighbours!'
>   (*i.e.* there is so little meat on you that it will not suffice the guest).

And the hare, turning, sat up on its hind quarters and shouted back to the gazelle:

> '*Hubi!* O father of forgetfulness,
> O rimmèd hornèd one,
> If thou seest the wadi green
> Thou becomest partner of it with the jinns!'
>   (*i.e.* the sight of pastures makes you mad).

And they parted ways.

The camp-fires would have been replenished if firewood had been available, for the poor Badawin were numbed with cold and the night was cruel. As the fires flickered out beneath them, they one by one lay down with their rifles, only the night watch alert against surprise by an enemy, while I went off to do my 'star taking.'

22nd December had been a long, uneventful day, marching through the sands of Yadila, and whenever we had to turn south in avoiding obstacles, the full blaze of the sun burnt my face.

We were floundering through heavy dunes when the silence was suddenly broken by a loud droning on a musical note. I was startled for the moment, not knowing the cause.

'Hanaina! Hanaina!'[1] shouted my companions. 'Listen to that cliff bellowing, Sahib!' and a man at my side pointed to a sand cliff, a hundred feet or so high, and perhaps a hundred yards or more away on our right hand. I was too much absorbed to reply. The hour was 4.15 p.m., and a slight north wind blew from the rear of the cliff.

Before this, in similar winds, we had passed many such cliffs, but they had emitted no sound, only the light surface sand being carried up the gentle windward slope to spill like smoke over its top. The leeward face of the cliff was a fairly steep slanting wall and I looked in vain for a more funnel-shaped sand gorge that by some rushing wind action might account for so great a volume of noise. The usual term, 'singing sands,' seems to me hardly appropriate to describe a sound indistinguishable from the siren[2] of a moderate-sized steamship. The noise continued for about two minutes and, like a ship's fog-signal, ended as abruptly as it had begun.

A suggested explanation of the phenomenon, that the sand had been heated all day and the fall of temperature in the afternoon set the whole face sliding, came to my notice too late for investigation: the volume and nature of the noise did not suggest it, nor did it occur to me to ask my companions at what other times of the day it happens, though, from the implication of a remark made later to account for a night alarm, 'singing sands' after dark would not in their minds appear to be abnormal.

---

[1] *Hanaina* = bellowing. The two tribes of the sands use different terms for singing sands. The Rashid call it *Al Damam*, and the Murra *Al Hiyal*.

[2] The modern use of this word is equally unfair to the enchanting voices of the Sirens of the *Odyssey*.

There are other varieties of sand noises. The sands of Umm Dharta—'Mother of Wind'—(the name may be generic) to the northward of Umm al Hait, I am told, have a springiness which causes wheezing when camels walk upon them. And I myself was to be startled a month later in the sands of Suwahib on hearing a sharp 'phut' under my camel's feet like the falling of a spent bullet. It was instantaneous, and I did not hear it again. A Murri riding at my side who was familiar with the phenomenon, though it was rare, could only suggest some dark activity in the uppermost of the seven underworlds; but this has no direct connection with the loud and continuous bellowing which happens, according to the Arabs of the sands, only in heavy dune country.

And now, after two long slow days in Shu'ait, we were to bid adieu to the fair and gentle, if hungry, shivering camps between steppe and sand. On the 24th December we turned north-west and struck into the great dune-country, whose near edge stretched away from us to the west-south-west. Before us rose red mountains of sand.

The going at once became more difficult, and recalled to me my struggles a year before in the sands of Mugshin, nearly two hundred miles to the east-north-east, which I had tried to get through with mountain-bred camels, and after two abortive days had been forced to beat a retreat.

Very impressive is a great dune region at first sight—a vast ocean of billowing sands, here tilted into sudden frowning heights, and there falling to gentle valleys merciful for camels, though without a scrap of verdure in view. Dunes of all sizes, unsymmetrical in relation to one another, but with the exquisite roundness of a girl's breasts, rise tier upon tier like a mighty mountain system. No contrasting

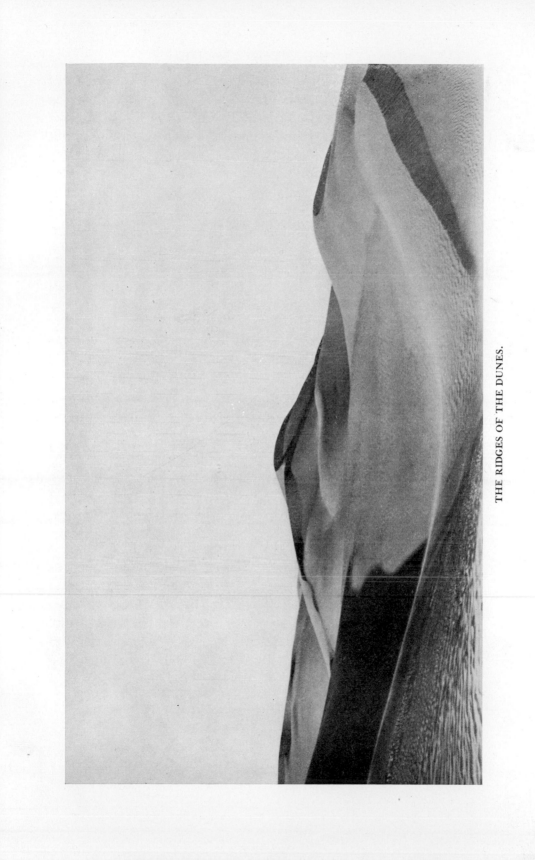

THE RIDGES OF THE DUNES.

shades are afforded by the sun's almost vertical rays in this tropical latitude, and the resulting impressions are soft planes and an exquisite purity of colour. So smooth from a distance, the sands are in reality lined with faint coruscations like tiny wavelets on the shore, and what from afar is a sheet of pure red colour, when approached sparkles with glints of green and gold. A breeze blowing from the north sweeps up gentle slopes to spill a filmy wisp of sand over the brink and thus builds up a flat rim along the upper leeward edges. The effect from near at hand is that of the Hellenic helmet of Flaxman's Heroes, but in the far distance the winding ridges of the dunes look like the walls of some fair city built upon a hill.

The Vigil of Christmas was a night of excitement. We had arrived late in camp, camels had been hobbled as usual and driven off to the scant bushes, from behind some of which came the brisk noises of merry camp-fire parties. There came a sudden scream. To me it sounded like the hooting of an owl or the whining cry of an animal; but it spread instant alarm. My camp was at once in a ferment.

'*Gom! Gom!*' 'Raiders! raiders!' shouted the excitable Badawin, leaping to their feet, their rifles at the ready; my servant came running across to me with my Winchester and bandolier. Our *rabias*, of the 'Awamir and Karab tribes, rushed out shouting: 'We are alert! We are alert! I am So-and-so[1] of such a tribe. These are my party and are under my protection.' The object of this was to save us

---

[1] *abu fulan.* In Arabia a man will often call himself and be known as 'the father of a son's name,' a commentary on the honour in which parenthood of males is held. Indeed, Saiyid Taimur bin Faisal, the Sultan of Muscat, almost invariably signed himself in private correspondence, 'Abu Sa'id,' his son, Saiyid Sa'id, being the heir apparent.

from raiders of their own factions, if these they were. It is said that the cry is never abused.

Others ran out on all sides, though in the dark night they were not in touch with one another, and it seemed to me that friend might easily be taken for foe.

An hour elapsed and there was no repetition of the sound and, indeed, no sound at all, though my party were by no means reassured and the stalwarts who were out remained out to keep night watches.

I was thoroughly tired and hence very ready to believe that the alarm had been raised by a wild beast and not an enemy, so my vigil fell short of that of my companions. My assumption was correct. Next morning the tracks of a wolf were traced near by; its whoop had, it seemed, been suspiciously like the *'awan*, the war cry of raiders making the attack.

The technique of desert raiding should be studied by all travellers. An approaching party may be friend, but is always assumed to be foe. Had the wolf cry betokened what we feared, my party would have responded with a fusillade in the air in that direction—a procedure calculated to damp the ardour of oncomers of whatever disposition. All *rabias* present would have shouted their names and tribes as my Karabis had done. The shout would have been recognised, for almost every tribe has some vocal peculiarities. Some friend would have shouted back his name and if reassured, he and the *rabia* of my party would have advanced from opposite sides and the approaching party have been led in.

If two parties meet by day, *rabias* on both sides will ride forward to within a few hundred yards to identify and be identified, while both main bodies halt apprehensively. The discovery of an enemy will send the *rabia* fleeing back to his companions, who will open fire at long range: or in the case of a sudden appearance of a supposed enemy, men will couch their camels and run out in front of them in extended order and fire upon the oncomers. The object in both cases is to frighten away the other party.

The party numerically stronger, better mounted and better armed must prevail, and flight is seldom practicable for the weak. If the raiding party enjoy only a slight advantage a war of attrition will ensue until one or other has no more ammunition, for by desert canons none should submit while he has a round left: but if the attacking party are in preponderant strength there will be no dallying; they will sweep down upon their victims.

Surrender to the first oncomer is the only hope for an individual. '*sellemni!*' is the desert equivalent of the schoolboy cry of *pax*, and as a token of submission the rifle is held above the head, or thrown to one side. '*fi wijhi*,' 'In my face,' is the victor's reply if he wishes to show mercy.

If the would-be prisoner has reason to expect good terms he may say '*sellemni*—with my 'rifle,'[1] or 'dagger,' or 'camel'; but this is a risk seldom taken; probably his adversary is covering him with a rifle, and the best he can hope for is to be spared to return empty-handed to his kith and kin. But if one of the attackers has been killed, the law of the blood-feud must operate and his life be forfeit. So also if the answer 'by my face' is not returned, he may expect no mercy. Thus raiding parties are of two kinds, that whose tribe and yours have no blood-feud, that where a blood-feud exists. Both want your camels and arms, the

---

[1] I found the word *bunduq* (pl. *banádiq*) in common use in the sands for 'rifle.' This confirms Yule's note in Hobson-Jobson that the Hindustani derives through the Arabic.

second your life as well. 'We would show our "face" to one section of the Sa'ar but not to the other—God is the All-knowing'—Khuwaitim had said to me as we rode along.

It was Christmas morning as we left behind us the 'alarm' camp (said to lie due north of Wadi Urba) and set out across what was to prove the loftiest and vastest of all the sands met with on my journey—Uruq adh Dhahiya. For the first four hours came a succession of mountains, cliffs and intervening gorges of sand. Our camels, wretched beasts, climbed arduously to knife-edge summits and slithered knee-deep down precipitous slopes. Here and there we turned back for very fear and tried a better way, and all dismounted to scrabble with our hands in the soft slopes to make a path for the camels to climb.

As we walked the soft sand came well over our ankles at each step; shoes would have been out of the question; nor was riding any comfort for the body must be bent, now back over the camel's quarters, now forward on the neck, at acute angles. Alarming too it was to look down a steep slope of a hundred feet and more where we must pass, yet our ungainly brutes, resolute and surefooted, braved a diagonal course across its face, their great pads sinking up to the shanks with every step, and throwing up clouds of sand as they were withdrawn.

No horse could possibly negotiate these southern sands, even if it could be brought thus far through the waterless wastes of the borderlands, and for a motor car they would be quite impassable.

Our toil had its compensations. There were moments when we came suddenly upon a picture of sublime grandeur, an immense and noble plastic architecture, an exquisite purity of colour, old rose-red, under the cloudless sky and

A GYPSUM PATCH IN THE SOUTHERN SANDS.

brilliant light. A winter's day in Switzerland affords a comparison—the feel of the yielding substance underfoot and a glorious exhilaration in the air.

At last, after passing a dune system called Thurub bin Imani, which was said to mark the half-way point between the sweet water of Khor Dhahiya and the brackish water-hole of Bin Hamuda lying to the north-east, the going became easier, for we changed course and steered north for long stretches along the sand valleys that here have a north-easterly axis, between the mighty dunes.

Just before sunset a halt was cried.

'Khor Dhahiya!' shouted my party as we couched our camels. I ran to the brow of the hill before me and, concealing myself, looked down into a mighty sand valley running north-east and south-west, and here perhaps a mile wide. In its bed, three hundred feet below, a green patch marked our objective, the famous water-hole, where Shaikh Salih was to have met me with a fresh relay of camels on the fourth day of the moon. To-day was the fifth, so that I was a day late, but signs of Salih or his party there were none—only silent naked spaces.

For prudence' sake we halted short for the evening, in scanty pastures, while two of our number took their water-skins and at once trudged off by a wide detour down into the valley to spy out the land. I watched with my telescope their microscopic figures at the hole, and wondered whether an enemy lay lurking near. But after a careful search of the whole area they turned back unmolested, while I, waiting expectant for their news, watched their foreshortened figures growing as they climbed the sands until the sun went down and darkness came over the scene. The tidings were at once good and bad news. Neither friend nor foe had recently watered there, tracks made by themselves two moons ago still stood; Mubarak, Shaikh Salih's companion, had visited the water-hole but yesterday, God was the Knower!, and they would show me his footmarks on the morrow.

My Christmas dinner consisted of desiccated soup, made with the water of Dhahiya, which thus needed no salt or pepper, and one of the few tins of baked beans I carried for special occasions—festive fare after a strenuous nine hours' march without solid food. A midday meal was an indulgence I never allowed myself. It would have been quite out of the question to cry a long halt at noon—for the rule of life in the heart of an arid desert demands rapid marching from pasture to pasture. Instead I carried a flask of camel's milk and a daily ration of malted milk tablets, and short stops for our camels to graze or for the Badawin to pray afforded me the opportunity to slake my thirst.

In the desert, halts are always and rightly called in the camels' interests. The poor beasts, which the traveller starts by despising and learns to admire greatly, are the means by which he moves forward to success or away to safety. In remote waste places if the camel die, its master dies. The invariable consideration my companions showed for their beasts was noteworthy. Often I found myself the only member of my party in the saddle, while the others walked for long hours to spare their mounts, and ran hither and thither to collect occasional juicy tufts of camel-thorn with which to feed them as we passed along.

Our camels were tired out. Their humps, large and full at the outset, told a story. The hump is the barometer of the camel's condition, and ours had all fallen miserably away. This was only to be expected after an eight days'

WATERING AT KHOR DHAHIYA.

journey under loads through these barren and waterless southern borderlands.

On the following morning we were early astir. The Badawin led their camels down as best they could, chanting merrily a promise of the water that the thirsty brutes so sorely needed, in measures the animals most surely understood. I went on foot, avoiding their monstrous tracks in the soft slipping slopes, avoiding, too, the sight of camels pushed to acrobatics, carrying precious chronometers on their backs. When I reached the bottom, watering had already begun, to the sound of brisk happy noises that are heard at no other time. The hole, scarcely more than a yard in diameter, was rimmed with a heap of new yellow mud, the débris thrown out by a Badu who at the commencement of operations had descended as always to clean it out. As I looked down into it I saw another Arab standing below, up to his knees in water, replenishing the leathern water-buckets that were lowered to him. Near by a Karabi held bucket after bucket to the lips of his eager animal, talking to her the while, until a raised head and fat belly denoted she had had enough, when he playfully dashed the water that remained over her neck or threw the bucket into the air to catch it as it fell.[1]

But where was Shaikh Salih and my expected camels? I spent an anxious day wondering, though Kilthut, the Shaikh's son, was ready with explanations. Khor Dhahiya was a notoriously unhealthy spot, he said, being known and used by the Sa'ar and other raiders from the Hadhramaut, and there were here no pastures, as I could see for myself.

It was late afternoon before we left the water-hole.

[1] I have heard that the local gypsum is used to build a water-trough in summer round these water-holes.

[177]

Sunset found us on a high sandy flat, thick with *zahar* and *abala*, fat pastures indeed, and even better ones were reported ahead. There Shaikh Salih would surely be. And so an early morning start. The party scanned the immediate sands for signs of his tracks, and soon there arose the now familiar explosive thanks to Allah. I shared their heartfelt joy, for among the footmarks that had been identified were those of Hamad bin Hadi, a son of the Murra whom Salih had mentioned as one sufficient for my purposes, could he be persuaded to turn guide and *rabia*. There were marks of many more camels, twenty others—encouraging discovery—for our animals, exhausted after their forced marches to Dhufar and back, could not have moved on under loads for three more days without a rest.

'Look, Sahib! That is So-and-so,' my men said, pointing to a foot impression that looked like every other footprint to me. 'That is his camel; he was leading her. She is gone with calf. See how deep are her tracks.' I was astonished at the accuracy of my party's description of those that were ahead of us, the amazing facility with which they read the evidence of the tracks we followed. In comparison the finger-print methods of the West seem a slow, laborious, technical process.

The sands are a public diary, that even he who runs may read, for all living creatures go unshod. Each of my companions not only knew at a glance the footmarks of every camel and man of my caravan, but claimed to know those of his absent tribe, and not a few of his enemies. No bird may alight, no wild beast or insect pass but needs must leave its history in the sands, and the record lasts until a rising wind bears a fine sand along to obliterate it. Snakes,

[178]

MARCHING IN THE MIGHTY URUQ ADH DHAHIYA.

hare, a sand fox, and numerous lizards owed their undoing to such tell-tale marks; their hiding-holes were in vain.

And now the sands with the crisp imprints of identified friends became our guide, and led us at right angles to our old course on a north-easterly bearing through rugged dune country, the aneroid steadily falling. As we breasted the tops of sandhills I scanned with eagerness each new horizon for Salih's camp. Suddenly there was merry chatter as black specks ahead were detected and pointed out to me as the object of our quest. A doubly welcome sight! for now our combined strength would relieve the tension of the recent anxious marches, and means become available, I hoped, for the onward march into the sands.

XIV: A GEOGRAPHICAL NOTE ON RUB' AL KHALI

A T the cost of breaking into the narrative for a few pages, it may be convenient here, where my route leaves the perimeter of the sands, to refer the reader to my map and consider briefly the shape of these sands and the configuration of Rub' al Khali.

The entire area of south-east Arabia, bounded by long. 48° 00 north of the 20th parallel, and by long. 46° 00 south of it, is, except for a narrow coastal belt, marked on our maps Rub' al Khali, Arabic words that may be translated the Empty Quarter. The meaning is sufficiently literal to have an application, and the term is one that is familiar to literate Arabs elsewhere who have learned geography from text-books, but the tribes who live in the Rub' al Khali neither use the term nor understand it in its geographical sense.

Rub' al Khali consists of desert, the eastern and southern portions of which to the extent of nearly a third of the total area are steppe lands; the rest an ocean of sands stretching away to the north and west. The southern steppe is known as Nejd, the eastern steppe as Sih in the north, Jaddat Harasis in the south; the sandy region is known as Ar Raml or Ar Rimal. Tribes are within large limits localised and for them particular areas both in sands and steppe have individual names. A steppe region sometimes derives its name from that of the tribe that habitually occupies it, but more usually from the name of a wadi.[1]

---

[1] The word *wadi, i.e.* 'valley,' or here a 'dry water-course,' is used by these Badawin not so much in a topographical sense but as a term for pastures. *Al Wadi al kabir* (there is a Moorish relic in the Spanish Guadalquivir), meaning the big wadi, often stands in the colloquial tongue for good pastures, and not necessarily for a huge valley, or stream.

The southern edge of the sands which in the course of my last two journeys I skirted for nearly two hundred miles, I have already shown to stretch almost parallel with the south coast of Arabia from Mugshin to north of the Hadhramaut, and to be falling from south to north and from west to east.

The eastern edge of the sands runs north-north-east from Mugshin, a four days' march to Qarn as Sahama, thence it turns due north and approximately follows long. 55° 40', passing thus within a day to the westward of Ibri, skirts the west side of Jabal Hafit and extends thence onward as a spur to bisect peninsular Oman.

Within the sand borders, the mountainous gypsum system of Uruq adh Dhahiya is said to form a mighty horseshoe range whose base rests on the central south borderlands in the regions of Umm Gharib, Kharkhir, Uruq adh Dhahiya, Miniyur and Raga'at; its western arm approximately follows long. 49° as far as lat. 20° N., embracing the regions Ga'amiyat, Huwaiya and Shuwaikila: its eastern arm follows long. 53° E. approximately as far north as lat. 22° 30' N. embracing Uruq Mijora, Tamaisha, Shaiba and Maraikha.

Within this horseshoe will be found only the tribes who are essentially dwellers in the great sands, i.e. (i) the Murra approaching from the north-west; (ii) the Rashid and Bait Imani sections of Al Kathir approaching from the central south; (iii) the 'Awamir and Manasir (to a more limited extent) approaching from the north-east.

Outside the horseshoe and between it and the steppe are the border sands used seasonally by particular sections of the steppe tribes. In the east these tribes are Albu Shamis, Daru', Harasis and Afar: in the south Bait Kathir, Manahil,

'Awamir (southern elements) Sa'ar and Karab, but they severally keep within a safe distance of their own water-holes.[1]

Altitude readings recorded along my four routes covering altogether some two thousand miles in the north, the south-east, the south centre and the centre of Rub' al Khali, together with the recorded direction of wadi beds (either observed or ascertained from Arab information) furnish the means of establishing the slope of this part of the continent of Arabia.

The general configuration of Arabia which rises abruptly on the west side in the Red Sea and Dead Sea rift escarp-ments to decline gently eastwards to the plains of Iraq and the waters of the Persian Gulf does not extend through-out the Rub' al Khali. Here the land mass rises abruptly on three sides: on the north-east, the Hajar range of Oman; in the central south, the Dhufar system; in the south-west, the mountains of Hadhramaut and Najran. Low levels mark the Persian Gulf and Arabian Sea littorals on the south-east side of the desert. That the sands are sloping down to the Persian Gulf on three sides is thus apparent: so also must there be a depression in the central south-east.

The altitudes of the eastern edge of the sands already delineated are approximately as follows: in the northern spur which I crossed in 1926 the reading was 1200 feet. To the westward of Jabal Hafit it is about 1000 feet. Sir Percy Cox recorded Ibri as 1600 feet, so that the edge of the sands in that latitude, bearing in mind the south-westerly fall of its wadi Al 'Ain, must be considerably lower. The height of the sands at Mugshin was about 400 feet. Hence

[1] There is an isolated island of sand to the eastwards in the Ja'alan triangle, which is the habitat of the Yal Wahiba tribe.

[182]

it may be deduced that the eastern edge of the sands is falling from north to south.

East of this long eastern edge of Ar Rimal is a steppe which rises slowly north-eastwards to the great Hajar backbone of Oman, whence the drainage wadis Al 'Ain, Al 'Aswad, Al 'Amairi and Musallim follow almost parallel courses to the south-west to lose themselves in the eastern borders of the sands. To the south-east of Mugshin is another steppe having no discernible slope but said to be bounded on its north-east side by the isolated ridge of Jabal Hugf. On its south-eastern side the wadis Qadan (Ghudun?), Raunib and Haitam (I crossed the mouths at sea-level in 1928) fall south-eastwards into Sauqira Bay.

On its south-western side, Jaddat Harasis receives the system of Wadi 'Ara, the inland drainage of the northern extension of Jabal Samhan. Where I crossed it in its sources on an earlier journey the wadi heads were running north-east, and aneroid readings varied between 1100 feet east and 1400 feet west. To the eastward of Jabal Hugf the only considerable wadis, Halfain and Andam, fall away from the eastern Hajar of Oman and run due south, in part to drain into the Gulf of Masira.

There is thus an area of depression at the south-eastern extremity of the great sands forming a corridor running south-east and extending from the coast of Sauqira Bay through Jaddat Harasis and thence on into the sands, probably in long. 54° E. to 55° E., lat. 20° N. to 22° N. Within it, water comes to the surface at Mugshin and Hamaidan. North of this corridor the general slope is upwards towards the north and east, south of the corridor it rises to the south and west.

An item of much geographical interest is the presence of

[183]

desert quicksands on the northern side of the corridor, where it meets Ar Rimal. The extent of Umm as Samim, as the area is called, is said to be a two days' march in every direction. In appearance a sheet of salt plain, it gives no indication to the unwary traveller of its treacherous bogs. Many have perished here and only certain Daru' Badawin who come to collect salt on its borders are said to brave its secret passages, raiders, as might be expected, giving it a wide berth.

Von Wrede, the Bavarian soldier of fortune, who in 1843 penetrated the Hadhramaut in Muslim disguise, records a similar phenomenon, its place-name Bahr as Safi. He marched towards one of the white patches armed with a plumb-line of six fathoms. 'With the greatest caution I approached the border to examine the sand, which I found almost an impalpable powder, and I threw the plumb-line as far as possible; it sank instantly, the velocity diminishing, and in five minutes the end of the cord had disappeared in the all-devouring tomb.'

While I do not wish to impugn Von Wrede's veracity I should record that most of the companions of my journeys had raided in the sands to the north of the Hadhramaut, in fact the Karab *rabias* hailed from there, but none knew of Bahr as Safi, and all averred that the quicksands described exist to-day only in Umm as Samim, lying between sand and steppe to the north and east of Mugshin and south and west of 'Ibri. Many Omani Badawin and others told me of the Umm as Samim quicksands.

XV: THROUGH THE SANDS OF DAKAKA: THE SECOND RELAY OF CAMELS

'Haiya bi wusulkum, sahib!
Marhaba wa haiya bikum!'

THIS was the desert greeting of Shaikh Salih as I eagerly rode up some distance ahead of my party to the new camp, and, couching Gerainha, slipped off her back for the last time to grasp Salih's outstretched hand. With him was a man I recognised—fat old Muhammad who had been with me on my last year's expedition. But only these two; the rest of the party of strange Badawin looked on from their sandy eminence a little way off without bothering to come forward to meet me, and I scented a coolness in the atmosphere which seemed to augur ill for my plans. Was this to be the limit of my journey? Was I not to be allowed to move forward?

But as my party straggled in the cold faces took on a kindlier expression, and men sprang up to meet their returning kindred and salute them in the manner of Badu meeting Badu. This nose kiss[1]—it is also the lovers' kiss—in its attenuated form before me consisted of three brushing nose to nose movements, left to right, right to left, centre press, while each placed his right hand over the other's left shoulder.

[1] Between desert men the nose kiss takes the place of hand-shaking. With Bait Kathir under the mountains it is observed after a five or six days' separation, but seldom oftener; here in the sands Badawin salute each other thus if separated for only one day.

The Mahra in the steppe, though a Badawin tribe, are peculiar in using amongst themselves not the nose kiss but a triple cheek kiss, right, left, right.

[185]

A circle of squatting Arabs was soon formed and I ordered three bowls of dates to be set in the midst and the coffee cup to go round. The new Badawin eyed me silently, giving me a feeling that I was being weighed in the balance as they spoke in low tones to right and left with members of my old party. The last-named disdained the coffee and dates as these went round the first time—unusual for those who had been so insistent for *fuwala* on the march—and it was amusing to me to find in the Rub' al Khali an application of the time-honoured principle of 'family-hold-back.' The delicacies received the nominal patronage usual on such formal occasions and there was plenty when it came to my party's turn to stick fingers into the common dish.

'*Marhaba wa ehlen ya haiyakum!*'

Thus old Saif, the rightful shaikh of the tribe by blood[1] but an effete branch (and consequently superseded by the Kilut family, not of shaikhly lineage on the male side but resolute, brave and effective), as he took off his ammunition belt and threw it into the circle. This was an invitation to my party whose visit to the coast and hunting activities on the march had brought them a few rounds of ammunition apiece, to spare of their bounty for the titular chief. Now one, now another threw a round into the pool, as it were, and when all had done Saif was ten rounds to the good.

Shaikh Salih had not failed me. He came along bringing a man of consequence for introduction, walking in Badawin fashion hand-in-hand with him.

'This is a shaikh, Sahib! shaikh of the Murra' (it is well

---

[1] If Bait Imani is excluded from Ar Rashid (and they are now regarded as having achieved autonomy), the tribe consists of two sections, Mat'ariba and Sa'adna, the latter the shaikhly house of which Saif was the head.

to promote your friends thus in the desert, though in point of fact the description was not very wide of the mark).[1] 'No better guide in all the sands than Hamad bin Hadi, no doughtier fighter, no more skilful hunter; and loyal, I call God to witness, for did not my brother take his daughter to wife; none knows the pastures and the water-holes like Hamad; he knows a way across the sands and agrees to be our *rabia*.'

Hamad was a middle-sized man of dark complexion with shifty black eyes, a hawk-like Armenoid face thickly bearded and a curious quick voice which bespoke him a man of greater vigour than Salih, but on first impression not so inspiring of trust. The dweller of the desert like a child or an animal requires a very slow and careful approach, and Hamad, who had never before seen a man of my colour or heard an accented voice, would not improbably be suspicious; so I decided that leisureliness in coming to the point was the right policy. The first meeting was therefore an occasion only for the coffee cup and amiable conversation about hunting; likewise the second, which was profitably reinforced with the present of a head-dress for his son.

'What do you make of Hamad?' said Salih to me the next day.

'The very man.'

'Didn't I tell you so? But he wants a lot, Sahib!' The greed of the Badu is proverbial, but I had made a sworn pact with Salih before leaving the coast, and now he was to observe the conditions scrupulously by persuading Hamad to accept the terms we mutually considered fair.

The new party, now reduced in numbers, had become

[1] Hamad was the headman of the Hathalain, a subsection of Al Ghuferan, one of the divisions of Al Murra.

more friendly to me. The antipathy I thought I had detected in our first meeting was but their native sullenness: in truth they had come here with Shaikh Salih expressly for my purposes. The plan was that they would bear me westwards through these sands of Dakaka to the water-hole of Shanna. There I must dismiss them and engage a third and still further reduced party of men and camels, which Shaikh Salih would go ahead to select and bring to the rendezvous after ten days if God willed, and neither of us met an enemy.

These central southern sands of Dakaka were indeed the key to the problem of my journey, for they had received the rains of last year and were therefore blessed with exceptional pastures so that the herds had concentrated here. This had made it possible for a large party laden with full milk-skins to come to the coast for me; here I could find an escort to take me on, and hence a party would avail at the most advanced point towards the inmost sands for a jump off into the unknown. Had Dakaka itself been hungry, had last year's rains fallen not here but to the north-east, the camel concentrations would have been too far removed for the system of relays by which alone I could hope to cross the deserts in quick stages carrying scientific instruments.

Pay-day was a day of excitement, for a hired Badu is the most difficult person to satisfy on dismissal. His contracted pay was fifty dollars for himself and camel and forty dollars for a pack animal; of this he had drawn half at Dhufar, in advance; the other half he was getting that day, so that my camp table glittered with Maria Theresa dollars (each worth about 1s. 4d.), the only coin the sands know, and that but infrequently. The chink of silver, a sound rare in

Dakaka, was a necessary accompaniment to setting up piles of twenties and twenty-fives, which would facilitate payment, for then all I had to do was to put so many piles into each man's hand as he came along. But I was reckoning without my host. Each laboriously counted and recounted his share and a horrid infection spread amongst them, of each looking up and declaring he was one or two short. A companion would take the money out of his hand and count it back in fives, generally to the man's ultimate satisfaction. My method of counting 6, 7, 8, etc., or even omitting to count at all, appeared to puzzle them. Their practice was to count 1, 2, 3, 4, 5 and then begin at 1 again —an object lesson in the human appeal of the decimal system. At the end of an hour my table was bare, every name on the pay-roll of my escort had been ticked off; two hours later I was congratulating myself that on the whole pay-day had passed satisfactorily, when suddenly there was much shouting; a serious row started and it looked as though the old party, with whom my relations had been so cordial, were going to spoil this record by a free fight on the day of parting. It seemed they had incurred mutual debt obligations at Dhufar and the liquidation of these demanded a standard of mental arithmetic and of patience in discussion not vouchsafed to them; hence the heated words and the possibility of the dagger as an honourable arbiter. Peace only came when Shaikh Salih gathered up all the payments that I had made into a large common heap on his head-dress laid out on the sands, for a complete redistribution by himself. Thus I had to witness all my pretty work of the morning brought to naught.

Peace prevailed at last—but not contentment. For they must have rations, they said, how else were they to get home with their exhausted animals not in milk? They would die on the way. Their demands seemed to me to be three times in excess of their legitimate needs and to be inspired by the approach of Ramadhan, when the fast by day is compensated by gorging at night. Other Badawin not of my party also gathered round imagining a vain thing in their hearts. For before me by the most favourable computation was a six weeks' march, and my stock of food represented a bare six weeks' supply and thus had become more precious than gold. To dissipate it must lead to certain failure. I had guarded it most jealously on the march; it was the only matter over which I could afford, when seriously challenged, to show temper, for I knew that the end of my rations meant the end of my journeyings. Normally camels in milk are taken along at grazing speed; not on raids or forced marches, which would run them dry or exhaust them. Thus the great desert before me, with camels of necessity not in milk, would provide, in the last event, nothing but the flesh of our own mounts; and to take that would be *propter vitam vivendi perdere causas.*

Camp must be broken with all speed, for so long as I remained my old party and the stray starvelings of the sands that came along would batten on me; so in lieu of food they were sent away cheered with two or three dollars apiece. Similar treatment was accorded to the master of Gerainha— she, patient brute, having carried me from the Qara Mountains, was now returning to her home in the steppes to the south. Her mistress there was reputed to be the most beautiful girl in all the land, one that troubled the hearts of not a few of my escorting Badawin; indeed, she was the subject of a romance of which she would learn in due course after her fate had been decided. She was now nineteen and unmarried, an unthinkable state of affairs in polygamous Arabia, and Bin Aksit, her father, was twitted by the rest of his companions on the march for his selfishness.

'Why not give her to the Sahib?' they would say mockingly, 'he's young and strong and look at his dollars, why you could buy all the camels in Rub' al Khali.' And behind his back they would accuse him of miserliness for he was passing rich in the possession of fifteen camels, and as he had no close male relatives, the daughter would inherit his all, which made her doubly attractive in their sight.

'How much do you want for her?' I asked him one day in the dispassionate way which a Badu would tolerate from the lips of a man not like himself.

'Three camels,'[1] he said. 'Why, the daughter of 'Ali brought her father three, and who can compare 'Ali's daughter with mine? All know she is worth it, but no one has offered me more than two, so I will not agree and she is content to stay with me.'

[1] This marriage-price would go entirely to the father. With Bait Kathir in the mountains the marriage-price of a virgin bride may vary between twenty dollars and three hundred dollars, according to her family, face and fortune, but a half only goes to her father, the remainder being divided between the other near relatives. I have met a case of a two-hundred-dollar bride (which places her high in the scale of social values) where the division was as follows: father (half), one hundred dollars; brother, thirty; mother, twenty; sister, nothing; paternal uncle, twenty; maternal uncle, ten; paternal aunt, five; maternal aunt, four; paternal grandfather, four; paternal grandmother, three; byes, *i.e.* unaccounted for, four.

A widow or divorced woman on remarrying would herself get the marriage-price.

In Oman the bridegroom pays half the marriage-price in advance to the father, and the remaining half after marriage by slow instalments. In theory it goes to the bride for her jewels, bedding and personal adornments.

That was a fortnight before. Later I had seen that Bin Aksit and Ma'yuf sat round the same camp-fire together overmuch, and now and then withdrew from the general circle to engage in rapt conversation, and the gossip of the camp when Gerainha had departed was that Ma'yuf was the lucky man.

Private conversation is achieved by two persons rising from the circle and betaking themselves fifty paces or so from their companions, but even then they are not safe from intrusion. It is amusing to watch a third Badu come along and instead of sitting in the general circle, go up and salaam the whisperers and sit down with them—a flattering if gratuitous indication that he thinks their talk more likely to interest him. There is so much community of life amongst them, however, living as they do in the open, always cheek by jowl for mutual protection from a common enemy, that familiarity, and the impulse to act without too sensitive a feeling for others is ingrained in them, and a European who would travel happily must be prepared to adapt himself to their standards. On one occasion, for instance, a Kathiri, seeing the milk bowl at my side, suddenly held it to his lips and drained its contents; they were dregs, it is true, but a European could not afford to show resentment. Even my heart-to-heart talks with Shaikh Salih were not undisturbed, for one or other of my party spotting us from afar and finding the attraction irresistible would come up with a hearty salaam and sit down without a 'by your leave,' to hear what it was all about.

With my party reduced in numbers to twenty men, nearly all strangers to me, we started off again on a westerly course, meeting no encampment on our way. I suspected that the main body of the Rashid tribe was grazing to the

MARCHING IN DAKAKA.

north, and it was essential that I should escape their importunities for food. I should thus also avoid the consequences of any religious objection some fanatic among them might take to my presence on the sacred soil of the Faithful.

The first day, as usual, was a short march—the fresh, untried camels bellowing protests against unusual burdens, and their masters quarrelling among themselves about alleged inequalities of loads. My Bikaner-pattern saddle was the subject of universal disapprobation for its size and weight, wherefore I suffered the humiliation of being given a different camel to ride each day.

In this region of Dakaka the sands were somewhat milder in mood than the mountains and valleys of Uruq adh Dhahiya, for which they form an exaggerated crossing of the T. The basic formation was a hard red sand, in immense undulations, like a troubled sea many times magnified. Occasional superimposed sandhills of a paler colour (that became less lofty as we went on) were sometimes solid, sometimes horseshoe-shaped—termed *hugna*, and of very curious shape. They appear to arise from reversible wind action and in their depressions lay often a white patch of gypsum and not infrequently a water-hole.

Here there was no lack of sweet water—sweet, that is to say, judged by the other waters of the sands—and amidst improved pastures we deliberately made slow going, so that I now found more opportunity for collecting of zoological specimens and photography than during the recent long nervous marches when such things had to be neglected. We dawdled in fact while bin Kilut and bin Ham went scouting the country-side about my business.

The important member of the new party was Hamad bin

[193]

Hadi, whom I grew to respect as the days wore on. His companions showed towards him much respect, as befitted the son of his father, a Murri known throughout the sands, who had slain eight men of the rival Manasir tribe during his lifetime and had died in venerable old age beside the eponymous well of Bir Hadi, one of many water-holes dug by him. With Hamad came his nephew Marzuq, our *mu'edhdhin* on the march, and a cousin, another Hamad, of rather unstable temper, who appeared with two strings dangling from his nose (suggestive of the physician's stethoscope with nostrils for ear-holes). This practice of plugging the nostrils with cotton is common throughout Arabia and Persia, as a protection against evil smells which are supposed to aggravate most maladies. Hamad clearly suffered from ophthalmia, which, however, he ascribed to an evil spirit, a *zar*. I attended its exorcism that evening, a simple ritual compared with the elaborate performances practised in the coastal villages of Oman,[1] but presumably of the same nature and lacking nothing in the frenzied display of the possessed. The chief differences were that the desert audience were not women, but men, who did not play a hysterical part in the proceedings: the Master of Ceremonies was a man and not a woman; and fire was used in place of blood.

Hamad, the afflicted, knelt before the fire within a circle of squatting companions, the Master of Ceremonies, Muhammad bin Shughaila, seated himself next to him, and between them on the sands was placed a cup filled with fire. One or two of the party brought their cooking-pots and thus was the stage set.

Hamad now took off his head-dress, folded it once

---

[1] See my *Alarms and Excursions in Arabia.*

TYPICAL DAKAKA SANDS.

diagonally and used it as a shawl and veil combined, holding the ends with outstretched arms. He began to bob and sway his body, while his companions around chanted,[1] clapped their hands, and drummed with their fingers on upturned pots. The *zar*-possessed put more and more frenzy into his movements as the minutes passed, bowing blindly over the fire on to which he must have many times fallen but for the care of a neighbour, who held out a cane before him; now and then he took up the cup of fire to hold it under his veil and inhale it as though it were the incense burner, an act that seemed to impel him to more feverish activity, and so it went on until his voice became tremulous and his mood hysterical. An hour may have passed thus; and now the Master of Ceremonies began. He had a series of questions to put to the *zar* (who speaks by the mouth of the patient), but the *zar* seemed to share my view that the exorcism had been too summary or so it seemed by the tardiness at first of the answers.

M.C.: 'Are you *afera?*'

Zar: (No answer.)

M.C.: 'Are you *jinn?*'

Zar: (No answer.)

Chorus of Badawin: 'It's a *zar* of course. Has not Hamad said it is Saif Shangur?'[2]

Hamad went on swaying and gibbering. A pause on the part of the M.C.

Badawin: 'Go on, Muhammad!'

M.C.: 'You are a shaikh. What do you want? Tell us.'

Zar: (No answer.)

More vigorous drumming and hand-clapping. The

[1] See Appendix VI for the chant.
[2] There are many *zars*. This is one of the most popular of them.

patient whispering to himself: 'Saif Shangur! When are you coming?'

M.C.: 'Do you want money?'

Zar (at last on the move): 'A ring.'

M.C.: 'Must it have a stone in it?'

Zar: 'A ring.'

Chorus of Badawin to M.C.: 'Don't ask unnecessary questions.'

M.C. to Badawin: 'Who has a ring?'

Ma'yuf parted with his poor possession, which the Master of Ceremonies now introduced into the cup of fire and then put on one of Hamad's fingers, and so continued holding his hand while he put his final question.

M.C.: 'Will you remove the evil from the eye?'

Zar: 'Yes.'

M.C.: 'There is no other evil except that in the eye?'

Zar: 'No.'

M.C.: 'Swear that you will remove it.'

Zar: 'Eh, eh.'

M.C.: 'Swear by the oath of a *qabaili*.'

Zar: '*Fi wijhak*.'

M.C.: '*Shered*.'—It has fled.

And thus the proceedings were at an end, and the no-longer afflicted one rose unsteadily and went off to his sandy couch for the night.

We left our camp that lay to the north of the water-hole of Bil Ashush and moving westwards came two hours later to a great horseshoe hill named Hulaiyil, the red sands here clothed unexpectedly with generous dark green *abala*. It was our New Year's Day—a festival unrecognised of course by Badawin (indeed, only two of my Rashidi companions remembered the days of the week)—but the place pleased us all for its pastures, and I decided to halt and spend the day shooting. Hamad, the subject of last night's exorcism, came up as I dismounted. His eyes were no better, though he would have me believe that they were, pointing in proof to the nostril wads that had been withdrawn and hung about his neck—but still kept in reserve, I noticed. Perhaps he was of too recent a generation of believers for a faith-cure, for the Murra tribe are said not to practise magic, with the exception of the isolated southern groups, having learned it from the Rashid, who use it in common with every tribe of the southern steppe.

I spent the remainder of the day with my rifle under my arm, making a circuit of the camp at some two or three miles' distance, but to my surprise came upon no track of any animal bigger than a hare, for, despite the hungry marches of the southern borderlands, we passed tracks of antelope and fox there every day. Animal imprints became easy to identify, and I soon learned without any conscious effort those of every wild animal of the sands and when it had passed. Dakaka was overrun with the golden hare, and almost every bush bore signs of a recently scraped hole beneath. Into these the passing Badu would thrust an arm and draw out the wriggling creature, while we would often spy one sleeping in some leafy shade and easily get quite near to it upon the soft noiseless sands.

Hare for dinner produced another animal story. If you would hear how the hare became lawful for man to eat, it is necessary for you to know two things: firstly, that in the ancient days the brute creation could speak; and secondly, that it was customary for the women of the time to bind into a faggot the sticks they had gathered and ride it home like the witches of Europe with their broomsticks.

One day, then, the Prophet (upon him be prayer and peace) said to some women:—'Go and gather me firewood.' And off they went as they were bidden, but in the wilderness they fell to gossiping overmuch and dallied.

And the Prophet (upon him be peace), when they did not return, became impatient, and said to the hare that sat at his side:

'Go out into the wilderness and you will see some women gathering sticks; tell them to bind up their bundles, and ride home at once.'

So off the hare went and found the women, but instead of conveying the message as it was delivered to him, he merely said:

'The Prophet says, "Put the firewood on your heads and return home." '

Thus the women, gathering up their sticks, came, returning by the slowest way.

As the hours passed and they did not arrive, the Prophet grew angry; but at last he saw them approaching, and as they came up he cried:

'Why did you not return riding as you always do?'

'Because the hare said you wished us to return this way, O prophet of God.'

Then the Prophet turned his wrath from the women to the hare, and picking up a brand from the fire, he struck the now fleeing animal on the tail, which to this day bears a small black mark. Then he raised his voice so that all could hear and called after the hare, 'Henceforth you are *hallal*, for all men to eat, every bit of you—even to your bowels.'

We made an early start next day and soon passed two mighty horseshoe hills that marked the water-holes of

Mashruma and Dhiraibi. Hamad the *rabia* and I were riding ahead when he suddenly halted, his eyes fixed on some distant object; and he stretched out his hand towards me for my telescope. We dismounted while he pointed out the hill that aroused his fears and motioning me to remain where I was, crept forward towards it, using the cover of the folded sands. Later he returned reassured, for the suspicious thing proved to be a knoll and not an enemy.

Hamad, it seemed, was a marked man. He was famous for raids, sometimes single-handed, into the Sa'ar country; he had in fact shed Sa'ar blood, and so could not expect to survive his next meeting with a superior party of them; this and the Manasir blood-feud he had inherited gave him many ghostly fears. Again and again he held us up while he searched the horizons with my telescope, and whenever we halted for the night, he would slink back over our tracks for some miles lest we were being tracked by an enemy, and return just after nightfall, when tracking was no longer possible, with the glad news that our camp-fires could now be safely lighted.

To our immediate north was reported the water-hole of Waraiga. There my two original emissaries sent from Dhufar to find their tribe had come upon them.[1] And there it was that the main herds of the tribe were now grazing.

---

[1] The route they took is of interest in showing Rashidi's probable line of retreat before Sa'ar depredations. From Shisur my messengers had moved north-eastwards along the Umm al Hait, struck through the sands of Umm Dharta to those of Ghanim, where they watered at Khasfa and Ablutan, thence north-westwards through the salt-pans and sand-mountains of Mijora to the sands of Hibak, watering at Zughain, thence southwestwards to the bordering water-hole of Fida, on through the sands of Dakaka to the water of Waraiga.

The rearing of the camel is in this environment the pre-destined life to which every man-child is born. He is her parasite: her milk provides almost all his food and drink, her wool his shelter and clothing. Life is the quest for green pastures, rain the gift of God, and lightning man's pillar of fire. The great changing world without; the rise and fall of kingdoms; science and art and learning; spiritual forces at work for human betterment—'the oppositions of science falsely so-called' and immoral systems making for human degradation; the welter of races, tongues and classes—of these he is unaware. They have no meaning, and there-fore no existence for him. He follows the primitive life his fathers have led for ten thousand years, and his sons must live for as long to come. He abjures the soft and sedentary ways of life; his code knows only pitiless ferocity for his enemies, and for his friends the heights and depths of human courage and the milk of human-kindness.

Pastures[1] and water are the two elemental needs of nomadic life. In winter pastures come first, for herds require water infrequently—once in fifteen or twenty days perhaps, or where rains have produced sodden grazing they may not return to a water-hole for two months, during which time the Badawin never taste water but live exclusively on milk. In summer,[2] on the other hand, when the great heat and

---

[1] Pastures = *mar'a*, *akl*, but generally *ma'ash* (Rashid dialect). To the Badu the best camel-fodder is the *samr* acacia found in the steppe at altitudes above 1200 feet. Next come *abala* and *zahara* shrubs of the sands and *gasis* after rains or dews. *dhu'ya* and *dha'ut*, both steppe flora, follow, and then *markh*, found between steppe and sand. Next in the order are *ghaf* acacia and *selem* (known locally as *hardhai*). There are many other kinds of camel-fodder, but these are the mainstays of the southern deserts.

[2] Parties of Murra are said to come from time to time and spend the summer in Dakaka on account of its comparatively sweet water.

glare make the sands almost unendurable, herds are restricted within two days' radius of a water-hole, for they
require watering every other day.[1] In the higher altitudes,
however, and amidst the perennial pastures of the southern
steppe against the mountains, camels are herded into caves
by day to escape the effect of the summer sun, and are
turned out to graze by night in the cool. In these conditions
watering every fourth or even sixth day will suffice.

In the sands themselves man must be forever on the
move. In summer, movement is by night in sharp marches
from one water-hole with adjoining pastures to another.
In winter, water not being a pressing consideration and
pastures being eaten up as they are found, movement is by
day with a halt of perhaps two or three days over each; the
herds move slowly across the great spaces in unending cycle.
The direction of the march is decided by scouting parties
of two men (*towuf*), who must ride fast and far. Their
reconnaissances in winter may last for several weeks, the
men living on milk, with which their water-skins have been
filled at the outset.[2]

In summer the great heat of the sands is a torment to
them, for it makes sleep impossible once the sun is high,
and by night little time avails for sleep, for they must
protect their camels by riding in the cool. An honoured
task is theirs, given to good guides and men who can be
trusted, at need, to calculate not too nicely the time their

---

[1] Camels which are frequently watered are called *shuwarib*. Camels
away from water in winter for long periods:

(sing.)	(pl.)
jazi	*juwazi*, by Murra.
nash (*neish*)	*nuwash*, by Rashid.

[2] After the first few days, of course, the milk curdles; where marches are
long, it is diluted with brackish water.

[201]

milk-skins will last, so that they often return a day or two late and fasting. Shaikh Salih and many others of my escorting Badawin had known such experiences. Small wonder that in their minds milk (which alone makes their life possible) should be honoured above every other meat. The Prophet himself held this. Witness the language he held with a companion who had returned from a feast:

Prophet: 'And what was set before you?'

Companion: 'We had camel's flesh.'

Prophet: 'Your host killed for you.'

Companion: 'And we had rice.'

Prophet: 'He honoured you.'

Companion: 'And dates.'

Prophet: 'He pleased you.'

Companion: 'And we had the milk of the camel.'

Prophet: 'Ah! Enough, he feasted you!'

On the fourth day we continued our westerly course towards the *hugna* of Khudhfiya, a large hill that had been in sight of the camp overnight, and which we passed after half an hour. In its great gypsum-lined hollow facing south-west—as do all these horseshoe hills—was a cluster of straw-like sun shelters beside the water-hole, unusual erections to find in the sands.

Presumably they were relics of some summer watering. Hamad slipped off his camel, as the Badu manner is, without couching her, and handing the headrope to his nephew as we passed on, descended into the hollow to look for traces of watering by possible raiders. He caught us up later with the news that all was well, and only the camel marks of bin Ham (of my recently dismissed party and now on his way to Huwaiya on a recruiting campaign) showed that he had passed three days before. We pressed on to

arrive three hours later at the water-hole of Shanna, our
immediate objective. My advance guard of two Badus ran
up from the water-hole as we arrived crying, *'Gom! Gom!
Muhammad bin Mubarak the Karabi! Muhammad bin
Quwaid the Sa'ari!'* (names of two notorious Hadhramauti
raiders between whom and my companions there was a
blood-feud). Hamad, with whom I now went to the hole,
scrutinised the sands and gypsum bed about it, then looked
up smiling and reassured. The attempted befooling may
have been to tease him or perhaps to encourage me to
disgorge a little of my supposedly large stock of ammunition, or it may only have been a joke. In the last event it
succeeded, though it reminded us that we were still very
much exposed to the raider; indeed, Hamad forthwith
borrowed my telescope and made off for the tallest hill
and that was the last I saw of him till the hour of evening
prayer.

XVI: AT THE WATER-HOLE OF SHANNA—THE HALT BEFORE THE NORTHWARD DASH

IT was the full moon before Ramadhan, and a full moon is a mixed blessing. It makes star observations with an artificial horizon troublesome. It is an ally of the raider, for tropical skies are so bright that he can see to track by night. Its advantage was that I could see to record my notes with no other aid as I lay near a camp-fire.

That night camel flesh was for dinner. One of our camels was found to be ailing, some said mortally, and the one way with a worn-out camel in the desert is to kill and eat it.

The old *fatira's* tribal brand[1] showed her to be of Janaba origin, she had indeed been part of the booty of a raid, a *dhalul* and lady of high degree before coming to this sad inevitable end.

'How does the flesh compare with beef?' I asked Khuwaitim, a Rashidi now domiciled in Dhufar, my original emissary, in fact.

'Incomparably better,' he said.

'And mutton?'

'Likewise it lacks the flavour of camel meat.'

'And what are the prime parts?'

'In a young camel the lower ribs; to-day the legs.'

'What of the marrow of the thigh bones?'

---

[1] Each true Badu tribe has a particular mark, usually very simple in design, but with significance of an armorial bearing: it is branded on each camel of the tribe on the face, neck or quarter as may be the particular tribal custom. Sections within the tribe sometimes have their own particular *wasm*. A complete list of those met with in Rub' al Khali is given in Appendix V.

'Delicacy of delicacies! Wait and you shall see.'

'And how are we going to have it cooked—stewed or grilled?' (In the steppe where a heap of stones could have been gathered they would have grilled the flesh in the Stone Age manner.)

'We shall boil it. But alas! there is no salt. *W'allahi*, if we had salt, you should judge of the soup.'

O blind lover! I thought. I will also record my own view that camel flesh is very tough and stringy, and that boiled, as it has to be, in brackish water and without fat, it is a weariness both to the palate and to the digestion.

Poor bint Shantuf was brought along and couched. Two holes were hastily scooped in the sand under her forelegs, which were then bound, and one Badu holding her tail, and another twitching her upper lip to bring her head back along her body, made her powerless to resist. Muhammad, better butcher than exorciser, had sharpened his dagger expressly and now bending close to the ground on her blind side, gave her a sharp stab in the pit of her neck. A torrent of blood gushed forth as he quickly slashed across her great throat, muttering as he did so, 'In the name of God, the Compassionate, the Merciful,' and then continued sawing with his dagger blade through her veins and windpipe back to the bone, his hands and arms streaming with blood. After her first desperate lurch and a few feeble gurgling grunts she lay still, with her monstrous neck tilted over like a falling tree, and her eyes of a glassy pallor. Never have I seen Badawin more elated; the prospect of a hearty meal cheered them all and with little axes and knives they all fell gleefully skinning and jointing. Five heaps of fresh meat soon lay on the sands—for the five camp-fire parties composing my caravan, and a shout

[205]

of joy announced the moment to cast lots for them—ever the desert way. Five representatives stood forth, one for each party. A head-dress was produced and into it each put a marked round of ammunition. The four corners were bunched together and the contents shaken up. A by-stander was invited to grasp one round through the head-dress, which was then opened and the owner of the chosen round given first choice of heaps. Four times the performance was repeated, each time with a round withdrawn, and when the last had gone so had the body of bint Shantuf. Eagerly the Badawin scattered in search of firewood, for no sooner is an animal slaughtered than straight it goes into the pot, neither Arab climate nor Arab nature suffering it to 'hang'; within an hour of the time when the beast walked up to the place of execution she was sizzling to content the hearts and noses of the Badawin sitting round their camp-fires. Not that all of her was to be cooked and eaten that day, for much of the flesh was kept back to relieve our scanty store of food. The surplus meat my companions cut into strips and later dried, like biltong, merely by carrying it on their saddles exposed to the sun, and as they went they nibbled it and declared it to be very good.

As soon as afternoon prayers were at an end the party addressed themselves to the great shining stomach of the beast. It was perched on the top of a convenient *abala* bush beneath which a circular hole about a yard in diameter was scooped in the sands, and lined with bint Shantuf's own neck skin as for a waterproof sheet. The bladder was now pierced and the contents trickled down to make a pool of yellow liquid.

'It is delicious,' they said, as each in turn went down on

SLAUGHTERING A DYING CAMEL FOR THE POT.

MY MURRA GUIDES, HAMAD BIN HADI AND TALIB.

hands and knees setting his lips to it to drink his fill; 'far better than the brackish water of the sands.'

I was not astir at dawn, but learned later from my servant Muhammad that the *mu'edhdhin's* call no sooner woke them than the Rashidis made a joyous dash for a drink at the pool[1] before lining up for prayers.

At Shanna one of my party brought me a perfect flint arrow-head saying that he had found it at the water-hole, but this was untrue. The arrow-head, like a large flint spear-head in possession of another Arab, had come from the sands of Sanam. The owners from whom I acquired them had no knowledge of their original use, but I gathered that such flints are sometimes picked up in the sands and used as firelighters. Hamad bin Hadi, to whom I showed them, that he might search for others to our common advantage, considered them intrinsically uninteresting, for he with an eye less for archæology than for the picturesque, declared that at but a day's march west of Shanna there were 'stones' in abundance and, more interesting by far, graven images—'God was the Knower!'—and the work of the sons of Adam in the Days of Ignorance. The name of this spot amidst the dunes of Ga'amiyat he called Shag al Masawwar, a name which seemed to promise much, 'the Valley of Images.' It was deemed unwise for me to leave the main party, so I sent Hamad to bring me specimens against the promise of reward. Thirty-six hours later he returned with a rib-like stone two feet in length, another of symmetrical circular shape, one and a half feet in diameter, that looked

---

[1] *Ilfadh*. The Murra, according to Hamad, contrary to South Arabian tastes, do not greatly relish it, and drink it only when suffering from thirst that cannot be satisfied in any other way. The Rashidi word for it, *althudh*, seems to have substituted *th* for *f*, a peculiarity I noticed in other words.

like the pelvis of some ancient reptile and various small specimens of quaint shapes, resembling Losspuppen or Fairy Stones. These were clearly Nature's work. The two big ones looked like fossil bones, but proved to be mere sandstone concretions.[1]

'Here you are, Sahib!' said Hamad, as he laid them on the sands before me, while his fellow Badawin looked at him disapprovingly for having brought along what must be added burdens for the camels.

'I don't know what they are, Hamad, what do you think they are?'

'The work of Bani Hillal, *Allahu alim!*' said he, and the onlookers nodded their assent.

Bani Hillal, through the length and breadth of Arabia, and indeed of North Africa, is a name to conjure with, a name that stands for an ancient but now extinct tribe to which every well or other relic of past days is ascribed; its name is ever on the lips of men. Bani Hillal is the fount of the whole folk-lore of the southern desert. Every Badu has something to tell of its legendary heroes, often in the simple rhymes of his beloved tongue, and when I have heard one story from different lips, I have noticed that the version hardly differs by one word.

The great traditional hero of Bani Hillal was one Bu Zaid, so named not that he was the father of a son Zaid, but because he was 'the possessor of excellence'—a man of superior qualities. The name Antar was strange to these remote dwellers in the Rub' al Khali, but legends of Bu Zaid and of his kinsman Dhiyab bin Ghanim, another hero of the tribe, these they have in abundance.

They place the ancient home of Bani Hillal in Wadi

[1] See Appendix II.

Markha in the land now occupied by the Daham; there the mighty well Bir Jaufa with its thirty rigs remains to this day, men tell, as their glorious memorial. Every member of my party knew some verses—Salih knew them all—of the poem, a typical heroic, of Bani Hillal in their spacious days and their decline. It recounts how one hundred thousand, nay, two hundred thousand, had been the number of their horses; it told of Bu Zaid's two thousand forbears, of the great drought that befell the land, so that there was no rain for thirty years and camels ate of the hair of each other and perished miserably while their masters were vainly digging in the earth for roots with which to feed them; nor was there even a breath of wind so that the finely powdered *waris*[1] they had placed on the Peak of Markha was found undisturbed a year later; and the sons of the shaikh of Bani Hillal approached their father and said, 'The people die of hunger and we must take from the merchants to feed them,' but he would not, though he himself went hungry and the fort walls groaned with grief.

Most of the stories, however, have to do with a later generation, when Bani Hillal had become a poor nomadic tribe and were waging war with the settled people of Risha, whose king was Zeniti.

Bu Zaid, their champion at this period, owed a charmed life to his mother's descent from the *jinniya*, which made him impervious to iron, whether it were arrow, sword or the spear, till the day he bore witness '*La Illah, ill' Allah*,' whereupon the *jinns* who had hitherto protected him from front and rear withdrew their protection from the front, so that he became like other men in that he could be killed

---

[1] A vegetable product of south-west Arabia used in Oman as a skin-dye; it is brought as a fine powder, canary-yellow in colour.

from that direction. Some of these stories that I thought worth recording will appear in subsequent chapters, as they were told me from time to time on the march or round the camp-fire.

My position here at Shanna I calculated to lie north-eastwards of the Hadhramaut, lat. 19° N., long. 50° 45′ E., altitude 990 feet. Our objective was to be Doha in the Qatar Peninsula on the Persian Gulf 330 miles distant as the crow flies across this barren ocean of interior sands. Hamad claimed to have been there once, pointing his cane in a direction a shade to the east of north, which fitted exactly with my traverse and astronomically worked positions. But I had to be careful not to appear too knowing.

A plan of action had crystallised, thanks to the Murra *rabia*. The size of our party would be reduced to twelve picked men and mounts and five pack animals all in perfect condition. This would make my rations good for thirty days, less the five days which must elapse before the arrival of the new party; but meanwhile to seek relief by reducing my present escort was impossible for fear of raiders. My resources thus allowed none too great a margin, and to loiter in these sands meant death. Perfect health in camel and man was essential; marches must be long and sharp; loss of camels, sickness, treachery or tribal opposition involving a hold up of ten days or too slow progress might spell disaster. The great consideration was to get out of the hunger stricken wastes as soon as possible. Such were the themes of Hamad's daily homilies.

A successful crossing was by no means certain; if the pastures in our way failed, we should have to face the question whether to tempt the Fates further by going on, or to turn back to certain sustenance, but with men

[210]

physically fit and fresh camels in good fettle at the most advanced jumping-off point, the problem was well on the way to solution. This was the stage I had reached. The Shanna was a strategic point in my crossing, and the starting post for the last relay.

The improvement in the ration situation which came from the slaughter of the camel was now offset by the arrival of untimely guests—a party of five Karab and Manahil that had crossed the sands by easy stages from Abu Dhabi. Like all their kind on first acquaintance, they maintained an icy reserve and, in answer to my enquiries as to their route, waved a general direction, a matter I found it politic not to press.

I had hoped that they would not dally, but the dates and coffee which they must receive seemed to encourage them to stay for more. It soon became clear that they had no intention of moving so long as my Rashidis' bounty was forthcoming. Hamad the *rabia* alone realised how necessary it was to husband our rations, especially in the light of an approaching Ramadhan, but to withhold food from the passing strangers so long as they chose to remain in my camp would have been to infringe the sacred rules of desert hospitality, if not to incur the odium of my companions. How my men would have wished to regard a parlous situation was reflected in another story to the credit of Bu Zaid.

'Bu Zaid was most famed of his day for generosity. Camel by camel he had killed his immense herd to feed the stranger and the poor. So the forty sections of Bani Hillal took counsel and said, "We will each give Bu Zaid a camel so that he may possess a herd again." And this they did. But the numbers of his guests and the largeness of Bu Zaid's heart

led once again to the day when he had no camels left. The
Bani Hillal saw there was no profit in Bu Zaid having a
herd, so they said, "We will make him a present of only one
camel on which to mount his wife when the tribe is moving,
and this we will do on the one condition that Bu Zaid swears
not to slaughter her for the guest, as he otherwise most
surely would."

'And Bu Zaid agreed to their stipulation.

'Several moons had come and gone and Bani Hillal were
encamped with their vast herds and their numerous tents,
when there arrived a party of Arabs from the side of Mecca,
and they enquired, "Where is the tent of Bu Zaid?"

'And none would say.

' "Tell us, where is the tent of Bu Zaid?"

' "It is before you," and so they passed on and on.

'And Bu Zaid hearing them called to his wife and said,
"Bind my eyes that I see not the faces of guests for whom
I cannot make a feast." So she brought a strip of date
basket and covered his eyes with it.

'And after a while he said to her, "Look out and see has
anyone taken them in."

'And she looked out. "No," she said, "they are before
the tent of So-and-so."

'And a little later he asked, "See! who has taken them in?"

' "No one," she replied, "they have now moved on to the
next tent."

'And again and again he asked, and again and again
received the same reply, so that his heart grew hot within
him, and at last able to contain himself no longer he rose,
and tore the covering from his eyes, and taking a knife
slaughtered his only camel where she stood at the entrance to
his tent, and sending for the strangers made for them a feast.'

I could feel no such sentiments for my unwelcome guests from Abu Dhabi, who proved leech-like in their attachment. They were on their way home to the steppes north-east of Hadhramaut, which led me to question them about the mystery of their famous Bir Borhut, supposed scene of volcanic activity, the only one on the mainland of Arabia, and quoted by Dr. Hogarth as 'that great well cursed by 'Ali, according to the Jihan Numa.' They, like earlier escorts of mine who knew the country, were emphatic that no volcano existed. But various superstitions attach to the wadi wherein the well exists, the most persistent that it was the place of the departed spirits of wicked men, so that to this day none dare approach it by night.

One of the Hadhramautis made a deal with a member of my party—a young camel in exchange for a rifle, ammunition and dollars, but from the noisy arguments that accompanied the transaction, it appeared to lack the grand manner which marked an exploit of Bu Zaid in his boyhood as told me that afternoon:

'Bu Zaid was an orphan and brought up by his uncle the shaikh, Husain bin Sirhan. One day while yet a boy he was grazing a small herd of two bull and seven cow camels, and there came passing by a party of Arabs, and with them was a camel, and on the camel's back was a massive sword, *shahman*.

'And Bu Zaid, regarding the sword, enquired of the Arabs whether they would sell it.

' "Yes, if you wish to buy it," they said mockingly, because it was so large and heavy that no ordinary mortal could wield it. And so the camel was couched.

'Bu Zaid now took up the sword, sighing, "I would have wished it a little heavier, but perhaps it will do."

[213]

'Then he laid it aside and went to his camels and brought and couched a cow and over her he placed one of the two bulls to serve her.[1] This was to be the target for his aim, and the test of the sword. If it cleft through the bull into the camel he would buy it.

'Then he picked up the sword, and standing a little way back he lifted it above his head and brought it crashing down upon the hump of the bull with such force that it severed the two camels into four halves. And turning to the Arabs he gave them his bull and six cows that remained in payment for the sword, and the sword he placed over his shoulder and so came joyfully to the side of his uncle.'

It was the forenoon of 8th January at Shanna and I was sitting exchanging stories with my companions when suddenly a small party of Arabs and camels appeared from behind the shoulder of a hill in the middle distance. My Arabs leapt to their feet and loaded their rifles, though it was only as a protective measure, for we were expecting the Bait Imani Shaikh. My telescope and the leisurely approach of the small party restored confidence and my companions were able soon to recognise Shaikh Muhammad bin Ham and his five companions.

They dismounted a little way off, and leading their camels passed one behind the other along our line of welcomers, for the usual nose-kiss salute; thereafter all sat

---

[1] Camels are thus exceptional in the animal kingdom in the performance of the act in a sitting position. The Badu master is necessary to the operation, scooping the sands round the cow's legs for her comfort, inserting the penis—the formation of which is in reverse axis to nearly all of the rest of mammal creation, and interfering after a few minutes to drive the bull off. After ten days if no result is apparent, the cow's master will find another bull to serve her. The sign of pregnancy is the flag-wagging of her ridiculous tail when approached by a rider to mount.

down in a common circle to exchange the desert news—camels, pastures, raids and the like—over the delicacies of coffee cup and dates that I provided. Amongst them was Musellim, a member of my last year's expedition. His appearance now was a pleasant surprise, but alas! he had not been enlisted among his shaikh's quota, and only came to importune me in the eager hope that I would enroll him separately or instead of another. In the morning he made his plea; he was a typical young Badu with large irregular teeth, tattooed gums[1] and a wealth of long narrow black plaits that fell from under his greasy head-dress; he talked, as the Badu does when excited, in a wild torrent of words, repeating himself over and over again, but never faltering; he knelt at my side, his left hand over the crook of his upright riding stick, his right hand outstretched, the middle finger and thumb making a letter O with which he kept tapping an imaginary door-knocker to emphasise his points, though his voice, which could be heard half a mile away, would never have conveyed to a stranger, unaccustomed to his tongue and mind, that this was his appealing mood. He called God to witness that what he said was true—he was a better fellow than the next, and his mount was my mount! a glory to behold and a joy to ride. His impassioned peroration was typical, so that I thought it worth recording. 'Ya Sahib—*tshuf*—look here—I want to come with you—do you hear me?—I am like your servant Muhammad to fetch your firewood and obey your orders—do you hear me?—I know the sands' (a deliberate falsehood) 'and I'm

---

[1] A series of short black tattoo lines on the upper and lower gums between the teeth. It is a universal practice of both sexes in South Arabia, carried out in childhood, and is said to arrest the growth of long teeth and to prevent them from becoming loose.

more favoured of God than others. I call God to witness—Listen! O long of life, I'm not like Sahail or other—Are you listening to me?' (Sahail was!)—'If you enrol me—pause—*tshuf*—I do not want money in advance, I can be patient—*tshuf*—O long of life, look at my camel, fat, *rahaim*, glory be to God. She will arrive at Qatar or where you wish—do you hear me?—I'm your servant *dhil hin* and *ghair dhil hin*—*tshuf*—O long of life—if you won't take me take her, *waja'in fidak*—I am your servant like Muhammad, you know me—have you thought about it?—I'm a good lad—Glory be to God' (here he touched my sleeve with his hand which he then carried to his lips and kissed). '*wa hadha! salamtak.*'

Musellim's eloquence ended. He sat back looking up for my decision. I liked the wild ruffian, but the ration question forbade my increasing my party without some strong reason, and so against my personal inclinations I told him, No.

Next day Musellim came to say farewell, and so departed to his tribe, smiling as he went, without a semblance of ill-will towards me, confident only in the wisdom of Allah's inscrutable ways.

My party for the onward move was now complete, for Shaikh Salih and his men had already arrived. He too had brought with him an extra recruit, one Talib, a Murri herdsman of the Shaikh of Qatar, thus raising the number of my escort to thirteen. Both Hamad, my *rabia*, and Salih pressed for Talib's inclusion—the number thirteen is not unlucky in Arabia—and so a party of thirteen Badawin it had to be. Talib was indeed a most valuable acquisition, for he had crossed the sands this year, whereas my *rabia* had not done so for many years and the bulk of my escort never at all in this longitude. Talib's still greater qualification was that he claimed to know the recent whereabouts in the Jiban, where our course must lie, of Ikhwan tribes,[1] with whom we must at all costs avoid collision.

These Ikhwan are religious zealots, the puritans of Islam, distinguished amongst their co-religionists for bigotry and intolerance, and the militant nature of their creed. In their eyes even my companions, members of orthodox sects of Islam (the South Arabians, Shafi', the Murra, Hanbali) were heretics, while to me, a non-Muslim, they were likely to be very hostile, and here, being only nominally under the rule of Bin Sa'ud, they might be emboldened to attack us. Smoking is to these Ikhwan a serious and punishable offence, and the nomadic life anathema, because the absence of water it entails must lead to infringement of those religious rules of Islam that prescribe ablution before prayer and after bodily functions. And being for the most part recent converts themselves from Badawin life, they display all the fanaticism of the proselyte.

My own servant, Muhammad, a Muscati and no paragon, put the Ikhwan case succinctly to me one day as his own sceptical view of the acceptability of the nomad's religion.

'These Badawin,' he said of my companions, 'are not fashioned after the manner of God's creatures at all.'

'How?' I said.

'They go for months without water. The sons of Adam would not tolerate it. And their women! they have intercourse with them and do not wash the greater ablution. How can their prayers avail?'

[1] The elements we feared were Bani Hajar and two sections of the Murra—Fuhaida and Al Adhaba.

XVII: THE NORTHWARD DASH

THE zero hour for the northward dash had arrived, and at four o'clock on the afternoon of 10th January 1931, my small party set out from Shanna. I should have preferred an early morning start, for I was tired after a busy day spent in settling accounts with my old escort and making advances to a new one. But there were two compelling reasons for delay: firstly, because of the necessity for moving camp before dividing up rations amongst my escort; our Hadhramauti visitors and relatives of my escorting Badawin, who ostensibly came to say farewell, had held on till the last in the hope of profiting; to have issued rations in their presence without giving them a share or allowing my Badawin to do so would have been impossible. Secondly, my *rabia* held Saturday to be the day most propitious for starting a journey, and Sunday entirely unacceptable.[1]

[1] Propitious and unpropitious days were constantly met with in South Arabia. The second and fifth days of the week were held to be good: Friday only moderately so. Sections of the Mahra tribe will never start on a raid or journey on a Sunday at all, or on a Friday until after the midday prayer. The first day of the moon is held to be a good day if it falls on any other day of the week.

Karab and other Hadhramaut Badawin have told me of the following superstitious beliefs which may or may not hark back to ancient star worship in South Arabia:

(*a*) During a period of five days, when the moon is in the constellation of Scorpio, action is unpropitious; no raid, journey or the like will ever be undertaken.

(*b*) The age of the moon is taken as a guide in the direction of a journey. The first, eleventh and twentieth days, called *duwar*, are propitious for movement in any direction.

The semi-circle east-south-west is divided up into ten

Passing the first high sand ridge sufficed to meet the twin requirements of self-preservation and superstitious belief, and we halted for the night. Camels were unsaddled, hobbled and driven off to the nearest camel-thorn while their masters gathered round to feast their eyes on the rare sight of bountiful food, and to take physical possession of it. Each drew his share of butter in a lizard-skin—a receptacle always found in a Badu's saddle-bag, while the other rations were divided up in bulk between the three parties that had been formed. The sight of flour, dates and rice had an exhilarating effect on these habitually hungry men and put them in the right mood for story-telling; so Salih, as he presided over the division of the dates, was easily prevailed upon to tell us another story of Bu Zaid.

'Bu Zaid had a wife but did not allow himself complete coition with her, and so he suspected that the two sons she had borne were not his, but another's. The tribe perceived that they did not resemble him and also had their suspicions, so came privily to Bu Zaid's sister and said that Bani Hillal must have a son from the loins of Bu Zaid. Wherefore one night she went secretly to her brother's bed and he, not knowing her in the darkness from his wife, lay with her. And as he was about to withdraw himself prematurely, according to his habit, she jabbed him with the bodkin that she had kept in her hand in readiness for this moment. The shock achieved its intent and in the fullness of time she bore a son, who came to be known as 'Aziz bin Khala,

divisions (bearings) coinciding with the ten days between the *duwar*. It is unpropitious to move on a bearing that coincides with its day, *e.g.* third bearing from east on third, thirteenth or twenty-second of the lunar month.

[219]

'Aziz, son of his uncle. And 'Aziz grew up into a strong youth, endowed with courage and other virtues.

'Many years had passed, and Bu Zaid wished to discover which, if any, of these three supposed sons was his. So he said to the eldest, "Come, we will go a journey." And Bu Zaid prepared a sack of flour and put into the mouth of it a single date. Then the greybeard and the youth prepared their camels and journeyed till they came to a plain which was as bare of pastures as the palm of a man's hand, except for a single *sidr* tree. And Bu Zaid said, "Here we will halt and I will sleep under the *sidr*, while you prepare me a meal."

'And while he slept the young man looked round but could find no firewood, for the *sidr* was green, so he opened the sack of flour, and seeing the single date within, took and ate it, for he was hungry.

'And Bu Zaid awaking, said, "Where is the meal?" "There is none," the youth answered, "for firewood is nowhere to be found, and I opened the sack to find but one date and that I ate."

' "Then we must return," said Bu Zaid.

'And after they had dwelt in their tents some days, Bu Zaid addressed the youth's brother, saying, "Come, let us go a journey." And again he prepared the sack of flour with the single date, as he had done before, and the two set out and came to the same plain with its single *sidr* tree.

'Said Bu Zaid, "I must sleep here while you prepare the meal."

'And the young man looked about for firewood and could find none, then he opened the sack and seeing the date, ate it.

'So when Bu Zaid woke and asked for his meal, there

was none, and the youth gave answer as his brother had done.

'And so they returned home.

'Some days had passed when Bu Zaid turned to 'Aziz. "Come," said he, "we will go a journey."

'Once more he prepared the sack of flour and put into it the single date, and the old man and the youth set off, and they came to the same bare plain with its single *sidr* tree.

' "I must sleep," said Bu Zaid, "prepare a meal." So 'Aziz searched the plain for firewood, but finding none, came back and sat down to think, and he saw that only the dry wood of their saddles and riding canes would serve. So he made a fire of these, then chopping branches from the *sidr* with his dagger he fashioned them into new saddles and riding crooks. Thus he baked two loaves of bread and set one for Bu Zaid and the other for himself, and discovering the date, he cut it in halves and set one upon his father's loaf, and the other upon his own. Then he awakened Bu Zaid, saying, "Arise and eat, O father."

'And his father roused himself and beheld what the youth had done, and jealousy entered Bu Zaid's heart,[1] and he said within himself, "I must kill 'Aziz, for he is a better man than I."

'Now it was planned that they should pass on next morning to the water-hole which lay at a very great distance. But at midnight Bu Zaid rose and crept stealthily to 'Aziz's camel and sticking a needle into her foot lamed

---

[1] Bu Zaid could not tolerate a rival; in his later days he murdered Dhiyab bin Ghanim, a mighty hunter and fighter, though Dhiyab had taken one of Bu Zaid's sisters to wife. Dhiyab's son, when he grew up, slew Bu Zaid to revenge his father, in the traditional Arabian manner.

her, and then quietly preparing his own camel, departed in the dead of night, leaving 'Aziz to perish of thirst.

'And 'Aziz woke in the morning to discover what his father had done, for the camel could not put her lame foot to the ground, and he realised the black design in his father's heart. Then he took a needle and stabbed her other three feet, so that when she put one foot to the ground the sharp pain would make her raise it again, and so bring down her other three feet. In this manner she would pick up one foot after the other and so move forward in this fashion. And thus, 'Aziz, taking another route than his father, was first at the water-hole; there he lay down to rest, but fearing Bu Zaid, placed his shield, hidden beneath his mantle, over his body.

'Bu Zaid, on arriving, found the youth thus sleeping, and taking his lance, gave a sharp thrust at 'Aziz's heart. The spear point, sliding off the shield, awakened 'Aziz, and he, springing up, wrested the spear from Bu Zaid's hand, saying, "I am stronger than thou, and have thee at my mercy, but thou art my father and my uncle, and so I spare thee."

'Thus did Bu Zaid know that 'Aziz was his own son, and they fell weeping upon each other's necks, and returned home together in contentment of heart.'

*

The end of the story saw the break-up of the party, for it was the hour of prayer before the evening meal.

The next day was our first proper day's march, and like all first days with new men and camels, was short and noisy. Halts at frequent intervals to adjust camel-loads, and Badawin bickerings about back and girth-galls kept delay-

IN NORTH-WESTERN DAKÁKA.

ing us, so that when we halted for the night we had made scarcely more than twelve miles. Around the camp-fires the wranglings continued until we evolved a system of changing loads from day to day in a regular order to ensure equitable treatment. This restored quiet.

One Badu, more peaceable than the rest, as he collected titbits for his camel from the *abala* under which I sat, snapped off a young branch and held it upside down. 'Look, sahib,' he said, as water dripped from within the stem, 'this is why your Agaba can go for days without drinking.'

Next day we made an early start on a north-easterly course, and passing the large white hill of Abu Akhshaba, came at midday to some isolated dunes which give their name, Gusman, to the locality and mark the north-westward limit of Dakaka.

Lying inside the great dune bulwark of the southern borderlands, Dakaka consists of these wide, sweeping red sandscapes of hardish sand with low dunes running in all directions. It falls in altitude from probably 1100 feet in the south to 785 feet hereabouts, and its long axis runs east-north-east for a seven days' march. As we moved westwards the aspect of Dakaka had grown more rugged and water-holes increased in depth from three fathoms in the east to thirteen fathoms at Shanna. Twin water-holes, Zuwaira and Turaiwa, even deeper than Shanna (which was within a day's march of its western extremity) were said to lie to the south-west. Beyond them to the west there was reported to be no water in the sands[1] of Ga'amiyat,

[1] The route of raiders from the sands into the Hadhramaut is therefore restricted, to the westwards, to a north-south route through western Dakaka and Kharkhir. It thence turns west along the southern borders of the sands through a famous corridor called Shaggag al Ma'atif.

Huwaiya and Shuwaikila that extend towards the Najran.

Our march that day had followed the camel-tracks of a small herd, and my *rabia* recognised them as a kinsman's and their direction to indicate recent watering. Soon we came upon the encampment. I was invited to dismount before two small tents to see a sick man, whom I found old and much emaciated; he complained of the almost universal stomach trouble. The Rashid ascribe it to *afera*, the most intractable of evil spirits, but my patient said it was 'from God.' The only palliative in my power was to cheer his heart with a handful of dates, the last I suspected the poor wretch would ever want. The urine of the young cow camel is taken in small quantities for such disorders, or preferably her vomit (said to be less thirst-provoking), which is obtained by ramming a stick down her throat. The urine has a second utility as a hair-wash, in that it kills vermin. All the desert beauties use it.

The only other occupants of the tent were two women and a boy. The women were both veiled, as are all the women of the sands, though they were not averse from talking with the stranger. They were the wives of the old man and of his son. The boy, the son of the younger couple, and aged about four, ran about the tent naked and uncir-cumcised.[1] Then the younger man came up, carrying a badly mauled hare, with its captor running at his side, a long dog of whippet size and dark brown colour.

[1] Circumcision with the Murra takes place at the age of about five or six. Ar Rashid, and to some extent Bait Imani, have of late years adopted the same practice, giving up the adult circumcision found among their Mahra neighbours to the south, but they still maintain certain rites the boy being taught to hold his head up bravely during the operation while the onlookers say 'Karim! Karim!'

A SMALL MURRA ENCAMPMENT.

The Murra all have these dogs, with which they hunt the hare and occasional *rim* for the pot (whereas Al Rashid and other South Arabian tribes have no dogs) and on our northward march we passed from time to time the footmarks of a dog, and, near by, the tracks of the Badu master. Sometimes they were in pairs and abnormally extended, a sign that the animal was then in full course.

The miserable tent where I sat was just high enough to give a squatting adult headroom. It consisted of two twenty-foot strips of very roughly woven dark brown and white wool, the dark colour of camel-hair, the light possibly from the sheep's wool of Hasa. Every thread had been spun and woven by the women within. Lying about was the bodkin used in its manufacture, a few iron camp-fire pegs, tent-pegs once the horns of an antelope, the long iron bars used for digging water-holes, a rounded stone from the northern steppe to serve as hammer, two camel saddles and a variety of crude leathern buckets on rough wooden frames, one a water trough, another a receptacle for skins. In such items are comprised the few poor belongings of the nomad folk other than the nobler possessions of camels and firearms.

We passed out of Dakaka (Lat. 19° 32′) into Suwahib, one of the most extensive regions in the sands. It derives its name from its character, for the word *sahaba* stands locally for parallel ridges, and the plural, *suwahib*, consisted of chains of sandhills in echelon, averaging perhaps half a mile apart, with a general north-east axis, the intervals between them bellying sands of red. The ridges seldom exceeded fifty to eighty feet in height though their featureless slopes exaggerated their size. They were reported to stretch south-westwards beyond Gusman to embrace the western Dakaka and reach to the high dunes of Ga'amiyat.

The pastures grew scant as we progressed on a north-north-easterly course, crossing the Suwahib diagonally at long intervals. A twin giant hill, called Khalilain, was the only noteworthy feature of the march on the thirteenth, till we came in the late afternoon to the water-hole of Bainha,[1] the aneroid showing a fall, to the senses imperceptible, of two hundred feet in the march of nineteen miles.

Water was at two fathoms. Its great brackishness and its beer colour were properties which, I was sad to find, were not disguised by desiccated soup. Indeed, from this stage onward the water was such that I gave up drinking it except when desperately thirsty in the saddle, or occasionally as cocoa when halted, for it acted as a violent purge. In the marches that stretched down and away to the eastward—the habitat from time to time of my Rashidi companions—the water was said to be too brackish for them to drink, while in places even their camels will turn away.

Camel's milk formed my chief diet, but the supply was limited, for the two milch-animals I had obtained with much difficulty were approaching the end of their lactation, and there were days when their milk had to be watered down to make enough. To these camels, however, I owed the fitness I enjoyed throughout, though I lost a stone and a half weight on the diet.

Bainha, where we watered, had been discovered and dug by my *rabia*, Hamad bin Hadi. I had already appre-

[1] Bainha, so named because it lay midway between the water-hole of Bir Hadi and the Buwah.

TYPICAL SU'AHIB SANDS.

ciated Hamad's great worth as a guide, for guiding in the
desert requires not merely memory for direction but an
intuition for water and pastures, and an ability to read the
sands and avoid the evil that may be impressed on them.
Not every Arab bred in these sands can guide, many in
fact lose their way and die of thirst, particularly when
camels stray in summer and their owners have to track
them. To return on his own tracks or to follow those of
others is regarded as a lost man's safest course to water,
but a wind arising will obliterate all tracks, and wind is
an ever-present menace. About seven years ago a party
of Mahra were raided in the steppe by two members of
Manahil, who made off with ten camels. Discovering the
loss while the tracks of the retiring raiders were still discernible, seven Mahri stalwarts went in pursuit, and the
tracks brought them to the sands of Dhahiya, previously
unknown to them. On came the bold pursuers, who
reckoned upon the pursued having to halt over a water-
hole, where they too would water. But the Manahil, fearing
pursuit, prudently avoided the water-hole of Khor Dhahiya
and went ploughing on northwards through the death-
dealing sands, one man alone cunningly going off at a tan-
gent to the water-hole to fill his water-skins and returning
by the same track to rejoin his companions. Thence they
proceeded. The Mahra, following hopefully on the main
camel-tracks of Manahil, were certain that their thirst
would soon be quenched, but before they could overtake
their despoilers a sand-storm came and obliterated all
tracks before and behind them. They were now lost in
the sands. Six months later one of my own party of Rashidis
came upon the seven skeletons and the bones of their camels.

I was filled with admiration for the consistency of Hamad's

direction. Twice and thrice during the hour I would compare my prismatic compass reading and find a variation
of no more than five degrees. The shadow cast by the sun
at our backs could give no more than a general direction,
and I was naturally quick to assume that he was led by
the orientation of sand corridors, here 45°-50°. Later,
however, in sands that had no such conspicuous tell-tale
features, his course showed scarcely less exactitude, and I
was driven to seek for some other explanation. Maybe the
faint corrugations of sand surfaces, presumably of some
constancy from prevailing winds, solved part of the mystery, but most I feel is due to an instinctive sense of direction highly developed in particular individuals, of whom
Hamad was one. He had not been over this country for
many years, and by the very nature of nomadic life, could
not have sojourned in any one place for long. Unlike all
but one of his companions, he had names[1] for the major

[1] The identity of his star names with ours, in the case of: Altair = Nasir
al Tair; Rigel = Rijl; Scorpio = Al Agrab, *i.e.* scorpion (Ar) recalls the
fact that many of our star names are derived from the Babylonians
through the Arabs.

I record below and on the opposite page some star-names given me by
a dweller in the Rub' al Khali who had not been out of the sands.

English	Arabic of Rub' al Khali	English	Arabic of Rub' al Khali
Altair	Nasir al Tair	Regel	Rijl
Vega	Nasir umm Wuga	Betelgeuse	Yid Sa'ad
Polaris	Al Jedi	Bellatrix	Yid al Kesha (Rash-
Great Bear	As Seba'		idi) Yid al Tib
One star			(Murri)
called	Banat Nash	Sirius	Mirzem
Capella	Al Imbari	Canopus	Sahail as Saduq

constellations and larger stars, and by night to this Theseus
the labyrinth of the sands had no mysteries.

On reaching Lat. 20° my companions observed with
keen interest our arrival into the *hadh* belt, *hadh* being a
small, sage-coloured bush, saline in character, which survives longer without rain or dew than any other desert
growth—whence, in times of exceptional drought, only the
hadh regions in the sands support life. There the sand
tribes are to be found, unless they are driven clean out
into the steppe borderlands, the Rashid in that event retiring
south-eastwards to Umm al Hait, and the oasis of Mugshin,
the Murra back to the northern water-holes of Jabrin and
the Jafurah-Jiban border-line.

Buwah, the first *hadh* region we entered, was well blessed
and the signal for an early halt to graze. Full bellies led to
an early start, and good going on a bearing of north by
east was made all the more pleasant by a light breeze in
our faces. The intervening trough of the Suwahib here
became red, rolling billows, gentle, but so soft as to occasion
dismounting now and then for a path to be cleared by hand
that the camels might pass. Hungry and desolate country

English	Arabic of Rub' al Khali	English	Arabic of Rub' al Khali
Pleiades	Al Thuraiyya	Achernar	Sahail al Kadhib
Aldebaran	Kelb al Ghanim	Scorpio	Al Agrab
Auriga	Ghanim	(Its tail)	Shola
Orion	Sa'ad	Venus	Zahra
Orion's Belt	Janbiya		
Three small stars	Ausa (*penis*)		

Venus was the only named planet. They had no name for Jupiter or
Mars.

[229]

succeeded, with only sprigs of *gasis*, which grew drooping as wind-blown trees parallel with the ridge-axis in testimony to a prevailing north-east wind. In the afternoon we passed by three shallow water-holes, Bahat Salama, Bahat Hajran, and Bahat Jamal. Water was reported everywhere on our right hand at an arm's depth, but so brackish as to be undrinkable by man or beast, and therefore named *khiran*, in accordance with a practice common throughout the sands.

The Badawin, who had not bothered to fill their water-skins in Dakaka, did so at Bahat Jamal. There also we watered camels for the water was held to be sweet, whereas that before us was saline, that would sharpen the thirst and cause disordered health. The saline pastures of these sands were equally lowering to the camels.

Next day we passed from the region of Buwah to that of Umm Malissa. The intervening sands became more rugged and the long, beautiful ridges grew less definite in character and broke up into small detached chains, which were reported to continue northward a day's march on our right hand, like an inverted letter S, through the *hadh* regions of Karsua' and Wasa' to the dunes of Sa'afuk north of the twenty-first parallel.

The heat was most trying even in this winter month of January, and for the first time on my journey I felt very exhausted, doubtless from the combined effects of the hot sun playing down on my back for nine long hours in the saddle, and acute thirst after drinking Buwah's beer-coloured water.

My note-taking was a week in arrear. There had been neither time nor opportunity, and had our margin of rations warranted the risk, I should have been well content to halt for the day, but the need was to press on. The Badawin, ever mindful of the welfare of their camels, were ill at ease in these drought-stricken wastes and anxious to press on with all speed to some expected pastures in southern Mazariq.

The menace of raiders had diminished as we marched north and was now left behind. True, the Sa'ar had in times past raided as far north as this, but to-day, with the main body of Rashid behind us in the south, a raiding party would come into contact with them there, or, in any case, would not be so foolish as to push thus far and expose itself to the risk of being cut off.

Sa'ar! The name is a word of terror to the Rashid and the southern Murra, whose boys are brought up to live to revenge brothers and fathers, and to redeem lost fortunes. The cause of raids and inter-tribal feuds is at bottom economic. Men kill and are killed in the fight for camels. Peace, or rather truce, alternates with war for periods of a year or two. In time of war it is the greatest shame for a young man to show no disposition to fight. *sharab al khumr*, 'wine-filled,' is a synonym for gallantry applied to the young man who sets out to kill or be killed with a gay heart, but a stay-at-home who shelters his life or makes excuses when the communal interests of his tribe are involved, is regarded as a white-livered craven for whom none will have respect, and to whom none will give a daughter in marriage.

Young Kilthut, Shaikh Salih's son, told me the story of his 'blooding' by the Sa'ar which is worth setting down, not merely as a true version of what happens when enemies meet in the Rub' al Khali, but for the light it throws on desert psychology.

[231]

War had been going on for a year and more between Rashid and Sa'ar, and the Rashid decided to make overtures for peace. Kilthut was one of four sent as an embassy to try to make truce for a year. They set out and came to the steppe, hoping to meet a Sa'ari *rabia* who would give them safe-conduct into Sa'ar confines.

But the tale will go better in Kilthut's own words, as he spoke them before the camp-fire, his face aglow, and he himself all animation, for a Badu talks with his eyes and hands.

'It was about the hour of the afternoon prayer. Near the edge of a wadi we dismounted and crept up to the edge, and peering down into it, saw five Badawin around a camp-fire and their camels grazing, and we knew them by their double-poled saddles to be Sa'ar. Greed took possession of our hearts, for although we came to make peace we had not as yet done so, and were still in a state of war with the Sa'ar. Also it seemed that Allah had delivered them into our hands, for it was near night and they must soon turn their camels to graze and sleep themselves. Then we could crawl up and kill our enemies and carry away the spoil. But now our own counsels became divided. I urged that we enjoyed a great advantage, having seen them first while they were yet unaware of our presence. However, the two chief members of our party, one of them my Uncle Saif, the Sa'adna shaikh, would not agree, saying that the party below were probably from a bigger body close at hand, and their advanced position here showed them to be themselves on the war-path, so that they would be in no mood for peace parleys; our mission must therefore end, and we must fly. In our pride, we two young men, Musellim, a Bait Imani, and I, said that we would not return except with the camels of our enemies. Our elders strove with words of prudence to persuade us to return with them, but we would not listen and they left us.

'Musellim and I tethered now our camels at a safe distance and crawled to the brink of the gorge to watch the enemy's movements. Presently one of them took the camels off to some grazing down the wadi as we had fore-seen, and then returned to his friends. We saw them make up their camp-fire for the night. But with our number reduced now to two against their five, we decided it would be impossible to overcome them; instead we would creep down at dead of night, steal the camels, and depart, thus getting such a start that in the morning there would be no chance of their catching us up on foot. And so we prayed the evening prayer and returned to our watching-places and waited; and about midnight when their fire had ceased to flicker, we crept stealthily down—we could have killed the men in their sleep had there been more of us—and we loosened the hobbles of the camels and thence turned up by an easy slope and found our own camels, and so we started off homewards.

'One of the Sa'aris awoke long before the dawn and discovered that their camels were missing. He roused his companions and they followed on our track by the light of the full moon. Meanwhile we pressed on till the next afternoon, but being then tired and supposing we had many hours' start, my companion and I stupidly halting for a short rest, fell asleep. Suddenly I awoke. There before me, at about one hundred paces, was an Arab, covering me with his rifle. I looked round hurriedly, and seeing no others supposed that he was alone; so I leapt behind a small rock to draw my own rifle from its jacket,[1] but before I could do it he had fired. The shot missed. I had now slipped a round into the breech of my rifle, but thinking that his action might have been defensive, and him perhaps a friend, maybe some Mahri who mistook me for a Sa'ari, I shouted, "We are Ruwashid. Fear not, we are Ruwashid."

'He answered, "By my face. I am so-and-so of the Sa'ar, and we (mentioning his section) are at peace with the Ruwashid. You have my camels, and we are stronger than you; thirty men are behind me."

'And I shouted, "Deliver me with my life, my camel, and my rifle."

'And he answered, "By my face."

'So I got up. But even as I did so his party came rushing upon me, not knowing what had passed between him and me. And one of them drew his dagger and lunged at me (here Kilthut put his finger in his mouth and rubbed the spittle along his forearm to discover the old wound-mark) and another stabbed at my companion, but he, jumping back, was only gashed across the forehead between his two eyes, though he bled much. But now, God be praised, the first man who had given us sanctuary came up and intervened and so our lives were saved.'

'Then you got the worst of it?'

'Yes! They took our two camels as well as their own, and our rifles and daggers, although I had been promised mine. But they honoured their word, for later when peace was

---

[1] Every Badu in the Rub' al Khali carries his rifle in a rude leather case to prevent sand from getting into the mechanism. He makes this case himself, usually from the skin of the antelope or other beast of the chase. Its tip is often decorated with a gay bunch of leather thongs. The well-to-do Arab of Oman decorates the stock of his rifle with bands of silver and gold from the same affectionate sentiment for it.

made I got my rifle back and a camel in place of the one they had taken from me—but not my dagger.' (A most unusual course, as there is no restitution between tribes traditionally hostile, and peace follows the usual formula of, 'The past be past.')

'But,' continued Kilthut, 'this Sa'ar party were themselves to be overtaken by misfortune. They moved on eastwards and came upon a Mahri and his wife and a single camel; they slew the man and took the camel, but when they had reached Manahil country they were caught by a large raiding party of Bait Kathir and Mahra and their shaikh was killed and they turned and fled in confusion, their booty falling into the hands of Bin Tannaf.'[1]

[1] Bin Tannaf is the hereditary title of the shaikh of the Manahil tribe. The present holder is one of the most famous leaders of the raid. The leader has always the perquisite of two or three of the best camels taken, otherwise there is equal division of the spoil as in 1 Samuel xxx. 25.

XVIII: THROUGH THE CENTRAL SANDS

SUWAHIB lay behind us. Gone were the big bellying waves of red sand with their white-ridged crests lit up in the brilliant sunshine, gone the green pastures of the early marches. In Lat. 20° 44′ a narrow rugged belt was succeeded by a wide expanse of pale sands in the mood of an ocean calm. Relief came here and there in patches of withered *hadh* scrub, which recent strong southerly winds had covered with a film of fine white sand. Otherwise the scene was one of utter desolation, extending over a great part of the central sands of Mazariq, Nuwasif and Munajjar, making them a hungry void and an abode of death to whoever should loiter there. Yet but four years before one of my Murris had grazed herds in this region. In the verbal extravagances so typical of the Badu, he told me these had been the most blessed sands. But the circumstances were illuminating; they explained why the secrets of poor, precarious pastures or water should be so jealously guarded, and why therefore suspicion is the desert man's dominant characteristic. To such climatic vicissitudes may well be ascribed those early Arabian movements of hunger-driven man, the Semitic invasion of Babylonia, the Canaanite invasion of Syria, the Hyksos invasion of Egypt, and even the Hebrew invasion of Palestine.

Animal life still persisted in these stricken wastes, indeed by a curious chance two of my most interesting specimens were obtained here, one a sand-coloured fox[1] scarcely bigger than a cat, yet full-grown according to my Arabs and the evidence of its teeth; it proved a new species, probably

[1] The fox was called *hirr*, which is classical Arabic for 'cat.'

BELIEVED TO BE A NEW FOX (SP. FENNEC).

AN EAGLE'S NEST.

an Arabian variety of the Egyptian *fennec*; the other find, eagle's eggs, discovered in a gigantic nest, like that of an English rook, but much bigger, and roofing a solitary leafless *abala*. The bird itself I did not see, but the eggs have been found to resemble very closely those of the Abyssinian tawny eagle. My Arabs regarded them as unlawful for food, whereas bustard's eggs are counted a great delicacy amongst them. Bustard the size of young turkeys were met at intervals throughout the southern central sands and were innocently trusting if approached under cover of a slow riderless camel and by a circuitous closing in upon it, but for unfamiliar unaccompanied man they showed a discriminating distrust, so that our many halts in the hope of a meal produced only the back view of birds in flight, and human disappointment over the claw-marks left in the sand—a handsome Prince of Wales feathers pattern. Bird life was scant in the sands, the fan-tailed raven being the commonest and most widely distributed and next after him a tiny pied-wagtail-looking creature. Generally the birds met were solitary, or at most in pairs. Once I saw four bustard together and once six ravens, but this was unusual.

My natural history collection[1] was made up mostly of small insects, beetles, spiders, a few moths, butterflies, and a single dragonfly; it included a new mantis and a new locust.

The fox and the hare, both sand-coloured, were the commonest mammals, particularly in the southern sands, and there was a sand rat, wild cat and wolf, though un-

[1] The specimens collected in the sands numbered one hundred and twenty-five. Notes by members of the Staff of the British Museum (Natural History) are given in Appendix II.

happily the last two eluded me. The wolf is said to be small and sand-coloured, and to live chiefly in Suwahib, where it can readily paw a hole to shallow water.

Among reptiles there were twelve varieties of lizards, all alike endowed with pointed snouts for diving in the sands. The most numerous sort was a skink, with a sand-coloured square-sectioned body, and black markings along its sides. Its smooth shining snake-like skin did not dissuade one Arab from indulging a childish trick of putting the wriggling tail and half its body into his mouth. The biggest lizard was a monitor, much too strong and vicious to be handled except by being picked up, like a snake, behind the head. The monitor, unlike most of the big lizards of the steppe, is not eaten by Badawin. On cutting one open, I found a skink almost his own size within. The scorpions of the sands were small and of pale green colour in contrast to the big black-and-white varieties of the mountains and steppes. Only three different snakes were met with—all of a sand colour, boa, horned viper, and colubrid.

The stimulus of promised rewards made my Arabs enthusiastic workers for the Museum. Their reduced numbers on this northward journey allowed me to get to know them individually in a way that had been impossible with my earlier and bigger parties. The Badu—unless a religious bigot, in which case he is secretive and sullen— can be a most pleasant companion if you will but simulate a passion for saddle and rifle, praise the virtues of camels and be cheerful. Distant at first, he will after a week or so become, if cultivated, a cheerful fraterniser, and if there is something he wants, ingratiating. His conversations, how- ever, are liberally interspersed with the woes it has pleased

TYPICAL SANDS OF SANAM.

Allah to afflict him with—a stomach pain for certain.
'Fever! there was none in the sands, thank God,' and my
companions were incredulous of the infection by mosquito-
bite which evoked only a few and, I thought, insincere
expressions of 'There is no god but God,' the usual ex-
clamation when anything that astonishes is encountered.
But mosquitoes, Salih agreed, were a great nuisance at
Dhufar, so that his visit there had been a mixed pleasure,
for while he was used to flies innumerable around some
water-holes in the sands, it was only in Dhufar that he and
his camel spent nights of torment that made them glad to
turn about. Fleas and lice the sands have in plenty, and
whenever two of my Badus found themselves unoccupied
at the halt, they would take part in a mutual flea-hunt, each
in turn lying face downwards on the sand, while his companion sat by his head and scraped away with a dagger in
the long tousled locks.

'You have found none in your baggage!' one would say,
looking up at me. And then with pride, 'These bags of straw
we use for pack-saddles do not attract them, whereas the
double-poled saddle of the Murra is their favourite haunt.'

I was ready to change the subject for a more pleasant
one, and found myself listening to a delectable Bani Hillal
entertainment.

Would I like to hear how it fared with that ill-starred
youth 'Aziz, son of his uncle?

Yes, I would.

Then he would tell me the story of the self-imposed
immolation of 'Aziz bin Khala to forward his father's
amours.

'Bu Zaid loved a girl named 'Aliya of a neighbouring
tribe. One day he set off on a visit to her, taking with him

'Aziz, who had not yet seen her. And Bu Zaid described her great beauties as they went along and said, "But you shall know her, O 'Aziz! by this token. If she is sitting with other women she will be taller than they; but if standing she will be shorter than they." And father and son came to a well where women were drawing water, and 'Aliya was in their midst; and 'Aziz beheld them first sitting over the well and then rising to go away, so that he knew her. But alas! for Bu Zaid, 'Aliya had been affianced by her male relatives to another, and that very night was the nuptial night, when her new husband would come to her. But 'Aliya was unhappy, for she loved Bu Zaid.

'Now it was that 'Aziz dressed himself in her bridal raiment and set her jewels upon his neck and arms and took her place in the bridal bed, while she went out into the wilderness to the place where Bu Zaid was and spent the night in the embraces of her lover.

'And the new husband came by night to 'Aliya's chamber, but whenever he drew near to his imagined bride, 'Aziz turned a deaf ear, and a silent tongue to his entreaties, and pushed him away. So the angry bridegroom betook himself next morning to the 'Alim and explained his plight, adding, "I am not sure in the darkness that it was 'Aliya, for I am strong and never have I met anyone who could resist me except 'Aziz bin Khala."

'And the 'Alim replied, "Go to her again to-night and take with you a needle. And if you receive no better accommodation, pluck a hair from her head and drive the needle into the vein *urqal akhal* of her left thigh. If it be 'Aliya or a woman she will live, but if a man he will die, and by the hair you will know her."

'So the bridegroom came again that night to 'Aliya's

chamber, only however to meet with the same resistance, and in his struggles he plucked a hair from 'Aziz's head and drove the needle into the vein of his loins, and so departed.

'Before the dawn, 'Aziz rose as was his wont and came to his father's place in the wilderness, and told him of what had come to pass. And 'Aliya was affrighted, but Bu Zaid plucked a hair from her head and drove a needle into her thigh so that her husband might find the marks, and thus not suspect her.

'Bu Zaid and 'Aziz then mounted their camels and departed, 'Aziz with the needle still in his thigh, for whenever he should withdraw it, he must bleed to death.

'And they came to a plain, and 'Aziz said to his father, "Father, what is this place good for?"

'Said Bu Zaid, "It is a place good for grazing camels."

'And they passed on and came to some other herbage, and 'Aziz asked, "And what is this place fit for?" Bu Zaid replied, "This, my son, is a place good for raising horses."

'Again they moved on and coming to a place of desolation, 'Aziz asked, "And what, O father, is this fit for?"

'And Bu Zaid answered, "It is a place meet only for a graveyard."

'Said 'Aziz, "Let us dismount here and help me to dig a grave."

'So Bu Zaid and 'Aziz dug a grave and 'Aziz withdrawing the needle from his thigh died, and his father buried him.

'Bu Zaid went on and came to his tents, and his sister, the mother of 'Aziz, saw him a great way off, and alone; and she ran out saying, "Where is 'Aziz? Where is 'Aziz?"

'And Bu Zaid answered, "We have been raiding and many camels have fallen into our hands, and I have come on ahead bringing the good news, and 'Aziz follows with the spoil."

'Some days went by, and the mother grew anxious; and as more and more days passed and 'Aziz did not return, she moped about the tents and wept for her son's fate, nor would she be comforted.

'And Bu Zaid was sad at heart, and murmured to himself:

' "Have come to thee, old dame, forebodings of evil?
    For thou understandest our house
    As the wolf knoweth where the flocks are gathered
        for the night."

'And then aloud:

' "O my grief, if I should say he is dead, she dieth,
    And if I should say he lives, I lie."

'And so 'Aziz's mother knew that her son was dead.'

The story ended, the cry of the *mu'edhdhin* brought my entertainers to their feet and they went off to join the long line of worshippers that habitually fell in behind Hamad bin Hadi for common prayer.

An early start was made on the 19th January, our course still north-west. The absence of grazing in our way and our camels' thirst from their recent saline pastures made for fast marching. Leaving Umm Quraiyin on our right hand—a reported water-hole that marked the northward limit of Munajjar—we came to the sand region of Sanam, white and rolling in a gentle swell. This region—the word itself means camel's hump—is conspicuous for the comparative sweetness of its water-holes and their abnormal depth,[1] an

---

[1] A crude pulley-block formed part of the Murri kit: its use is nowhere necessary in the south.

average being eleven fathoms, and some there are of fifteen and seventeen fathoms in the west.

The shallower wells of the southern sands are sometimes filled in after watering to obstruct a possible pursuer. But here the water-holes are roofed to protect them, for great labour, skill and courage have gone in their making. Indeed the deep water-holes of Tuwal exact a toll of life, for the soft sides are prone to slip and entomb the miners, and all that avails for revetment is the coiled branches of some wretched bush of the sands. As we passed Safif, a Murri turned to me. 'Four of my brothers' (*i.e.* Murra tribesmen) 'lie in the bottom there. Two of them had descended to clean it out and were overwhelmed by slipping sand, and their companions, following to rescue them, were engulfed too. Safif is a tomb; we have abandoned it.'

The fasting month of Ramadhan was upon us. No crescent moon had been seen on the morning of 20th January, so hopes were set upon the evening. We halted in good time, all eyes towards the western sky in the wake of the setting sun. The first appearance of the Ramadhan moon excites intense eagerness on the part of the Faithful, and in Oman its entry and exit are accompanied by the booming of more than a monarch's salute. This evening disappointment was in store for us. The saffron sky turned to slaty grey and then to darkness, but there was no moon; to-morrow my companions would not be glorifying God in the Fast.

Farajja, our next water-hole, lay a nine and a half hours' march distant, and we were obliged to make it because our water-skins were empty. We were thus still in the saddle when just after sunset rifle shots rang out from ahead, and a faint wisp of the crescent moon showed in the pale sky.

[243]

With cries of 'Glory to God,' my companions couched their
camels and prostrated themselves in prayer, one or two of
them first sticking their rifles barrel downwards into the
sands. Our course had veered due west in the track of
our advance party and thus continued until after dark, when
the flare of a distant camp-fire was the beacon for our night's
halting-place. My companions being on a journey had a
right to break or postpone fasting till they regained their
homes, but none elected to do so. They all fasted[1] on the
march, as my Bait Kathiris had done at Mugshin a year
before. Hitherto they had availed themselves of the prayer
concession of the march, running the five occasions into
three, but now in Ramadhan they observed the entire
number. Scarcely in keeping with this increased religious
zeal was the change in the food *régime*. Dinner had formerly followed the joint evening prayer; now it followed
the sunset Credo of the *mu'edhdhin* and was sandwiched between it and the prayer that normally would follow.

Scouts for pastures may postpone the Ramadhan fast, but
the rule for the raider is different. He may enjoy the concession only on the return from the raid; during the approach and the attack he must fast.

The sand tribes have also a peculiar marital observance.
In Ramadhan sexual relations are only permissible if ablution can follow, that is, when near or carrying water.

At other times of the year the religious injunction

---

[1] The Sa'ar, according to the Rashidis—perhaps a tainted source in
view of their relationship—neither pray nor fast. And they mock a
Rashidi visitor (in times of peace) who does so, though they swear by
Allah and claim to believe in Him. 'They say, God is the Knower! that
their ancestor saved the Prophet from the hands of infidels who were intent on slaying him, and the Prophet granted to him and his heirs exemp-
tion from prayer observances. They say so! May God forgive them!'

HALT FOR PRAYER.

regarding this greater ablution is disregarded. When they are away from water, sand is used before prayer, but nothing after the sexual act. It thus comes about that while there is no rule against marriage in Ramadhan such marriages in the sands are rare, if not unheard of.

The months of the desert are lunar months, but known by names not always according with the usual Muslim calendar.[1] The word Muharram, for instance, is never used by them, and they reckon the year, so far as they date it at all, from the Fast month or the Pilgrimage month.

Here in lat. 21° 30' the sands of Sanam must be shallowing because for the first time the hard flat floor emerged in circular patches from the sands.

One of my Badawin found and brought me some potsherds and bits of broken old dull glass from the surface of one such place. I looked but could see no trace of an artificial mound, but only apparently natural undulations, and I was incredulous that the region could have had any considerable settlement,[2] preferring the theory that *dibbis*—syrup of dates—had been brought out here in pots from Hasa, for some bygone Ramadhan perhaps, before the kerosene tin became the common receptacle of Arabia. The possibility of archæological remains in Sanam should not, on the other hand, be ruled out. The Murra indeed

---

[1] The months of the Arabs of the sands are: Ramadhan; Id Fitr al Awwal; Id Fitr al Thani; Arafa (pilgrimage month); Ashur (or the month of Zakat); Sifr; Tom al Awwal, Tom al Thani, Tom al Thalith, Mithalil (sometimes Tom al 'Urba), called Tuwam; Rijeb; Qusaiyir. Qusaiyir and Mithalil are held to be unpropitious months for the raid or a journey. Ramadhan also unless a start has already been made.

[2] Salwa, Iskak and Mabak, ancient sites in the base of the Qatar peninsula, are ascribed to *Fuwaris*, that is, the Persians. They are now in Ikhwan hands, and for this reason I could not explore them.

[245]

have a tradition of the foundations of a fort once to be seen but now covered over by sand. Umm al Hadid, a water-hole, is also said to have a tradition of remains—two large blocks of so-called ironstone—whence its name. These, however, may have been meteorites.

I had collected a fragment of black meteorite in the Buwah region of Suwahib. It was found lying on the sands as we passed, the Badu who picked it up calling it an 'iron stone' presumably on account of its great weight. Its nature proved difficult to establish at first on account of its irregular shape and sharp angles, for the meteorite is commonly a rounded stone, sometimes pitted with holes. My Buwah specimen is thought to be part of a much larger meteorite which burst into pieces on its passage through the atmosphere.[1]

At Farrajja[2] our camels were taken off to water in the forenoon, and this provided me with an opportunity of collecting data for my map—the names and direction and distance of sands and water-holes that must be recorded as we went along and worked out by a process of arithmetical triangulation. But Badawin are apt to fret under too close and long cross-questioning and the most profitable information is obtained when the Arab can be encouraged to discourse. The occasion was one for a story too—the tale of Bu Zaid and his two brothers Yusif and Baraiga and their encounter with a *Jinn*. It ran in this wise:

'One day Bu Zaid, Yusif and Baraiga set out on a journey and at night they halted at a habitation where was a man, and his mother and their sheep. And the man

---

[1] A description is given in a Note by Mr. Campbell Smith (Appendix II).

[2] Farajja, named after its digger Faraj, a Murri, who is said also to have dug Shanna.

said to them, "I would fain come with you on your journey."

' "No," they answered, "you are not equal to the feats which are likely to be demanded of us on our way, else we would take you."

'And the man, wishing to show what manner of man he was, walked over to an acacia tree close by and seizing it by the trunk in his two arms uprooted it as though it had been a tamarisk, and hurled it to one side, saying, "Yet am I strong?"

'So it was decided that he should accompany them and the four set forth. And they came to a place where they met a young girl and she was leading a ram and carrying on her head a dish of rice that was drenched with melted butter. The girl was the daughter of the governor of a town close at hand. And they asked her where she was going. Said she, "I am going as an offering to the Jinn in yonder wadi, for the town is under sacrifice, and a virgin, a ram and a dish of rice must be brought to the Jinn each evening; and if these are not forthcoming the Jinn will destroy the town."

'Now Bu Zaid and his companions were famished, and the smell of the savoury dish increased their hunger, so they said to the young girl, "But we want our supper. Give us the ram to slaughter and the rice to eat, and we will attend to the Jinn and ensure that no evil befalls the town."

'And she answered, "The Jinn will surely dry up the water and my father's people will perish."

'But they paid no heed to her words, and taking the ram they slaughtered it and cooked and ate it. Then they turned their thoughts to the Jinn; and they divided the night into four watches, that each of them should in turn go and

[247]

occupy the haunt of the Jinn for an equal space of time.

'The first watch was given to the strong man who had uprooted the *ghaf* by the wayside. And so he went, but as he approached the Jinn, which was in the form of a huge serpent, it cried out, "Oh! Ha! you who bring my dinner— first the ram!" And the man, full of fear, fled, and returned to the three brothers, Bu Zaid, Yusif and Baraiga, saying, "Surely the Jinn will eat you up," and he ran off and was seen no more.

'Next went forth Yusif with sword, buckler and stick. And the Jinn, hearing someone approach, opened its great mouth, and Yusif making the form of a cross with his sword and stick passed through the buckler handle for a centre, jabbed it into the Jinn's mouth so that the sword stood on its tongue and reached to the roof of its mouth, and the stick lodged between its two jaws, and the Jinn could not close its mouth, or indeed do anything. Thus Yusif spent the whole of his watch until it was time for his relief, when he withdrew his weapons and departed to the side of his brethren.

'Then went forth Baraiga, and Baraiga's skin was so white that he had only to take off all his clothing to become transparent. Thus the Jinn was unable to see him, and spent its time vainly groping about for its prey, and while doing so it bumped its head against a stone, so that one of its eyes was struck out. And thus the third watch was kept.

'Last of all came Bu Zaid, and approaching the Jinn boldly he said, "Close your other eye, stretch forth your neck, and open your mouth that I may enter it for your dinner," and the Jinn did so, and Bu Zaid drew his sword and striking at its neck slew it. Then bending down he

[248]

wetted the palm of his hand in the Jinn's blood and ran at great speed to the Governor's Fort in the town, and he leapt from the ground almost to the roof and struck his bloody palm against the wall above the doorway, leaving the mark of the Jinn's blood there. Then he returned to his two brothers and the Governor's daughter in the wilderness.

'And when the morning came the people of the town saw the stream of the Jinn's red blood, and the bloody mark of a man's hand on the fort walls high above the doorway. And the Governor called all the people together to discover who had killed the Jinn, saying, "*W'allahi!* he who has killed the Jinn shall be governor, and I will hand the fort over to him."

'And there were many present that answered, "I did it," and "I did it."

'He answered them saying, "Come then, leap up and touch the place of blood above the portal."

'But none could do so.

'Baraiga and Yusif now came into the town to see what manner of place it was, for they had left Bu Zaid with the young girl and the camels in the wilderness.

'And the Governor, hearing of the arrival of strangers, commanded that Baraiga and Yusif should be brought before him. And he said to them, "The town has been under bondage to a Jinn, and now it is delivered and no more have we to sacrifice a girl and a ram and a dish of rice. Now which of you brought deliverance? Tell me, for he shall be the governor in my room."

'They replied, "We do not know."

'But the Governor did not believe them, and he said, "You must both leap as high as you can for me to see which of you it was."

'Then they did as he bade them, but their hands reached

[249]

to a point that fell far short of the bloody hand on the fort wall, so the Governor knew it was not one of them. He turned to them again and said, "And where is the rest of your party?"

'And they, fearing evil consequences, said, "We have only a slave" (a part that came easy to Bu Zaid on account of his black colour)—"and he is outside the town with our camels."

'The Governor replied, "I shall detain you till I have seen him." Then he ordered a camel and a slave girl to go out and bring in Bu Zaid. And he said to her, "When you arrive where he is, tell him to mount behind you. If he is a slave he will, but if he is a free man, he will surely desire to come to this place riding in front and will put you behind him."

'So the slave girl set forth on the camel and came to the wilderness where Bu Zaid was, and she said, "I am a messenger from the Governor, and he requires your presence before him at once, and you are to ride back with me upon this camel," and she motioned him to his place behind her. But he brushed her aside and sat her behind him and thus they came to the fort of the Governor and dismounted.

'Then said the Governor to Bu Zaid, "Jump, O slave, and place your hand against the bloody hand above the doorway." Bu Zaid replied, "I am a slave, how can I? I can do nothing."

' "Jump," said the Governor, "you must." So then Bu Zaid leapt into the air, and his hand reached higher than the mark of the Jinn's blood he had left there overnight. So the Governor and all the people knew that it was he who had slain the Jinn.

'The Governor now turned to the people and said, "It

is meet that the man who delivered you should be your governor," and then to Bu Zaid, "This fort is yours!"

'But Bu Zaid answered and said, "I want neither riches nor power, give me leave to go about my pleasure."

'And so they gave to him of treasure and horses and *rizk Allah*—the bounty of God—and he departed with his brethren in the fulness of joy.'

Before the story was ended our camels, coming back from water, appeared across the sands. Hamad and I walked out to meet them. As we went we crossed many recent camel tracks which showed Farajja to be a popular water-hole. The grouped tracks of four camels walking in line arrested my companion's attention, and he turned to me and asked me in play which camel I saw in the sands to be best. I pointed—pardonably, I persuaded myself—to the wrong one. 'There,' he said, 'do you see that cuffing up of the toes? It is a good sign: but not that skidding,' pointing to mine, 'between the footmarks.' 'That,' he said of the third, 'is an animal that has recently been in the steppe. Do you see the rugged impressions of her feet? Camels that have long been in the sands leave smooth impressions, and that' (pointing to the fourth) 'is her baby. Your camel is big with young—see the deep impressions of her small hind feet.' And thus and thus. It was not the least important part of Hamad's lore—a lore shared by nearly every dweller of the sands in varying degree—to read the condition of the strange camel, as yet unseen, from her marks, and hence to know whether to flee or to pursue.

Tracking in Arabia is an exact science, beside which the finger-print methods of the West are limited in scope, for the sands are a perfect medium.

In the more sophisticated parts of the peninsula—Oman, for example, a Court of Justice acts upon a foot-tracker's evidence, though there the *qaffar*, as he is called, has gifts not possessed, as in the sands, by the world at large. A case occurred during my service in Muscat. A Chinaman who had come to buy pearls and sea-slugs was murdered one night while he slept on the roof of his house in the Muscat bazaar. The murderer had apparently been surprised in the act, for he had jumped from the roof (it was a single-storey building) in his flight. The imprint of his foot remained in the lane beneath. On discovery next morning a pot was placed over it, sentries were posted at either end of the lane to prevent people passing that way, and a famous foot-tracker sent for, from up country. Meanwhile the days passed and the town grew nervous, for the murder had been a particularly brutal one—the neck had been cut with a sharp dagger from ear to ear—and the murderer was still at large.

The foot-tracker arrived and visited the footprint two or three times, on each occasion spending some minutes down on his hands and knees over it, as though to memorise it.

The next day the Council ordered that every male in the town must pass for inspection by the *qaffar*; quarter by quarter sent their tale of men. Some days had thus passed, till at last the *qaffar* gave the sign.

It was a young man in his twenties, an African slave, indeed a Court slave, and therefore not a safe person to charge in error. He was immediately arrested and sent to the Prison Fort, where charged with the crime he flatly denied all knowledge of it, and affirmed his innocence.

The clothes he was supposed to have been wearing were sent to the Public Analyst in Bombay and no blood stains were found, but other circumstantial evidence supported the foot-tracker. The slave was a notorious character; he was the sole occupant of the next house, so that he could have kept a careful watch on the movements of his intended victim; he could also have jumped easily from his upstairs veranda on to the roof where the murder took place, but he could not have jumped back.

The Indian Apothecary looked at the foot-impression too. There in the middle was an edge of splintered stone, and his opinion was that the man who had dropped from the roof on to the stone must have a slight cut in the sole of his right foot.

The prisoner was brought before me and I asked him to show me the bottom of his foot. He lifted the left one promptly. Examination of the right foot showed the cut mark there, and my head callipers confirmed that the position of it corresponded exactly with the position of the splintered stone in the foot impression. The slave suffered the prescribed penalty in public at the hands of a firing squad. The foot-tracker had not read the marks in vain.

And now six months later, in the centre of Rub' al Khali I was enjoying serener moments studying the tracks of the smaller animals. To a Badu, their simple story is immediately intelligible. For a European they have another appeal, the charm of graceful line or subtle invention; the sweep of drooping *gasis* in the wind makes a tiny picture of the prayer-ring the Badu sweeps with his cane towards the setting sun; the straight stride of birds' claws spaced one immediately before the other, a contrast with the earthy meanderings of some small quadruped; the neat little rosette pattern of a rat leads to a thicket, where you will find its tiny hole, a heap of newly turned red sand at the entrance; the crooked but beautiful intricacies of a lizard like a miniature arabesque lead to a sprig of herbage where it has played maypole and rolled over in joyous repletion; that futuristic riot marks the fallen twigs bowled over and over by the whims of the wind.

The morrow was intensely cold. Our course at first due east obliquely across the strong north wind, then turned into the face of it, and I was glad of my greatcoat. A large hawk, the first I had seen in the sands, circled about our heads to sail swiftly down wind as we passed an encampment of Murra with some fifty black camels. The great camel herds of the Murra are said to be mostly black,[1] whence the tents of the sands are generally of that colour, in sharp contrast with the colour of the wild animals of the sands, particularly the mammals, which is that of their environment.

We made a wide detour to avoid these Murra. They were ostensibly a friendly section, but it was declared unwise that I be seen or heard of, lest news of me get ahead with mischievous results.

Shaikh Salih as he rode at my side shivered, but would not bemoan the cold, lest he affront the Almighty, the All Knowing, who had sent it. I told Salih of the cold of an English winter.

'Do you hear that?'—he turned to Mubarak. 'In the Wazir's country the water that is cut off from the sea (a pond) becomes solid with the cold so that the Arabs and horses and donkeys can walk upon it.'

'There is no god but God,' returned Mubarak, and I

---

[1] A herd of camels is called *jaish* by Murra, *nishera* by the Rashid, and *bosh* by Oman tribes. The Badawin of the sands have five colours in camels: white, red, black, yellow, green. These are the dictionary equivalents. In reality: white=fawny cream colour; red=gazelle colour; black=a black-brown colour; yellow=between fawny cream and gazelle colour; green=a dark wood-smoke colour.

detected in his expression a fear lest I be the advance guard of a party of invaders, anxious to forsake such misery for their own delectable sands.

Long hungry hours in the saddle and the cold north wind made life at this stage uncomfortable, the night temperature falling to 40° F., and having no tent or other overhead covering, I found it necessary to sleep in all my clothes plus three blankets.

On 22nd January in the red rolling sand-hills of Ubaila we met the first of a series of sandstorms. We were sitting round the camp fire after the evening meal. Two nights before there had been a heavy dew, our first since leaving the Qara Mountains. To-night a cold wind from the north was blowing, but nothing presaged a coming storm. Suddenly the flames swept this way and that as though the wind blew from everywhere in turn. We all covered our faces with our hands to save our eyes from the smoke. My companions leapt up and rushed off in the darkness to bring in their grazing camels, for the sandstorm is one of their worst enemies. The storm grew fiercer; the Badawin, with their poor mantles wrapped round them, huddled together for warmth.

I slept fitfully. The hissing of the sand-laden wind, the rattling of my camp cordage and the cold of my feet made sleep impossible. When my face was exposed the gritty blast struck it with the sharpness of a knife. The temperature fell to 37° F. dry, 35° F. wet. I dozed off just before dawn and woke soon after to find my saddle and baggage embedded in driven sand. The wind had dropped and round the camp-fires clustered huddled and shivering Badawin. Soon they were rousing their camels that had been rounded up overnight for safety, and the wretched beasts shuffled, shivering, away to feed and to feel the warmth of the rising sun.

To me the night had disastrous results. The sand had got into some of my instruments. My small cinema camera was out of action, and my two aneroids no longer tallied, so that I was obliged thereafter to record two different readings, not knowing which, if either, was right till the end of the journey.

'I bring you good tidings of the *shamal*! I bring you good tidings of the *shamal*!' shouted a young Badu next morning in ironical reference to the bitter north wind, the temperature standing within 5° F. of freezing-point.

> 'But for the north wind
> There would be no increase,'

retorted Shaikh Salih, quoting a desert rhyme upon the wind's stimulus to the bull-camel.

The rolling reds of Ubaila had given place again to the more typical white open spaces of Sanam as we approached the water-hole of Jahaishi. A chill depressing day with the plain a white smoke-screen that swept towards us and past us filming our camels' feet, the wind had stung my poor companions, who, muffled up in their scanty garments sat shivering as we rode along.

'Couch her, Sahib! Couch Agaba,' they cried, 'it is the hour of the midday prayer.' Here beside the abandoned water-hole of Duwairis were firewood and a little grazing, and I realised we were halting for the day. Sand filled my eyes, and my note-books; sand was everywhere; note-taking with numbed fingers was impossible, and all that could be done was to sit idly in the swirl of sand and cold discomfort, and wish for a lull.

IN COLD AND HUNGRY UBAILA.

The Badawin collected brushwood from the thickets and piled it in a strong hedge twenty yards long. It was *gadha*, a considerable bush which we here met for the first time. Behind this shelter the camels were couched huddled together, only a few hardy brutes electing to stand and graze. Later in the day when the sun made itself felt and the wind dropped a little, they hobbled off to some near pastures, but when the wind again rose they were promptly brought back, their masters fearing to lose them, if left out, for the wind immediately effaced all tracks.

The homing instinct of the camel—if the absence of an established home does not make the term a paradox—is amazing. Her fixed idea apparently is to regain the fat pastures and main herds she has just left. During the preoccupations of marching, she may forget, but when a halt is called and she is turned out to graze unfettered, she will wander back alone the way she has come. Her master means nothing to her. She has no affection for him and never learns to know more of him than the sound of his voice. Yet she is utterly dependent upon him for her watering, being powerless to fend for herself even at the shallowest water-hole. She is excessively stupid except for an uncanny sense of direction, but is none the less '*Ata Y'Allah*'—the Gift of God—in his eyes.

'If you leave Agaba[1] to herself,' said Shaikh Salih, 'she will go off across the sands directly under that star back to

---

[1] Every camel has an individual name by which she is known to her master, but a disinterested party will know her by one of nine names, according to her age: first to seventh month, Huwar (suckling); seventh month to second year, Inferid (*i.e.* is fending for itself); second year, Bint al Bun or Weled al Bun; third year, Madhriba (may be covered by bull); fourth year, Yadha (able to calf); fifth year, Thiniya; sixth year, Raba; seventh year, Sidis; eighth year, Shag al Naga or Nufi.

Dakaka and her companions, though she has never come this way before.'

'But how will she fare for water?'

'She will wander back without water and arrive safely in the winter time, but in summer she will perish of thirst before a quarter of the way.'

Our march during the past two days had afforded an instance of this. A strange camel, a cow big with calf,[1] had joined our party, or rather led the way, for she bounced along ahead of us, making straight for Qatar where her camel brand showed her to belong. She was presumably anxious for dates or sardines, the local delicacies she missed in the sands; lucky for her that the season was winter!

'Do not let your camel eat of this *gadha*,' shouted a Murri next day as we passed through a verdant plain of it; 'it is *jinn* haunted.'

'But only these *gadha* pastures of Al Hirra and Banaiyan,' explained Hamad to me, 'elsewhere it is good enough fodder. Here five camels died in one night, and on another occasion two became ill and their milk dried up.'

I had also found this idea, that *jinns* could affect the wholesomeness of vegetation, at Mugshin, where it caused a magnificent grove of acacias to be largely neglected. My Badawin's invariable habit of picking the juiciest herbage for hand-feeding their camels was there suspended, nor

---

[1] A cow in calf is known as *midini* (Rashid) al *algaha* (Murri). The period of gestation is twelve months. She may go thirteen months; or sometimes eleven, but in the latter case the calf seldom survives. Where it does it is called *saham*, the mother *jaret*. The cow calf, as yet uncovered by a bull is a *bakra*. The Murra call a bull and cow calf *ga'ud* and *hashi* respectively.

would they shoot the hares of this grove for the pot.[1] The Kathiris had another strange belief, that a camel hand-fed at Mugshin instead of grazing for itself would suffer misfortune.

The famous water-hole of Banaiyan lay but a day's march ahead. An hour and a half after leaving our overnight's *hadh* pastures, we breasted the red sand-hills of Khiyut al Buraidan that marked the northern border of Sanam. The wind had dropped and the pure smooth surface of the rosy sand-hills—here called Hamarur—was in refreshing contrast to the white smoking plains of the recent marches. Patches of vivid green *haram* lined the gravelly troughs in the sand-hills and our hungry camels occasionally snatched at a tuft as we passed, though without encouragement, for *haram* is a saline feed which does no good to the animal not used to it. 'Now the Manasir,' said a Badu with a sweep of his arm to the eastwards, 'have little else and their camels are reared on it and grow humps like this'—here he caught the elbow of one arm held out before him, the forearm bent upwards on the palm of the other hand—a favourite gesture to indicate a large hump and therefore a thriving animal.

Rare ridges of red sand in the plain, long and low, and patches of *gadha* growing out of elephant-mask accretions of sand about their roots, formed an area called Qadha Za'aza and brought us to more rolling red hills. In the midst of these we halted over the water-hole of Banaiyan. The caravan had dragged out, as all tired caravans do. Ramadhan was telling on the men, the saline pastures on

[1] A curious taboo peculiar to the Manasir tribe is that they will not eat hare or other animal that has been shot in the head, *i.e.* presumably if its brains have been disturbed.

the camels, and the long marches and cold north wind on both. Hamad and I were the first arrivals.

'Drink, Sahib,' he said, 'the water of Banaiyan is good.'

Hamad, even had it not been the fast month, would himself have forborne. It was their code after a thirsty day's march that when we arrived at a water-hole no drop of water should pass the lips of the advance party until those in the rear had come up, nor would any man eat a crust with me on the march unless his companions were there to share it. If this precarious condition of life produces savagery between enemies, it breeds none the less a fine humanity among friends.

Banaiyan was a real well, stone-lined and therefore unlike the mere pits in the sand that are the water-holes of the south. As my party straggled in there was a visible change in their mood. Cheerfulness prevailed with the merry shouts and noise of spilling water that they love to make, while their great thirsty brutes with long necks stretched down to the scooped-out water trough gurgled their fill.

The want of pastures forbade a halt in these barren, rolling hills, and the first animals to be watered were already on the march before the last had come up. I delayed to accompany the rear party. Soon we had to halt for the sunset prayer, and after that we found growing difficulty in following the tracks of our advance guard; the failing light soon made it impossible. So with Polaris before our left shoulder—as the Badu has it, with his hand over his corresponding collar-bone so that you shall not err—we made our way through the night. An hour had passed when there was a shout from a man behind me. Turning, I saw the glimmer of a camp fire away to the eastwards. We turned and made camp at seven o'clock. I was thoroughly exhausted after ten and a half hours in the saddle, but comfort came from the realisation that the great central wastes of Rub' al Khali lay behind me, the sea was but eighty miles to the northward, success was in sight.

XIX: AT BANAIYAN: A RETROSPECT

A T Banaiyan I had reached the northward, fringe of Ar Rimal.[1] It is a convenient point, therefore, at which to suspend the narrative for a brief chapter to consider in retrospect the shape and structure of the land; its nomenclature, and the sociological aspects of the life of its inhabitants, as revealed by my journeyings.

Arabia is divided geologically by the Rub' al Khali. To the west the preponderating mass of the peninsula is geologically part of the African continent, from which it is separated only by the depressed zone or rift valley of the Red Sea. It has been elevated to a height of several thousand feet, carrying marine rocks to the highest elevation, but within itself has not suffered much dislocation; even the volcanic rocks in the north were ejected without much force, so that no volcanic peaks were formed. On the whole therefore the country has remained relatively undisturbed during the vast spaces of geological time.

The eastern zone, that is, the massif of Oman, on the other hand, forms part of the Persian system of intensively folded mountains caused by pressure from the north against the more stable mass of Arabia Proper, at a time when active earth movements were forming the great ranges of south Persia and northern India.[2]

[1] In this Longitude 51° E., Banaiyan is regarded as the northward limit of Ar Rimal. To the eastwards the sands continue northwards through the regions of Batin, Liwa, Qufa and Bainuna to the shores of the Persian Gulf: to the westwards they continue through Jaub and Jafura to Hasa (see Map). But in the mouth of the true son of the sands these regions are not Ar Rimal.

[2] The reader interested in the subject is referred to *The Geology and Tectonics of Oman and of Parts of South-Eastern Arabia* (*Quart. Journal Geol. Soc.*, 1928), by Dr. G. M. Lees, to whom I make acknowledgments.

Dhufar, the starting-point of my journey, lends itself to the study of the geological structure of much of the Arabian plateau. Along the seashore are exposed granites and other crystalline rocks which form the massive basement of the peninsula. They are overlaid by red sandstones which form the lower slopes of Jabal Qara, probably like the Nubian sandstone found in Egypt, Sinai and Trans-Jordan, and over that again represented by the high cliffs of Jabal Qara are limestones of the Upper Cretaceous and Eocene Ages, but the southern face is in reality an escarpment forming the edge of the high sandstone plateau which slopes gently down to the edge of the sands where I found my Eocene fossils.

The great belt of sands lying to the northward for three hundred miles and more did not yield any indication of age, though the sand specimens[1] I brought back from the centre contain grains of pink and white limestone, indicating perhaps that the sand has not travelled from a great distance; otherwise they would have disappeared from the friction of the harder quartz.

Along the northern sand fringe to the north of Banaiyan I again found sea fossils of the same age as those in the south, but it is impossible to say from my single traverse whether the Eocene Sea once extended all the way across from Qatar to Dhufar, to be covered later with blown sands from the north-east, or whether the points approximately one hundred miles inland on both sides of the Rub' al Khali where I picked up fossils represent the northern and southern limits of invasion of the Eocene Sea.

It is possible that the basic floor of Ar Rimal is of some limestone formation, probably of Eocene or Cretaceous age,

[1] A list of sand specimens with analyses is given in Appendix II.

with exposures of the Nubian sandstone from which the blown sands have been formed.

The Rub' al Khali has been shown to be a zone of depression between high Nejd to the west and the Oman Mountains to the east, a depression that probably occurred at the time of the elevation of Oman—that is during the Upper Cretaceous and the Tertiary periods.

Of much interest, if of a negative kind, was the gentle character of the topography along my line of march—the general absence of any considerable folding to give rise to prominent features. Just over the Qara Mountains the steppe began roughly at an altitude of 2000 feet, and it sloped gently to 1100 feet at the edge of the sands, making a fall of only 900 feet in 100 miles. So also from this southern edge of the sands at 1100 feet to the northern edge at Banaiyan, 200 feet, the fall is but 900 feet in nearly 300 miles. Northwards of Banaiyan the same gentle slope is maintained towards the sea.

In describing the sands proper,[1] I have already noted that their greatest elevations, the dune country, lie along the southern fringe and swing north, according to Arab report, in about Long. 49° and again in Long. 53°.

The extension of these wings would approximately

---

[1] A résumé of the belts of main sand-shape I encountered from south to north is as follows:

		Miles.
I.	High, red, dune country	20
II.	Elevated, less rugged, red sands, with horse-shoe hills	40
III.	Parallel white ridges with intervening red valleys	100
IV.	Flat or gently undulating white sands	70
V.	Flat or gently undulating white sands, with transverse red hills	50
VI.	Steppe, salt plain, and red hills alternating	100

trisect Ar Rimal, and a reference to the map will show that it was through the middle section that my route lay.

The belief that the sands would prove waterless has been shown to be unfounded. Water, though very brackish, is found at any rate eastward of 51° E.[1] Indeed, throughout the middle regions in the low sands of eastern Suwahib and elsewhere, there seems to be abundant sub-soil water, but so saline as to be generally undrinkable by man. Such water-holes do not enjoy distinguishing names but are, as already stated, labelled generically *khiran*. Elsewhere, a water-hole which a camel or man will drink from enjoys a distinguishing name, often that of its digger; when necessary the camel plays the part of a distillery. She drinks the water and man drinks her milk.

So also the vegetation lay in zones from south to north:

Belt	Vegetation*	Latitude		Altitude	
		From	To	From ft.	To ft.
I., II.	{ Zahar Barkan Abala† }	18° 30′	20° 30′	1100	550
III., IV., V.	Hadh	20° 00′	23° 00′	600	250
V., VI.	Gadha	22° 40′	24° 00′	275	125
VI.	Shinan	23° 12′	24° 30′	200	S.L.

Lesser herbage was *Gasis* and *Haram* in the red sands of I., II., V., VI.

* *Zahar* (*Tribulus alatris*, Del.).
  Hadh (*Salsola sp.*).
  Shinan (*Arthrocnemum glaucum*, Ung.).
† *Abala* is the most considerable growth of the sands and by far the most useful. The framework of the camel saddle and tent utensils are made from this wood; it is also excellent firewood, unlike *Hadh* and *Shinan*.

[1] A chemical analysis of the contents of every water-hole is given in Appendix II.

The sweetest water lay on the westernmost points of my route in western Dakaka and Sanam, where the water-holes were as deep as thirteen fathoms and upwards, but the yield is said to be uncertain. Indeed sometimes, as with Turaiga, they dry up. The most brackish water lay on the eastern-most portions of my route, where it was shallow, as at Buwah, and the supply was apparently inexhaustible; this evidence would seem to support Arab information that the great sands rising towards the west and south-west are entirely waterless.

The regional names of the sands derive very often from some topographical feature,[1] or from some peculiarity of water or vegetation, or now and then from some association with camels.

The mode of human life in Rub' al Khali—the only life that short-lived pastures and inadequate or brackish water permit—is tribal and nomadic, a life economically pre-carious, politically unstable, but socially fixed and un-alterable.

---

[1] Mention has already been made in this sense of these categories of Dakaka, Suwahib and Sanam. So also are:

Buwah, plural of *Bah*, a shallow dipping-hole.

Munajjar from *Minjor*, where a water-hole has to be bored through hard rock.

Hadh al (Ga'ada), a region where *hadh* vegetation is predominant.

Khila(t Ajman), a region where *hadh* vegetation is not found.

Umm Malissa—'mother of smoothness,' a region in which neither *hadh* nor *zahar* grows.

Jaub, a wadi-like depression in sands—region Banaiyan-Jabrin.

Jiban, plural of *Jaub*.

Jafura from *Jifr*—a deep hole.

Shuwaikila—'strings of the udder bag'—hence two flanking areas of Huwaiya.

Tuwal—'length'—abnormally deep water-holes of western Sanam.

Aqal—'camel hobble'—the half-fathom holes of eastern Jiban.

The prosperity of the tribe is measured by the number and condition of its camels. The sources of wealth are good pastures and the manly prowess of its members who will aggressively acquire fresh camels at their enemies' expense.

Camels therefore fall into two classes, herds of milch camels (the assets and reserve) and the less numerous riding camels (working capital). The first may be worth one hundred dollars each, the second from two hundred to four hundred for an exceptional animal. The milch camel never knows a saddle, and is raised solely for breeding and to produce milk and wool. The female is therefore the valued sex, and the cow calf is always reared, whereas the bull calf is a luxury not worth his keep. In consequence he seldom survives the first year of life, and not infrequently is slaughtered for food on the day he is born without his mother seeing him. Normally two or three bulls will serve a herd of fifty cows; they also carry tents and the heavier burdens when on the move. Herds when wandering off to remote inaccessible regions split up over wide areas, each Badu family looking after its own; but the tribe will collect again for self-protection against the raiders of the steppe, whenever the need of grazing draws them southward into danger, as last winter.

The tribes strongest in camels are the Murra, Manasir and Manahil, also, to some extent, the Sa'ar. The Rashid have of late years decayed from the depredations of the Sa'ar, so that to-day a Rashidi with five camels is comparatively well off, with twenty he is rich, and one hundred is the limit of affluence; with the Murra averages are much higher. My envious Rashidi informant in emphasising their wealth, with a simile familiar to us of the West through the Old Testament, picked up a handful of sand and allowed it to trickle through his fingers. '*W'Allahi*! so-and-so has four hundred camels,' he said, 'and he is not a shaikh, nor has he money, nor clothes better than mine.'

'What happens to the milk?' I asked.

'Let a man have much milk,' was the answer, 'and he will have many guests. His neighbours expect it of him, and the passers-by. Any surplus milk will be given to the young camels.'

Camel hair provides almost all the few household wants of the nomad life—tent material, ropes, saddle girths, and miscellaneous trappings. Here again the cow is the more profitable sex. Her shoulders and back each year yield to her master's fist or dagger the raw material which his womenfolk will work up, for weaving is a feminine occupation; not milking, however, at least with Rashid and 'Awamir, who share the mountain taboo against the milking of camels by women; on the other hand, the Murra, Manasir, Sa'ar and Hadhramaut steppe tribes have no such ban.

Two types of saddle are in use in the sands. The double-poled saddle—the *shadad*—placed over the camel's hump. This, the normal saddle of the rest of Arabia, is used in the Rub' al Khali only by the Murra, the Sa'ar, and Karab. By the entire remaining tribes, as indeed in Oman and throughout the whole of south-eastern Arabia, the *zana* is used, a small light frame (without poles) covered with a goat skin and placed behind the camel's hump. The distribution of camel saddles is thus geographical; west of my line of route the tribes use the *shadad*, east of it the *zana*.

So also the sands know two dialects of Arabic, but here the division is latitudinal. There is a northern or Murri dialect and a southern or Rashid dialect, the latter also spoken by the 'Awamir[1] of the north-east. The chief distinctions between north and south dialects are word differences,[2] and a considerable difference of voice modulation. Hamad bin Hadi had volunteered the information that his people's dialect was peculiar, because Murra, he said, had sprung from an infidel; but in the presence of other members of his tribe he corrected himself, and all agreed to a common origin with 'Ajman, thence deriving from Yam. But the original maternal ancestor of the tribe was, God bless you, a *jinni*.

While polygamy is permissible, it is seldom that a Badu has more than one wife at a time, though if he is well off he may have two or may marry, divorce, and remarry. For a man and woman to live together out of wedlock is unknown, and would be impossible in a tribal society in which the liberty of the individual is subordinated to the interests of the clan and its posterity, and whose rigorous moral code is rooted in age-long experience, secure from the philosophical speculations of celibate professors. In theory no

---

[1] Kathir and 'Amr, the respective ancestors of Rashid and 'Awamir were, according to their traditions, brothers and the sons of Hamdan. A common expression on the lips of Shaikh Salih was: 'By the *sunnat* (*i.e.* rules) of 'Amr and Kathir.' The Hadhramaut tribes also have their separate dialects.

[2] *E.g.*

	Rashidi.	Murri.
Unleavened bread	Girus	Gadama
Wild cat	Khawenga	Idfa
Steppe	Jadda	Hadeba
Digging tool	'Atela	Ilhim

Reference has already been made of Y taking the place of J in the Rashidi dialect. The *chim* for a *kaf* is nowhere met, though common with the Ikhwan tribes of Mutari, 'Ataiba, 'Ajman, Dawasir, etc.: the g takes the place of q, a *qaf* sound is never met with amongst Badawin; the participle *qad*, noticeably absent in 'Iraq dialect, is universal in South Arabia. (In the Mahri and non-Arabic dialects its equivalent is *Bir*.)

marriage is valid, except it be 'knotted' formally by a Qadhi,[1] or adequate proxy, with considerable ceremony, doubtless designed to discourage its participants from breaking their bonds.

The prospective bridegroom and representative of the bride, usually her father or brother, go off together to the nearest town,[2] where a Qadhi will be found, for it is almost unknown for a Qadhi to come out into the desert. A system whereby certain tribesmen, who have taken advantage of a sojourn in the town to learn the formulae stand proxy for a Qadhi and celebrate marriages, has come to have a validity with dwellers in the remoter sands; the office is then hereditary. It is the custom after the 'knot' is tied for the bridegroom to pay over the purchase price to the father. Then he will bring to the bride some silver jewellery and a simple rug for the nuptial couch (and with the Rashid he must also make a feast) before the consummation can take place. The nose-kiss is the kiss of the marital bed.[3]

Man treats woman as an inferior, a chattel. This is

[1] An interpreter of Holy Law, sometimes a preacher among Sunnis, but among Shi'ahs, in Persia and 'Iraq, a priest. The institution of a priestly hierarchy is foreign to Islam, and is anathema to the orthodox, and especially to Wahabis.

[2] The Manasir tribe uses Abu Dhabi.
The 'Awamir tribe uses Ibri, Dhank and Biraimi.
The Rashid tribe uses Dhufar or Raidha.
The Murra tribe uses Hofuf or Jabrin.

[3] Intra decem primos matrimonii dies pudori habetur interdiu coitus. Corpus feminae ab umbilico usque ad genua nunquam detegere licet: si vir pannum qui ei pro tegumento est, removere velit, ilicet femina questa e tabernaculo excurrat. Pro lecto arenas habent; nam lectus, qualem nos habemus, eis ignotus est. Maxime usitatum est a latere vel a tergo cum femina coire, id quod etiam cum muliere praegnante vel paucis ante partum diebus nonnunquam fit.

[270]

perhaps natural in the desert environment, where un-interrupted physical fitness, brute strength, and an aggressive character are qualities which Nature demands and rewards. The beating of women for common, everyday lapses was approved by my Murra Badawin, but not by the Rashidis.

The politics of Rub' al Khali revolve round inter-tribal relationships. Geographical considerations make for three almost separate tribal groupings, the Rimal tribes, their neighbours of the eastern steppe and those of the southern steppe.

The true sand dwellers have been shown to be the Murra in north and north-west, the Manasir and 'Awamir in the north-east, and Ar Rashid and Bait Imani in the south.

Twenty years ago these tribes were at one another's throats. Murra and Manasir were old and implacable enemies; between 'Awamir and Manasir the feud was even fiercer. The 'Awamir, once a very great tribe in South Arabia, were the original dwellers in the present Rashidi sands of the Dakaka, Suwahib, Hibak and Ghanim, but unequal contests with the Manasir have impoverished them; while Murra and Rashid have many old scores. Yet to-day peace, the peace of Bin Sa'ud, prevails throughout the sands. The influence of the Ruler of Central Arabia, wielded through his able Viceroy at Hofuf, Bin Jaluwi, compels peace between all these old enemies, not through direct control, for there is and can be none, but through the immense personal prestige of 'Abdul 'Aziz himself. A belief in his strength and star has swept across the sands. Not love, but awe, serves this wise providence that so directs affairs. My own *rabia* Hamad bin Hadi had not yet made submission, but he was respectful in his fear of the mighty, the

[271]

belief that the ruler of Riyadh had power to despoil him of his spoils, or make him the prey of an enemy. Upon this conviction is founded peace in the sands to-day. Thus the sand tribes proper are in some degree leagued with Bin Sa'ud. They pay to him a nominal tribute and by that act are ensured mutual protection one from the other. In theory the tribute is an annual levy of one dollar on each camel. In practice, the Rashid have no money, and in any event they escape proper payment by reason of their remoteness. They do however send a camel from year to year as occasion offers in token of submission. When, however, rains fall in the northern sands and they migrate thither, the tax-gatherers' demands must be met, and a few camels are sold for the purpose.

Light as is the bond, the tribes grumble at it. They have no sympathy with the Arab proverb, that originated, we may be sure, in a town, 'A tyrannical Sultan is to be preferred to constant quarrelling.' They would rather have unfettered liberty than peace at a price; it is in their blood. They all swear that the existing peace shall last only as long as the present régime of Riyadh. Let Riyadh or Hofuf be thought to have lost its power, and raiding will be resumed immediately, and blood will flow again. This attitude of mind is not peculiar to the Rub' al Khali. The student of politics will recall many instances in the recent history of the British Empire.

It was the knowledge of this unprecedented suspension of blood feuds, springing from a determined but benign autocracy, that emboldened me to launch out across these ancient (and future) battle-grounds of the sands.

The politics of the eastern steppe are not unaffected by Bin Sa'ud's influence, though this varies from year to year.

Here the groupings form round ancient hereditary factions of Hinawi and Ghafari already referred to—'Awamir, Harasis and Afar belonging to the former, Daru'[1] and Albu Shamis to the Ghafari, but their strife has no echo in the sands.

The politics of the southern steppe are completely free from Bin Sa'ud's influence, and the great tribes of Sa'ar, Manahil, Kathir and Mahra, and the lesser ones of Karab, Yam, Nahad and Nisiyin are laws unto themselves. The most powerful single element is the Sa'ar. With them, Nahad and Karab may act in concert, while elements of the others are capable of uniting for a particular raid; but there is no long and sustained or organised warfare. There cannot be, for each man has but twenty rounds or so of ammunition and guards his stock jealously unless he is making a journey to the coast to sell a camel or two. Their wars are consequently sporadic with booty as the end and aim.

The Sa'ar tribe and its allies are to-day the serious menace to peace in the southern sands. Numerically powerful—perhaps two thousand rifles—they derive strength from their remoteness, and have hitherto refused to receive an embassy from Bin Sa'ud.

[1] Daru' and Manahil, supposed to have had a common origin, now by some odd chance belong (in name) to opposite factions.

XX: BANAIYAN TO THE SEA: THE LAST STAGE

JANUARY 28th was spent resting at Banaiyan after our eighteen days' dash across the central sands—a halt necessary to refresh tired camels and men. We gathered round the camp-fire at nightfall—it proved to be the last leisurely session the march afforded—and with the end of the journey in sight I was able to throw off my habitual restraint.

My electric torch was a source of wonderment to my companions. 'Could a strayed or stolen camel be tracked on a dark night with it?' that was the crucial question. The first Badu to place his hand over the lighted end discovered that there was practically no heat, and brought the miracle to the notice of his companions. They all followed suit and when, instead of feeling heat they saw the red hue of blood and shadowy finger-bones, they burst out in astonished cries—'There is no god but God. Surely the Sahib's tribe must be a wonderful people?' It was idle for me to declare that I had not made the torch, for did we not make still more marvellous works—rifles and ammunition!

'Who makes rifles?' asked one Badu, fondling his own.

'The Infidels,' said another without looking up.

'No,' I corrected them, 'we are Believers.'

'And if we came to your country, Sahib, would you be our *rabia* so that none should harm us?'

'There is no need for a *rabia* in my country.'

'But,' said Hamad, 'if one should slay me and you were my *rabia* what would you do?'

'But none would slay you. Nobody may carry arms in my country.'

[274]

'What a place!' I felt them to be thinking, 'fit only for women and slaves!'

'And should we get camels' milk to drink?'

'We have no camels,' I returned apologetically, for I knew I should get few marks for this.

'Then what have you got? Sheep? Cows?'

'Yes, sheep and cows,' I said, 'but we make ships and rifles and all manner of things from the iron of the earth.'

'True,' interjected Shaikh Salih with a sophisticated air, 'I've heard a Mansuri from Abu Dhabi say that one day a Nasrani came to the shaikh and told him that in his country a bar of iron like this,' and he flourished his camel stick, 'would make five rifles.'

Chorus of Badawin: 'There is no god but God.'

One picked up the torch again. 'It is heavy,' he said. 'God! it's heavy,' said another, as he took it out of his comrade's hand.

Salih: 'They are not an easy people' (*i.e.* not a weak tribe whose members could be treated as inferiors).

'Inside the torch is *guwa*—strength—' (a word they reverence) 'more potent than bullets, and such that it kills men,' I said.

'But why kill them?'

'Only bad men,' I returned—'murderers.'

'Yes, and very right too—"an eye for an eye and a tooth for a tooth"—'tis God's Law.'

'But have you no blood-money?'

'None,' I said.

'Then the murdered man's brother or cousin does not profit a single dollar.'

'Not a single dollar,' I repeated, conscious that I was scoring very few marks again.

'But have you no sanctuary?'

'No, our shaikh is strong, and no one would dare to give a murderer sanctuary.'

'But with us,' said Salih, 'sanctuary is honoured, unless there is shame in the murder, such for instance as a *rabia* who has betrayed his companion; what good man is there,' he continued, looking round his companions, 'who would withhold sanctuary from one who had killed his enemy?'

Chorus of Badawin: 'Yes, by God!'

'Which direction is your country, Sahib?' said one of them after a pause.

I pointed with my riding cane in a north-westerly direction.

'How far is it away?'

'*Hol*—a year's march, from Ramadhan to Ramadhan,' I said, 'at our pace.'

Chorus of Badawin: 'There is no god but God.'

'And which direction is it from Mecca?' interposed Salih, one of the few South Arabian Badawin I knew who had made the Pilgrimage.

I pointed as before, perhaps a shade more northerly.

'And how far is it from there?'

'Almost as far as it is from here.'

Chorus: 'There is no god but God.'

'Then it is beyond the sea, Sahib?'

'Yes,' I said, 'beyond the sea.'

'And what is there beyond it?'

'The sea again,' I said.

'Where is the Sea of Barlimul?' said Talib. 'I think you must mean the Sea of Barlimul.' He turned to tell his companions that there the world ended. Beyond was nothing. It was the seventh and last sea—*Allahu 'Alim!*

I felt I had done my share of story-telling, and was an
eager listener when one of them fell to telling a story about
Dhiyab bin Ghanim. Dhiyab was from the nobility of Bani
Hillal, albeit with the appearance of a slave. And on the
black day when Yusif was killed, and Dhiyab, Bu Zaid and
Baraiga were made prisoners, his appearance saved him
from close confinement, for he was thought to be of no
account.

He was first set to work with the masons repairing
Zenaiti's fort. But such was his lack of skill, that the stones
he slung up passed clean over the fort and landed on the far
side in the desert. So his captors said, 'This slave is no good
at this work, we will set him to tend herds.' And Dhiyab
was given cows to look after, but he neglected to water them
properly so that they came near to dying. And his masters,
seeing that he made a bad cowman, sent him with asses to
go forth into the scrub and fetch kindlings. There he cut
two long sticks and sharpened their ends and thrust them
through the backs of a pair of donkeys to make carriers for
his firewood. And so he brought a huge load to his masters.
Their first impulse was to applaud, not knowing by what
contrivance it had been brought, but as soon as the firewood
was off-loaded, the asses dropped dead. And the men of
Arisha shook their heads and said, 'Dhiyab's wits are weak,
he is fit for nothing but to tend camels; we will set him to
look after the Bani Hillal camels that we captured with him';
thus did Dhiyab attain the object of his desire. As the days
passed the condition of the camels improved, and Dhiyab
won favour in the sight of his masters. And each time he
watered the camels he chose a more distant water-hole, thus
lengthening his absences by degrees without exciting suspicion until one day he reached the point that favoured

[277]

his escape and thence made off back to Bani Hillal country
with the camels. And in order that the passer-by need
bring no alarming news of him to Zenaiti he sat on his camel,
facing backwards towards Arisha, and placed earth upon his
head and under his haunches.[1] And thus he came to the
Bani Hillal. There Shaikh Husain bin Sirhan, after he had
listened to Dhiyab's story, planned to rescue Bu Zaid and
Baraiga, and in the fulness of time the tribe set forth and
came to a fragrant pool into which fell three wadis. And
Bani Hillal took counsel together and decided to leave their
women and animals with sixty horsemen to protect them,
while the *gom* passed on to the country of Zenaiti, but on
the morrow they changed the plan, saying that in place of
the sixty horsemen they would leave Dhiyab bin Ghanim.

'The camels and the women are in thy protection,' said
the shaikh to Dhiyab in farewell, 'guard them with thy life.'

And Dhiyab replied, 'If one of them shall be missing,
then is my life forfeit.'

That night a *Jinn* came wandering down the wadi to see
who was encamped there. He carried in his hand a mighty
spear, and went in and out among the camels seeking for
the biggest and best, and having found it he speared it and
carrying the camel impaled over his shoulder returned up
the wadi. The next night he came again so that in the
morning yet another camel was missing. And when on the
third night there was still another visitation, terror seized
the camp, for none had seen the *Jinn* except the wife of
Dhiyab, and she was loth to speak for fear of the *Jinn's* revenge. Dhiyab, regarding his wife's strange silence, questioned her, but she would not reply. Then he drew his

[1] I record the story as told, but the allusion is not clear to me, and to
have questioned my narrator would have broken the thread of the story.

sword and tapped her with it, saying, 'Woman! tell me
what thou knowest or I will slay thee.' So she told Dhiyab
of the *Jinn* that came down a certain wadi and of how he
speared the camels and carried them off.

On the following morning Dhiyab despatched his slave
to follow up the *Jinn's* tracks and to bring tidings of where
the *Jinn* lived. And the slave came to a well that had been
caused by the falling of a star and saw the *Jinn* within it, and
the remains of the camels strewn round about the mouth
of it, and so brought back news to Dhiyab. So Dhiyab
mounted his mare and came to the well. As he approached
the *Jinn* stood up to show his monstrous proportions, for his
body was as much out of the well as within it.

And the *Jinn* shouted, 'Oh ha! Ya Dhiyab bin Ghanim!
hast thou come to eat or to slay?'

Dhiyab replied, 'I have come both to eat and to slay,' and
drawing his sword he struck lustily at the *Jinn* and cut him
in halves, so that one half stood within the well, and the
other lay fallen without.

Said the *Jinn's* upper half, '*Hain*'—strike a second time.
But Dhiyab replied:

'*Ma thinni,*	'I strike not twice,
Wa la zinni,	Nor go a-whoring,
Wa la akl al jins ni.'	Nor am I food for your kind,'

for Dhiyab knew what everybody knows, that whereas one
fell blow will kill a *Jinn*, two blows will surely bring two
Jinns to life.

And Dhiyab returned to the camp to find that the *gom*
was just returning, but alas! knew not that three of his sons
had fallen and also Amr bin Khafaiyat, a valiant and

beloved warrior whose mother had been of the Bani Hillal. And the *gom* were troubled in their minds as to which among them should convey the ill-tidings to Dhiyab, who would surely strike down with his spear such a messenger of woe. For Dhiyab's spear was never known to miss; once it was launched it must land in flesh; so 'it was written'; and should it not land in flesh Dhiyab would die in that same day.

And none being willing to tell him, it was decided to send Dalaiyan the slave, for they said one to another, 'Should Dalaiyan die he dies; and should he live he lives only to be a slave.'

And Dalaiyan asked for the speediest mare and they gave it to him, and he rode towards Dhiyab's place and drew rein at a great distance.

Dhiyab shouted to him, 'Tell me, O Dalaiyan, as I am of the sons of darkness, how went the fight, and tell me of the gallantry of my sons and how it fares with them.'

And the slave answered:

'Of our camels and our sons, the best have gone.
Thy three sons and bin Khafaiyat.
Bravest of warriors of their tribe and time.'

And as the slave now turned his mount about and galloped away, Dhiyab seized his spear and hurled it after him; but Dalaiyan bending low over his steed, the weapon passed over him and landed some paces beyond in the head of a snake.

'Great God!' cried Dhiyab, 'my spear has missed. Now must I pass to where the slain have gone.'

'*Selemni*,' shouted back the slave, 'save me unhurt and I will give thee good tidings.'

Dhiyab: 'By my face.'

The slave: 'The spear point landed in flesh.'

Dhiyab: 'God be praised! And mayest thou live long.'

We made an early morning start into Wahhabi territory[1] —the home of the Ikhwan (brotherhood) sectaries. Here we moved furtively. Every hour of the day the horizons were scanned for signs of the feared Puritans of Islam, intolerant men who hold it virtuous to fight not merely the infidel, but the heretic in Islam, by whom they mean every Muslim not holding their narrow views. My companions were emphatic that there should be no loitering, not even for my note-taking, between here and the coast, and that if suspicious tracks were crossed, we should take no risks but hide in the wilderness by day, and march by night. Fortunately for my map-making the second course was not imposed upon us, for it was Ramadhan, and the Ikhwan tribes had withdrawn to the regions of Jaub and Jafura for the Fast.

'God is sufficient for their Evil,'[2] exclaimed Hamad the *rabia*.

Our course lay at first through a hard gravelly steppe bright with pebbles coloured like camphor, cornelian or jade; thence through large white salt-fields, with dark damp patches here and there.

Fortunately the recent rain had not been enough to turn the crusted surface into a greasy mire and hold camels up as normally occurs. Beyond we came to light-coloured

[1] So named by us after the followers of the religious rules of Muhammad bin Abdul Wahhab of Nejd, a religious reformer of the eighteenth century. The Ikhwan, their twentieth-century successors, have taken their place and revived their doctrines.

[2] The word evil is used to mean every kind of misfortune, *e.g.* raids or disease.

[281]

sands and within them a wadi-like depression with vegetation,[1] Jaub Dhibi, our camping ground and a haunt, as
their tracks showed, of hyena, wild-cat, lizards and other
steppe animals.

The Jiban tract that lay ahead of us for the next few days
was of the same type; alternating ribbons of steppe, salt
plain and rolling sand-hills with a verdant sand depression
such as Dhibi at intervals of a half-day's march, Kharit,
Thuraiya, Sufaiya and Lizba. The steppes were dusted with
gravel of jasper and gypsum, pebbles of black, white, red
and green that shone in the sun; the northern salt plains
were studded by innumerable small shells[2] in an early stage
of petrification; the gullies in the sand-hills were here and
there bright green with *haram* scrub, or pink and white
with patches of gypsum rubble; and in these same gullies
we dug out the shallow holes at which we watered.

Before Lizba, however, was a considerable ridge, the only
one of its kind. It stretched east and west as far as the eye
could see, rose some two hundred feet on its southern side
and fell to the northwards through a quarry-like desolation
to rolling sands. In the sands many black-ribbed beetles
were crawling amidst sprigs of fresh grass, the green first-
fruits of the scanty winter rain. This grass, *ushub*, said to
produce the most delicious camel milk, gave us reason to
halt from time to time and graze our camels.

Talib, a northern Murri, had supplanted Hamad as our
guide in the marches north of Haluwain, a change for the
worse, though inevitable, as he alone of our party claimed
local knowledge. The compass directions and distances of

[1] The vegetation consisted of *shinan*, *gadha*, the stunted, bulrush-like
tarthuth, and *sa'adan*.
[2] See Appendix II.

water-holes that he gave me proved wrong, and when I took him to task, he swore that he spoke the truth 'by Him who created me and created the Sun.' I felt sure he had no mind to deceive us, but the pasture and firewood he promised for our night's halt did not appear. These were the chief considerations every afternoon in anticipation of the night's camp, and my company grew critical. 'Ya Arab,' said one, 'there is only cold and hunger ahead.' We veered to the eastwards, so that the conspicuous sand-hill, Alamat al Nakhala, formerly on our right front, appeared on our left; by sunset we had turned our backs upon it and were actually marching away from our goal in the hope of finding food and warmth that night. Had it been summer-time with its drought the mistake might have cost us our lives. One Badu in ten is a good guide, one in fifty a reliable informant. The mutual suspicion of the Rashid and Murra members of my party was of interest; it showed that neither believed their present peaceful relations to be lasting. So they would not disclose the secrets of their respective districts. Now and then a Murri would slip off to examine the state of some well or pasture, but it would never have done for a Rashidi to follow or enquire. Anyone contemplating such a journey as this is wise to collect all possible information beforehand; then the reliability of any particular informant can be quickly checked.

One day's march was very like another. Always an hour before sunrise I was awakened by the voice of Marzuq, sounding the Dawn call to prayer:

> 'God is great.
> There is no god but God.
> There is no god but God.

[283]

I bear witness that Muhammad is the Prophet of God.
I bear witness that Muhammad is the Prophet of God.
Prayer is better than sleep.
Prayer is better than sleep.
God is great.
There is no god but God.'

A chorus of sanctimonious groans from stirring Badawin was their Amen! There often followed Shaikh Salih's parental chiding of Kilthut who was ailing, and in consequence a laggard.

'Rise, O Kilthut, are you listening? Rise and pray!'

After prayers the Badawin, breaking up, drove their camels off to the nearest grazing, and then returned to breakfast off a handful of dates and a drink of brackish water. For the next eleven hours no food passed their lips, and during Ramadhan no water either; yet they seemed to thrive on it. My own breakfast-lunch, taken also at the first hour after sunrise, consisted of a bowl of camel's milk and a dish of oatmeal—my invariable diet for fifty-eight days on end.

If camel pastures were good I was allowed to finish my meal at leisure and to write up my natural history specimens and other notes before starting off, but if the camp had been a hungry one, then the moment I had finished my meal we would saddle, knowing that during the march we would have to loiter for grazing. My pack-camel was brought first.

'There is no god but God.
O God.
Him whom we supplicate.
O God.'

[284]

Thus a Badu picking up his cane lying on the sands between two toes, and leading my pack-camel over to couch her with a *kh kh* and a gentle tapping with his stick behind her knee or over her neck. Another would come to help him load up, and while the animal bellowed protestingly, they broke into a camel-chant suitably *agitato* for the occasion.

Badawin were everywhere loading up and moving off dismounted, each with the first foot forward muttering some pious invocation to the Unseen. The Rashidi formula[1] was as follows:

'In the name of God, the Compassionate, the Merciful.
Reliance is in God.
Peace upon the *rafiq*.
O God!
There is none other, and none equal to Thee.
And no escape from thy Will.
O God, by thy forgiveness
Make easy our path, and guide our *rafiq*.'

To which one of the party would return:

'There is no god but God.'

The morning routine was that we walked the first three or four miles, leading our camels; but I was usually first into the saddle, except for Bin Ham, a Bait Imani shaikh, and a doughty warrior among them still, in spite of a leg crippled by the old bullet wound of a raid.

[1] When starting out on a raid, the formula is sometimes as follows: 'God give to her back' (*i.e.* his camel's) 'good luck, and guide us so that we may return.'

[285]

The camel's great size and lethargic movements make her pace appear funereal, but the brisk movements of the small man ahead show that her average walking pace in easy country is about three miles an hour. Couched, her head swings superciliously from side to side and her filthy cud-filled mouth opens expectantly as her rider approaches, for she has been trained to rise instantly she feels the slightest touch to her back. Mounting has therefore to be a quick leap, which she often anticipates by a fraction of a second. Then she must be couched again with more knee-tapping. But so long as her master's riding cane is stuck in the sand by her head or his rifle lies on the sands in her sight she will sit contentedly. It is when he takes these things in his hands that she shows signs of nervous anticipation.

Mounted, she is always given her head, the halter being frequently unused, only a tapping on her neck with the cane, and a few guttural noises being required to teach her to obey her rider's will. Her own disposition tempts her to almost every tuft of food in the way; even she will crunch some fragment of white desiccated bone against her ridiculous toothless upper jaw unless her master urges her past in discouragement, as he normally will.

And so the Badu sits jogging along hour after hour with an occasional change of seat. In an Omani saddle he will not ride astride for long, but tuck his feet up under his haunches in a sitting-kneeling position, or ride side-saddle with his legs dangling limply. The double-poled Murra saddle admits of less variety, but is more comfortable to Europeans as the legs can be crossed to rest on her shoulders.

Most Badawin go bareheaded, a great shock of tousled dark brown hair being sufficient protection from the sun.

They will draw daggers as they ride along and scratch their own locks unabashed.

The rifle of a mounted Arab is generally carried in one hand across the animal's back; Rashidi saddles lend themselves to packing it; with a Murra saddle it leans up rakishly from a bucket, its bunches of tasselled thongs flapping merrily to the jogging. The Badu is a cheerful companion, generally humming some chant to himself. Occasionally he will burst forth *double forte* without any warning to his companions, who seem, however, always appreciative. Sometimes two would sing a duet, in unison of course. These chants vary between tribes; I was curious to record every one I heard so far as European notation[1] would allow. At other times they engaged each other in trials of strength, attempting to unseat one another while on the march, the loser's penalty being a ten-foot drop on to the sands.

Hamad, my *rabia*, was the strong man among them, and I had one or two indecisive tussles; then we tried a wrestling match with no better results, though I was head and shoulders the taller.

To dismount, a Badu will not normally couch his camel but side-slip off her; so also to mount, he will clamber up a fore-leg while she is on the move, gripping it just above the knee between his big and second toe, hauling himself up over her neck and thence vaulting round by means of the hump into a sitting position.

With such acrobatics were my smaller zoological specimens often collected. Now and again there would be a shout from behind, '*namuna*, Sahib, *namuna!*'[2] An Arab

[1] See Appendix VI.

[2] *namuna* = a specimen. With the Badu it often became *lumuna* or sometimes just *muna*, which is illustrative of the resilience of the desert tongue.

[287]

would come running up with some small creature to go into my killing-bottle and, not infrequently, some fairy-tale about it.

One day a podgy white slug—a repellent creature which lives in the nostrils of a camel till she sneezes it out—was brought along with the remark, 'It is this small creature that has brought camels to the service of man. But for it, the camel would have been as wild as the fox and the gazelle, fit only to be hunted and eaten.'

Another day it was a sand-spider of the kind that had woven a web over the footmarks of the Prophet when he fled before the infidels, so deceiving his pursuers and saving him.

My companions were ever punctilious about prayer, especially Salih, who would in the mid-afternoon look up:

'Is it the hour of prayer, Sahib?'

'After half an hour,'[1] I would say, looking at my watch and pointing to some pastures ahead. Halts for prayer were indeed determined where possible by the presence of camel grazing. Towards the day's end the party was usually stretched out over a mile or more so that my companions on the march would pray in twos and threes wherever they happened to find themselves, and not all together in line as for the camp prayer.

The camel went away grazing as her master made his devotions and ten minutes later there would be shouts of '*Hir-r-r*' (trilled) '*Shom*,' followed by her name. She would look up and wait, statuesquely, for him to come and fetch her; '*Muh Muh*' or '*Ra ra ra*' (rolled) are calls for an unled camel getting out of line on the march.

[1] The word 'hour' is meaningless to these Badawin. The only unit of time smaller than a day is the interval between prayers. Generally speaking, time is expressed in terms of distance.

The boredom of a long silence was often broken by an outburst from somebody. 'God is great and there is none other but He.' A pious answer is always ready.

'The day is cold!' I might say.

'It is from Allah,' would be the reply. To wish it otherwise were blasphemous. From God always, and everything. Never was there a firmer faith in the inevitability of events—murder, raids, disease, all are part of the Divine plan. Each has its written hour.

But there is also a merrier mood. Now and then a Badu will remember some favourite rhyme, perhaps about Bu Zaid or Dhiyab bin Ghanim, or other giant of antiquity.

Salih came riding alongside one day reciting the Bani Hillal's self-satisfied reflections concerning their enemies.

'These are sparrows, and Bu Zaid a *sidr* tree.
Them we put to flight; and to its shade return.
For wolf wound there is medicine,
For Bu Zaid's spear-thrust there is no medicine,
The blood gushes forth as from the well-bucket
Drawn up brimming and swiftly outpoured.'

'And swiftly outpoured,' came from another rider, characteristically repeating the last phrase. Then he turned to me, 'Our Lord Muhammad has said, "Bu Zaid will be found in Paradise." '

I showed no signs of surprise. Then another admirer broke in:

'O Bu Zaid! O Bu Zaid! Bu Mukhaimar!
Thy sword unsheathed, the stricken liveth not.

How many water-holes hast thou passed and not
    counted?[1]
In the watches of the night after the sun had set.
Seen how many waterings with empty bellies[2]
In the day when eyes were closed in sleep.'[3]

I confessed a preference for Arab prose to Arab poetry,
and so one fell to telling me the story of the combat of Dhiyab bin Ghanim and Alan the Slave of Risha.

'Alan was the slave of Zenaiti, and a much feared foe of
Bani Hillal, for whoever among them crossed swords with
him was surely killed. So they came to Bu Zaid and be-
sought him to slay Alan's mare. But Bu Zaid had given
his word that he would not, for when he was a prisoner of
Zenaiti's, Alan had come to him and said, "Let us swear
an oath that if we meet in combat neither of us shall harm
the other." And Bu Zaid had sworn. So when he escaped
and had raised a *gom* to rescue his brother Baraiga, he could
not take part in the attack but must stand aside. And it was
the custom for each party to send a champion to fight before
the walls of Zenaiti's fort. And the champion of Zenaiti
was the slave Alan, and death was the portion of whoever
entered the lists against him—thus the three sons of Dhiyab
bin Ghanim and the loved one Amr bin Khafaiyat died.
And Alan was mounted on a horse the like of which was
never seen before or since, and when it neighed the horses
of Bani Hillal became cold with fear and their riders
powerless to do aught with them. And Alan's stratagem
was to unseat his adversary by means of a long chain that

[1] Viz. from the speed of the raid.
[2] Viz. camels famished and able to go no longer.
[3] Viz. the enemies.

[290]

had a hook attached, and this he launched skilfully to catch in the chain-armour of his opponent, whom Alan would drag from the saddle and slay.

'The Bani Hillal took counsel together and they said, "As Bu Zaid will not fight this foe there is only one other who can, that is Dhiyab bin Ghanim." So Dhiyab was sent for and he came. And Dhiyab took three garments and boiled them so that they were reduced to pulp and these he donned instead of chain-armour. Then he filled the ears of his mare with mud so that she should not hear the neighing of Alan's horse. And now the field of combat was ready; it lay before the fort of Zenaiti and was fronted by a deep moat which Alan, after he had slaughtered a foe, must jump to enter the fort.

'The two warriors came on from opposite ends. And as they approached the centre suddenly Alan's horse neighed, whereupon Dhiyab cunningly turned his horse back upon Bani Hillal and retreated in order to draw his adversary away from the fort. Alan pursued hotly and when he came within striking distance hurled his hook. It caught lightly in the outer mantle of Dhiyab but instead of unseating him, merely tore a piece of the outer garment away; again Alan threw his hook only to catch in Dhiyab's second garment, and then a third time with no better success. Alan was now discomfited and himself turned to retire with Dhiyab racing after him. And when Alan's horse arrived at the edge of the moat it neighed as was its wont, but Dhiyab's mare, not hearing it, leapt the moat immediately after it and so Dhiyab came up with Alan at the entrance to Zenaiti's fort. Here Alan, who was arrayed in a suit of chain-armour, so that only his eyes appeared, turned his head to see where his adversary was, and as he did so Dhiyab launched his spear and it penetrated Alan's eye and passed through his head and buried itself to a half of its length in the wall of the fort.

'And Alan, as he lay dying where he fell, looked up and asked:

' "Dhib or Dhiyab?" for an 'Alim had told him that one of such a name would be his overcomer.

'Said Dhiyab: "Dhiyab."

'Alan (with his last breath): *"ufi al hisab"*—the day of reckoning.'

The night of 1st-2nd February was raw and cold, and I was awake before the Dawn Call to Prayer. The big moon in the western sky dwarfed proud Jupiter, whose glory had been unchallenged a fortnight earlier when she was young. From the procession of constellations across the bright tropical sky I had learned to know the hour. To-night were first Regulus and the Sickle (also suffering like Jupiter from a relative proximity to the Moon), then Spica and his Spanker and so on to Scorpio, a magnificent constellation in the east, with Venus to keep him company. I had watched her sliding down his body these last few nights. At mid-night I rose to take sights of Polaris, but found that the adjustment of my sextant, a daily requirement after the jolting of the march, had to-night passed finally beyond my power to effect. My star observations (which I had carried out in secrecy throughout) would have been prevented this evening in any case by the presence of a Badu, whose form silhouetted against the moonlit sky, now erect, now kneeling, showed him to be at prayer—surely an act of supererogation at this hour.

At dawn the eastern sky was awash in a sea of blood,

crossed by long purple clouds like ledging reefs, amidst which the stars soon paled and vanished.

We made an early start, returning at first on last night's tracks towards the towering hill of Nakhala through rolling sands that now and then obscured it. Two Murra guides, Hamad, Talib and I, clambered up its steep soft sides to the top, and were rewarded with a distant glimpse of the waters of the Persian Gulf. It was a sunny balmy day, and a glorious panorama lay about Nakhala, a waste of low sands stretching westward to the habitations of Jafura, and eastwards over ridges of bare sandhills to the sea. The vast, almost uninhabited wastes of Rub' al Khali stretched for weeks behind us; before us lay but a march of four days to the dwellings of men.

We descended. The aneroid registered below sea-level readings, as indeed it had done on the day before, and throughout the next day. Beyond some sandhills we came to Sabkhat al Manasir, a salt-field several square miles in extent, thickly strewn with sea-shells in an early state of fossilization.[1]

Keeping the sea a day's march on our right hand, we proceeded on a northerly course through quarry-like country of extreme desolation. A wolf was heard near the bluff of Farhud, where I collected other shells in a more advanced state of petrification.

The water-hole of Khafus gave rise to a dispute among my companions whether our camels should be watered there. The Ayes had it, and a halt of fifty minutes gave me an opportunity of climbing an outstanding crest to take bearings on hill-points said to be over the coast—a bold course that with pay-day now in sight I felt I could afford;

[1] See Appendix II.

also I had, perhaps, after these long weeks with my companions, gained a little of their confidence.

The following day our course, a shade to east of north, had taken us through more of this quarry-like wilderness, when, after a six-mile march, I beheld before me a large silver lake. I had learnt from my Badawin that we should pass on our right hand a certain Sabkha Amra, and had naturally supposed that it would be a dry salt-plain, like the *sabkhas* of the recent marches. Wherefore a lake some seven miles in length, and perhaps a mile and a half wide, came as a pleasant surprise. As we approached its southern end I picked up two large sea-shell fossils. Thence our course lay in a low flinty plain that edged its north side, its south shore appearing to be low sandhills.

While I photographed it, which I must needs do, straight into the sun under a yellow cloudy sky, my Badawin collected from its margin large chunks of rock salt, which they would use in cooking their rice.[1]

The border, some twenty feet broad, had a snow-like appearance, and at a distance it was impossible to see where the salt ended and the water began. Within some six feet of the water's edge ran a line of dead white locusts—desiccated specimens probably of the large red variety that is an Arab delicacy. The wretched creatures swarm from the desert in the spring and take a suicidal plunge into the first water they meet. The position suggested that the edge of the lake had receded during the year, but no explanation was vouchsafed by the two Murras, who alone of my party had been here before. The slope was so slight that a little rain, or summer evaporation, would account for the change of level.

[1] For chemical analysis see Appendix II.

HALUWAIN: AN AQAL WATER-HOLE.

A NEW LAKE: SABKHAT AMRA.

After leaving the lake a more north-easterly course towards the hog-backed Jabal 'Udaid led us through a plain sown with jagged splintered stones to another spacious salt plain, here called Amra. It is said to stretch westwards past the ancient sites of Iskak, Salwa and Mabak to the shores of Qatar Bight. Lake salt, and recent shell evidences and aneroid readings suggest that the base of the Qatar Peninsula was at no very distant time depressed below the sea,[1] Qatar making an island like neighbouring Bahrain,[2] but many times bigger.

My companions had halted in the plain for afternoon prayer. As I came up, Agaba, my camel, decided the place suited her. She refused to be urged on ahead alone and sat bellowing for bint Riman, her usual companion on the march—an irreverent accompaniment to the audible supplications of the Faithful. I was taken to task afterwards for making an elementary mistake, that of giving her the wrong signal. She had been taught to rise to a tap of the stick on her quarters, and my tapping her neck kept her couched. An unwilling camel is provoking, but no Badu will ever be seen laying a stick about her for fear of spoiling what good qualities she has. If annoyed with her, he will shout:

'Hai! (nasal) Come to thee kharash'—a wasting disease.

'Hai! Come to thee death, lawful or unlawful.'

'Hai! Come to thee a great burden.'

---

[1] It is perhaps not unreasonable to suggest that Gerrha, the ancient gulf port of Ptolemy, if it is not to be identified with Bahrain, may be looked for, not under the sea, as has popularly been supposed, but some miles inland.

[2] The name Bahrain—'two seas,' applied originally to the whole area from Doha to Qatif. The islands that are to-day called Bahrain were in early times known as Awal.

But in his heart he means nothing of the kind. He has a genuine attachment for her which he knows is not reciprocated. And so when she stumbles, it is more likely to be:

'Hai! thy deliverance.'

'Hai! Allah deliver thee from evil.'

Even when he has tramped for miles in pursuit of his straying camel, he approaches her with the words:

'Hai! God bless thee,' or

'*Ya hai b'ish fulana*'—greeting her by name.[1]

Fresh marks of camels identified with the Manasir tribe induced us to press on, for Hamad, the Murri, was in no mood to meet them.

A few distant grazing camels against the sky caused alarmist exchanges among my party. Talib, who was *persona grata* with local Manasir, rode ahead to spy out the land and conceal the constitution of our party if necessary, while we made a detour to avoid them.

'There is one thing I want from you when we arrive, Sahib,' said Sahail.

'What is that?'

'Tobacco.'

'But this is the Fast of Ramadhan.'

'Tobacco is the one thing I cannot do without, Sahib. I fast from everything but tobacco.'

'But is it not a sin?'

'By God it is, but what shall a man do—and it is only this Ramadhan, in no previous year have I drunk tobacco.'

Formalists would doubtless hold that Sahail had broken the fast by smoking, so that there was no virtue in the rest

---

[1] The Murra welcome of a stranger is: '*marhaba wa mas'hala;*' the Manasir, '*marhab-kum.*'

OUR LAST WATERING AT NA'AIJA.

THE SHAIKH OF QATAR'S FORT AT DOHA.

of his abstinence. Sahail, however—he was the only smoker in my escort—did not avail himself of the lawful privilege of the traveller to break the fast altogether. He was fasting in the spirit, though had any fanatic rebuked him he would doubtless have taken it humbly.

'God have mercy on me,' I heard him mutter as I pushed on ahead.

Talib our *rabia*, who had trotted off to investigate the unknown camels, now came riding back towards us. While yet a hundred yards off he was shouting:

'Have you prayed? Have you prayed?'

'Yes, God be glorified!' my companions shouted back.

He came closer to cry:

'*Ya haiyakum, ya haiyakum,* good news! if God wills,' and my party crowded round him for the latest gossip of the desert.

A few minutes later Shaikh Salih dropped back to ride by my side.

'Good news!' he said.

'God be praised.'

"Abdul 'Aziz bin Sa'ud is in Riyadh. The governors—a reference also to Bin Jaluwi of Hasa—are in their towns; still they rule!'[1]

'Thank God,' said a third.

'And in Jafura is life' (*i.e.* pastures from recent rains).

'God be praised,' came a chorus of Badawin, for fresh pastures at hand would let them turn aside on their return journey to rest and fatten their mounts for some weeks preparatory to the long march back to the southern sands.

Rain was indeed falling where we halted for prayer.

[1] The significance of this was that my Rashid and Murra companions felt secure from one another and from the Manasir.

Close by on a stone an owl sat blinking, and allowed a Badu to creep up within thirty yards of it, seeming to know how difficult a target it made, for the shot having missed, it calmly perched itself within close range of another rifle, and only took clumsily to wing when that shot also went wide.

My companions remarked the footmarks of asses an hour later when we passed the six-fathom water-hole of Zurga, the water supply of the well-to-do of Doha. Following the beaten track at a sluggish pace, we saw in the distance a large herd of camels grazing—sign that hereabouts were probably the most favoured pastures in the neighbourhood. Talib was sent ahead again to investigate, while my companions talked hopefully of a milk dinner. Unrealised hope—though Talib brought back a large clod of dates from the single slave herdsman he had found in charge of the Qatar camels. To me it seemed likely that he had deprived the poor wretch of the bulk of his food supply—the dates sufficed for the whole of my party that night—but it is desert pride and desert law to give generously to-day to the passing guest, and to-morrow to know hunger and be without the means of appeasing it.

It was a bleak, bitter evening; no stick of firewood anywhere availed, only miserable fires of dung were possible. Drizzling rain fell through the night, and I woke to find my blankets drenched; so that to breakfast in the dry I lay under my camp table. But it was to be my last breakfast in the desert, and so whatever the conditions, they could be supported cheerfully.

We were arriving. The Badawin moved forward at a sharp pace, chanting the water chants. Our thirsty camels pricked up their ears with eager knowingness. The last sandhill was left behind. After the next undulation we saw

A QATAR GROUP. THE SHAIKH (CENTRE); MY HOST, SHAIKH MUHAMMAD BIN'
ABDUL LATIF AL MANA' (RIGHT), AND HIS BROTHER.

MY PARTY.

in the dip of the stony plain before us Na'aija, where we had planned a final watering, and beyond it the towers of Doha silhouetted against the waters of the Persian Gulf. Half an hour later we entered the walls of the fort. The Rub' al Khali had been crossed.

APPENDIX I

THE RACIAL CHARACTERS OF THE SOUTHERN ARABS

BY SIR ARTHUR KEITH AND
DR. WILTON MARION KROGMAN.[1]

IN a letter written from Muscat early in 1930, and addressed to the President of the Royal Anthropological Institute, Captain Bertram Thomas made the following statement: 'From consideration of language, tradition and culture, there would appear to be little doubt that 1-8 of my list belong to non-Arab remainders in Arabia, and as I pointed out in my contribution to the Journal (*Journ. Roy. Anthrop. Institute*, June 1930) they would appear to be more kindred with Hamites on the other side of the Red Sea than the familiar Arab of Central and North Arabia.'

A year later, in his second paper to the Royal Anthropological Institute (July 1931), Captain Thomas again emphasised the Hamitic traits of the South Arabs. 'After an experience of fifteen years' service,' he said, 'living in close terms of intimacy with its peoples in Mesopotamia, Trans-Jordania, and the Persian Gulf, I am struck by the peculiarities of the inhabitants of the Central South.' He also cited opinions which had been formed concerning the racial nature of the South Arabs by Captain Richard Burton and by Maj.-General Maitland. Burton regarded

[1] At the time of this happy partnership Dr. Krogman was carrying out anthropological enquiries in the laboratories of the Royal College of Surgeons, being then (1930-31) a United States National Research Council Fellow.

the Arabs of the eastern and south-eastern wilds as representing the aborigines of the great peninsula. Maitland formed a very similar opinion. 'The Arabs of South Arabia are smaller, darker, coarser featured and nearly beardless. All authorities agree that the Southern Arabs are nearly related in origin to the Abyssinians, yet strange to say it is the Egypto-African race who are the original Arabs, while the stately Semite of the north is Arab by adoption and by residence rather than by descent.'

Thus Captain Thomas's own experience has led him to form an opinion of the racial affinities of the South Arabs very similar to that held by Burton and by Maitland— namely that their nearest kin is to be sought for amongst the peoples on the African side of the Red Sea rather than in the Semitic parts of Northern Arabia. Several questions which he put to the fellows of the Royal Anthropological Institute as he concluded his second paper reveal the fact that he awaited expert advice before coming to a final decision as to the racial nature of the unknown tribes he had visited and measured. 'Who and whence are these tribes?' he asked. 'Indigenous? Of African origin, or have they a common origin with African tribes, or are none of these hypotheses tenable?' In this Appendix we are to attempt to answer Captain Thomas's questions—so far as the limited evidence now at our disposal permits definite statements to be made—for, beyond a doubt, there lie buried in the sands of Arabia, materials which will yet help anthropologists not only to return definite answers to Captain Thomas's questions, but will also throw a new light on the history of early man in the East.

Before we set out to discuss the Anthropology of the

South Arabs in the light of Captain Thomas's observations and records let us see what the opinion of the expert anthropologist now is. This part of our task is made easy by the labours of Professor C. G. Seligman.[1] In 1917 he collected the few measurements which had been made on natives of Southern Arabia and examined the few skulls of Southern Arabs which had found a place in Museum collections. His observations on the racial nature of the South Arabs are of especial value because Seligman is also our leading authority on the peoples who live in that part of Africa which lies opposite to Arabia,[2] the Red Sea and Suez Canal separating the home of the African from that of the Arab. Now it was while collecting data concerning the Southern Arabs that Dr. Seligman made a discovery which greatly surprised most anthropologists. He found that a high degree of round-headedness—brachycephaly—prevailed amongst them. Why should this discovery have taken us by surprise? For this reason: the peoples of Africa, from the Egyptian in the north to the Bushman in the south, are emphatically long-headed. The Arabs of the north are also long-headed; the early inhabitants of Ur were long-headed. We expected that long-headedness (dolichocephaly) would sweep in an unbroken sequence over that part of the earth which lies between Mesopotamia in the north and Cape Colony in the south. Dr. Seligman's publication brought the orthodox anthropological mind up with a jerk. The people of South Arabia we expected to be long-headed. Dr. Seligman's data showed the opposite was the case; Captain Thomas's measurements proved that the

[1] *Journ. Roy. Anthrop. Institute,* 1917, Vol. 47, p. 214.
[2] Dr. Seligman has summarised his various contributions to African Anthropology in a small but most useful book, *The Races of Africa,* 1930.

[303]

South Arabs are amongst the most round-headed or brachycephalic of peoples.

Now the peoples of North-eastern Africa are long-headed and deeply pigmented, brown in the case of the Egyptians, black or nearly black in the case of the Somalis and other pure hamitic peoples. In India we again meet with long-heads and pigmented skins—varying from brown to black. The resemblances between the natives of North-east Africa and of the greater part of India are so numerous that we are tempted to believe that the countries which lie between Egypt and India had at one time been inhabited by a dark-skinned long-headed race. We were prepared, those of us who believed in this theory, to find that the Southern Arab would be dark-skinned and perhaps woolly-haired, but if he represented the original native we were in search of, he should not have been round-headed. We have to face this fact that the Southern Arabs are round-headed to a remarkable degree.

Now we do not rule out the possibility of round-headed-ness being evolved independently in widely separated peoples. If we are to look on the South Arabs as an evolu-tionary product of their homeland we have to suppose that a people, originally long-headed, became in the course of evolutionary progress round-headed. When, however, we look at the present distribution of round-headedness and observe that it is a characteristic of most of the peoples who occupy a tract of Asia stretching from Afghanistan and the Pamir in the east to Asia Minor and Syria in the west, we must keep our minds open to the possibility of a spread of round-headedness from the northern belt into the southern-most part of the Arabian peninsula. There is good reason for supposing that the whole of Arabia, instead of being as now a waste of sands was, in pleistocene times, even perhaps as late as the neolithic phase of our period, one of the most fertile and pleasant parts of the earth. There must have been, in this long period of time, many opportunities for a break through of the round-heads from the uplands of Western Asia southwards long before the historic period began. The Hittites, nearly allied to the modern Armenians, were of the round-headed belt, and they may have pushed colonies to the south. It was a solution of this kind which Dr. Seligman offered in explanation of the round-headedness of the South Arabs. He postulated an Armenoid admixture in the south bringing with it round-headedness. A number of other features, including a convex or parrot-beaked nose, is one of these. He looked on the South Arab as being no more Hamitic in character or origin than the North Arab. They were both Semites, both true Arabs. Now, in coming to this conclusion, Dr. Seligman was weighed by characters of the skull, whereas Captain Thomas, Captain Burton and Maj.-General Maitland, in attributing aboriginal and hamitic qualities to the South Arab, were weighed by skin, hair, language and a hundred other features the racial value of which we shall discuss presently.

No matter what our opinion may be of the racial nature of these southern tribes, we must regard them, and speak of them, as South Arabs. All observers agree in recognising a profound difference between the Arab of the north and the Arab of the south. It so happened that at the time Captain Thomas was measuring the heads of southern tribesmen, Mr. Henry Field, Curator of Anthropology in the Field Museum, Chicago, was applying callipers to a tribe of true Badawin Arabs in the neighbourhood of

Kish, Mesopotamia. How different the North Arab is from the South, in shape and size of head, will be seen from the appended chart, Fig. 1. In that chart the Kish Badawin (38 in number) are represented by o's, while Captain Thomas's Arabs (40 in number) are depicted by ●'s. The reader will quickly grasp the manner in which such a chart is constructed. The vertical lines indicate length of head, beginning at 160 mm., a very short head, and ending at 210 mm.—which is a very long head.

The horizontal lines, on the other hand, indicate width of head, beginning at 120 mm., a very narrow head, and ending at 160 mm., a very wide head. A man with a head 190 mm. long and 130 mm. wide is indicated on the chart at the point where the corresponding vertical and horizontal lines cross. Four diagonal lines, 70, 75, 80, 85, mark the boundaries between five groups of differently shaped heads. In such heads as fall above the '70' line the width is 70 per cent. or less of the length; such heads are very narrow—*ultra-dolichocephalic*. The heads which fall below the 85 line have a width which is 85 per cent. or more of the length; such heads are very round—*ultra-brachycephalic*. In the chart it will be observed that only South Arabs fall in the ultra-brachycephalic group; only Kish Arabs in the ultra-dolichocephalic group. The heads which fall between the '75'-'80' lines—whose width varies from 75 per cent. to 80 per cent. of the length—form an intermediate or *mesocephalic* group. In this intermediate group fall both North and South Arabs, but in the six South Arabs in this group two were Somalis. The normal long heads fall between the '70'-'75' lines, constituting the *dolichocephalic*

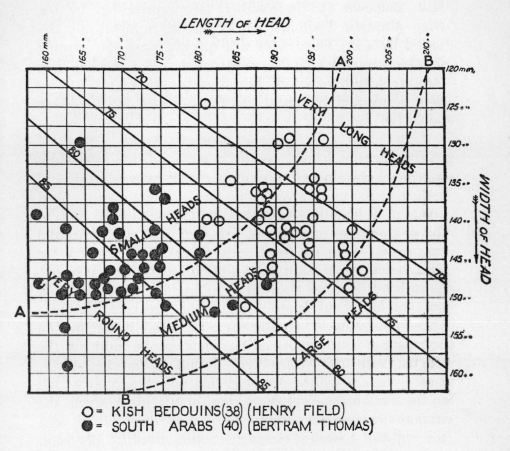

FIG. 1. CHART TO SHOW THE SIZE AND SHAPE OF HEAD.
(1) IN TRUE BADAWIN OF THE NORTH; (2) ARABS OF THE SOUTH.

group—men whose heads have a width which is over 70 per cent. and under 75 per cent. of the length. Not a single South Arab falls in this group—only the northern or true Arab. Similarly there is a round-headed or *brachycephalic* group whose percentages—or head indices—fall above 80 per cent. and under 85 per cent. Only two northern representatives fall in this group; all the others are of the south. Thus if we sum up the results depicted in our chart we find that the numbers in each head group are as follows:

	Ultra Dolichocephalic.	Dolicho-cephalic.	Meso-cephalic.	Brachy-cephalic.	Ultra-brachycephalic.
North Arabs	8	22	6	2	0
South Arabs	0	0	6	13	21

As regards head forms the Northern and Southern Arabs represent opposite extremes—the North Arab being an extreme dolichocephal, the South Arab, an extreme brachycephal. Indeed, as regards the proportion which the width of the head bears to the length, the North Arab is more hamitic than him of the south. We shall return to the value of head indices for the purposes of racial discrimination. In the meantime there is a further character brought out in our chart which deserves consideration. Actual size of head is, we believe, as important as shape of head in our search for racial affinities; even more so when we wish to make an estimate of the brain endowment of a people. The length and width of a head give only a crude indication of brain volume. Yet in a preliminary survey, such as this is, length and breadth dimensions do bring out a remarkable character of the Arabs—both of the north and of the south—namely the smallness of their head and brains. One of us (W. M. K.) has introduced two curved lines in the chart, Fig. 1. Head dimensions increase progressively from the top left-hand corner to the bottom corner on the right. The curved lines are so drawn as to divide heads into three size-groups. Those which fall above and to the left of the line A, A are *small*, 1325 cubic centimetres or under, those which fall below and to the right of the line B, B are 1475 cubic centimetres or over—*large* heads, while those falling between the two lines are intermediate or *medium* in size. As regards size of head the Badawin of the north stands to the tribesman of the south as follows:

	Small-headed.	Medium-headed.	Large-headed.
North Arab	10	25	3
South Arab	33	7	0

We thus see that Captain Thomas's tribesmen are not only very round-headed but also predominantly small-headed—when compared with the true Badawin. But as regards size of head even the Badawin occupies a relatively low position; only three of the thirty-eight fall into the upper group—fall above the cranial capacity of an average Englishman—which we may assess at 1475 cubic centimetres. Exposure to desert conditions may help to preserve or stimulate certain qualities of body and mind, but such conditions apparently have not encouraged brain growth. The men found in ancient graves of Ur by Mr. Leonard Woolley and assigned by him to the 4th millennium B.C. were both long-headed and big-headed.

Our chart has brought out very decisive differences between the shapes and sizes of head of the South Arabs measured by Captain Thomas, and the Kish Badawin measured by Mr. Henry Field, but our analysis has brought us no nearer to a decision concerning the racial affinities of the South Arab. To what great branch of the human stock are we to assign the people measured and photographed by Captain Thomas in South Arabia? Let us begin with the natives of the south-east corner of the peninsula—the Omani. In Fig. 2 an Omani is viewed in profile; the head above the ears seems lofty; its occiput rises steeply from the neck; the ears are planted very near to the back of the head—as in short-headed or brachycephalic peoples. This man's head index is 82.7—the width is 82.7 per cent. of the length. The nose is long, prominent and aquiline seen in full face, Fig. 3. We also note the full, prominent lips and the sparse distribution of beard under the lower lip and on the upper cheeks. The hair of the head is black and with no tendency to curl. The face is long, the colour a sallow brown, the stature 5 ft. 6½ in. In Fig. 4 is reproduced a profile of a typical Armenian of Asia Minor, one chosen by Austrian anthropologists to represent the Armenoid type. The head is more lofty, the occiput more flattened, and the nose more prominent and semitic, than the corresponding features in the Omani. There are a multitude of minor differences between this Armenian and our Omani yet there are resemblances in the points just mentioned which lead us to regard the two as members of the same basal stock—whatever name we may choose to give the flat-occiputed people of Asia Minor. Then in Fig. 5 is reproduced the profile of a peculiar tribe of Madras and numbered by Thurston amongst the tribes native to that presidency. Here again we meet with the leading Armenoid features—but the resemblances which link the Omani to this peculiar type of Madrasi are closer and more numerous than those which link him to the true Armenian of Asia Minor.

[310]

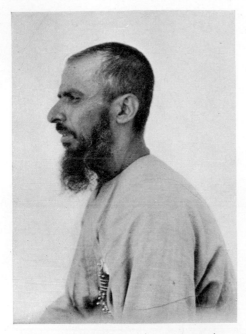

FIG. 2. AN OMANI (IN PROFILE).

FIG. 3. AN OMANI (FULL FACE).

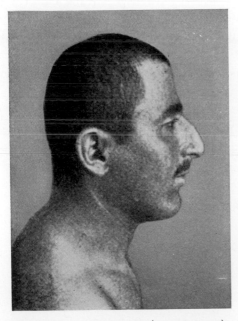

FIG. 4. AN ARMENIAN (IN PROFILE).

FIG. 5. A MADRASI (IN PROFILE).

Now although the Armenian is native to Asia Minor, the home of the Armenoid type—the people with flat occiputs, lofty heads, prominent aquiline noses and long faces—is a wide tract of Asia stretching from the Pamir to the Levant. How, then, are we to account for the prevalence of the Armenoid features at Oman and in certain districts of India, for we cannot suppose that the Armenoid type has arisen in India except by transportation. The only explanation which appeals to us is an early trade migration from Persia or an adjacent country along the Persian Gulf to India. The discoveries of Sir John Marshall in the valley of the Indus prove that Mesopotamia and north-western India were linked by trade as early as the 4th millennium B.C. We suppose that somehow the brachycephalic people of the Pamir-Levant tract broke southwards and implanted their predominant traits at various points on the Persian Gulf and further afield. We thus agree with Dr. Seligman as far as the Omani is concerned; this type shows certain Armenoid features. Yet besides these, it does possess many others which link it with Captain Thomas's tribes along the southern coastlands of Arabia.

It will be well that we should here break the thread of our argument which seeks to demonstrate hamitic traits in the South Arabs—in order that we may introduce a relevant piece of evidence derived from the study of skulls. In the Museum of the College of Surgeons there are two skulls which we must describe to bring out the fact that the brachycephaly of the South Arabian tribes is not the same as that seen in the Omani and in true Armenians. One of these skulls is from Oman and shows quite decided

Armenoid features. The other is a skull obtained by Captain Thomas from a pre-Islamic grave—in the central south—and which shows a form of brachycephaly very different from that found in Armenoid skulls (see Figs. 6, 8). The following account has been drawn up by one of us (W. M. K.):—

Captain Thomas was able to bring back with him only one skull, with jaw missing, representative of the South Arabian tribes. It was "unearthed from a rock tomb in South Arabia. Practically nothing else remained but dust. This form of burial in a bricked-up cavity in the rock was prevalent in pre-Islamic times, and is now only resorted to when a traveller dies and his companion has not the means to dig an orientated grave in the orthodox fashion." The skull is probably that of a young male adult approximately 25-30 years of age. The sex characters are very weakly developed. The forehead is smooth, with glabella only slightly accentuated; inion is only faintly indicated; the mastoids are small; the palate is very small and shallow; and the entire lower portion of the face is slight, though this impression is enhanced by alveolar absorption attendant upon the loss of the right first and second incisors.

The sutures of the vault are patent, with a suggestion of beginning closure in the posterior portion of the sagittal. They are all simple, with the lambdoid the most complex. It is worthy of note that there is a fronto-temporal articulation on the right side.

The skull is brachycephalic (C.I. 80·12; the index is 82·1 if corrected to the living by adding 8 mm. to length and 10 mm. to width), and moderately high, orthocephalic (H-L.I. 76·8; corrected to living, 74·16). The occipital arc is well developed, the post-auricular length being 53 per cent. of the total skull length. From its vertical aspect the skull is roughly ovoid, with the left parieto-occipital arc markedly more developed.

The face is low (upper face index 49·5). The zygomatic arches are comparatively slight and arise from the maxillae in a gradual upward and lateral sweep, and keep well within the contour of the cranium. The maxillary portion of the face is extremely short. The nasal aperture is of medium width, mesorrhine (N.I. 48·5) and is small and oval in shape. The inferior nasal margin is sharply demarcated and the nasal spine prominent. The nasal bridge is well elevated and the nasal bones meet at a fairly sharp angle. Seen laterally, however, the nose is not markedly prominent. Nasion is not depressed. The orbits are of medium height, mesoconchic (O.I. 81·5). They are rectangular in shape, slightly oblique, and everted infero-laterally.

The palate is very small, shallow, and parabolic in shape. All the teeth are missing, right upper incisors having been lost ante-mortem, the rest post-mortem.

The face in its entirety is orthognathous (Gnathic Index 88·3).

In order to emphasise the uniqueness of this type, it will be well to compare it with that of the skull of an Omani preserved in the Royal College of Surgeons Museum, as representing a possible "Armenoid" influence in southern Arabia (see Figs. 7, 9).

This skull, complete with mandible, is that of an adult male approximately twenty-five years of age. The sutures of the vault are patent and of average complexity, the lambdoid being most complex, the coronal next, and the sagittal quite simple. The sex characters are, in general, weak, though not so faint as in the preceding skull; the supraorbital ridges and inion are not strongly marked, the mastoids are rather small but glabella is fairly prominent.

The skull is markedly round, brachycephalic (C.I. 86·9; corrected to living 88·7), and is high, hypsicephalic (L-H.I. 84·1; corrected to living 80·2). The most prominent feature, however, is the strongly flattened occiput, so that the post-auricular length of the skull is but 45 per cent. of its entire length. Seen from its vertical aspect the skull is asymmetrically round, the left parieto-occipital area being greater than the right.

The face is long, the upper face index being 93·7. The zygomatic arches are strong, but do not project beyond the cranial contour to give "high cheek-bones." They arise abruptly from the maxillae, sweep laterally, and are deeply notched at the maxillo-malar suture. The nasal aperture is narrow, leptorrhine (N.I. 43·6) with a sharp inferior margin and a well-developed nasal spine. The nasal bridge is narrow, forms a sharp angle, and is prominent viewed from the lateral aspect. Nasion is not depressed. The orbits are high, hypsiconchic (O.I. 89·7), and while only slightly oblique laterally, are strongly everted at their infero-lateral margins.

The palate tends to be U-shaped and of average depth. The teeth are small, particularly the third molar.

The entire face is orthognathous (Gnathic Index 89·4).

The mandible has a robust corpus and a broad ascending ramus. The sigmoid notch is shallow and the coronoid process projects but little above the level of the condyles. The chin is well developed. The arch is U-shaped and the teeth small. The first molar has a rudimentary fifth cusp, while the second and third are + -shaped.

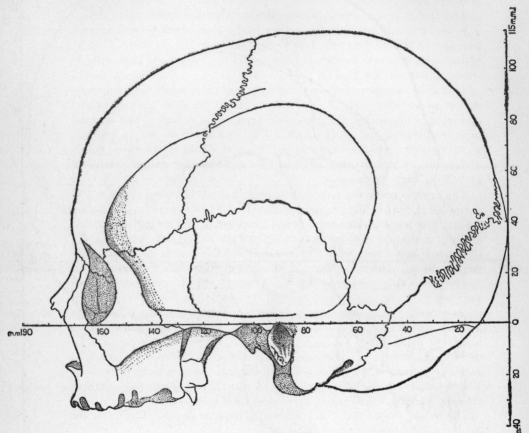

Figure 6

PROFILE OF SKULL OF SOUTH ARAB (HASIK) TWO-THIRDS
NATURAL SIZE.

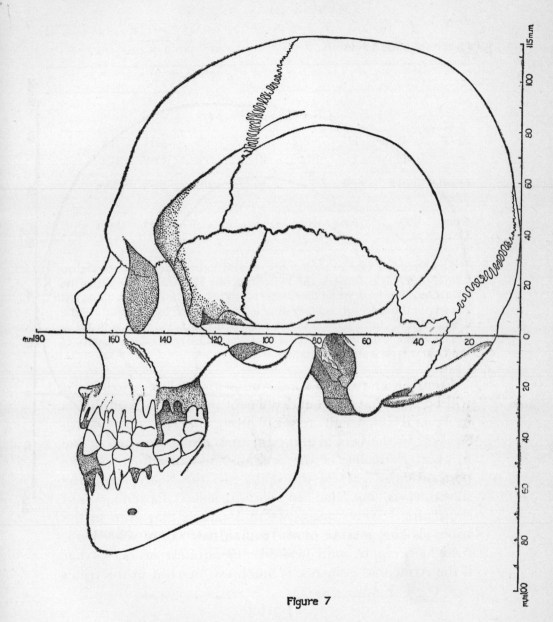

Figure 7

PROFILE OF SKULL OF OMANI (ARMENOID TYPE) REDUCED
TWO-THIRDS NATURAL SIZE.

CRANIAL MEASUREMENTS

Skull	L	B	Ht.	OH.	FL.	UFL.	BIZY.	NL	NB	OW	OH	BN	BA	Capacity.
6·088 Hasik	171·0	137·0	133·5	114·5	—	61·0?	123·2	47·0	22·8	39·5[1]	32·2	94·5	83·5	1365 cc
6·093 Oman	162·8	141·5	137·0	116·5	119·0	71·0	127·0	56·5	24·6	39·0[2]	35·0	113·0	101·0	1300

CRANIAL INDEXES

Skull	$\dfrac{B}{L}$	$\dfrac{H}{L}$	$\dfrac{FL}{BIZY.}$	$\dfrac{U\text{-}F\text{-}L}{BIZY.}$	$\dfrac{NB}{NL}$	$\dfrac{OH}{OW}$	$\dfrac{BA}{BN}$
6·088 Hasik	80·12	76·8	—	49·5	48·5	81·5	88·3
6·093 Oman	86·9	84·1	93·7	55·9	43·6	89·7	89·4

The foregoing cranial measurements and indexes demonstrate the essential differences between the two skulls, the Hasik approximating the South Arabian type, while the Oman is typical of a group with a marked Armenoid influence. It is interesting to note that the hypsicephaly of the Oman skull is chiefly gained by sub-auricular depth, the two skulls being nearly of the same auriculo-vertical height. The cerebellar capacity of the Oman type is thus the greater.

From Dr. Krogman's measurements and comparisons it will be seen that the roundedness of the Omani skull differs in several important respects from that of other South Arabs. In the Omani and Armenian skulls shortness is due to great flattening of the occiput and curtailment of the post-auricular part of the skull. In the South Arab the shortness is not due to post-auricular flattening and shortening. Nevertheless, we must admit that even in the tribes of the central south—individuals occur with high, straight occiputs, with beak-like or aquiline noses, so that if the Armenoid influence is much less marked in the tribes

---

[1] Dacryon, left side.   [2] Dacryon, right side.

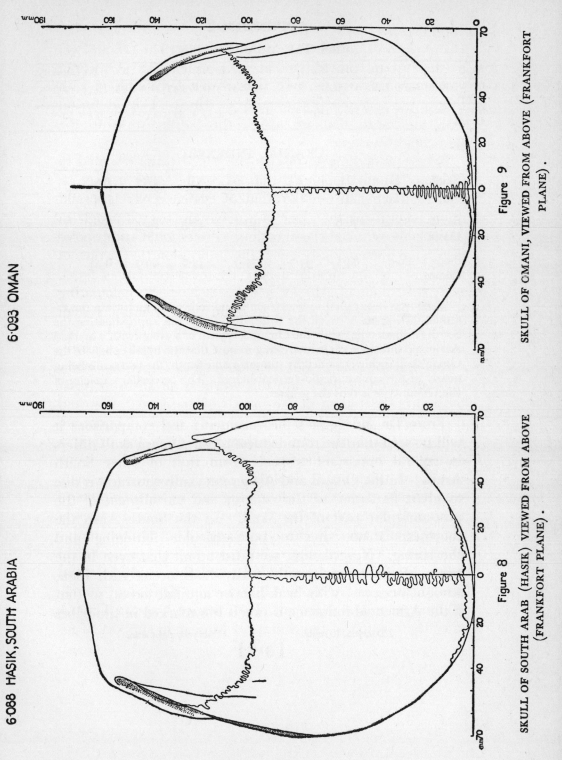

6·093 OMAN

SKULL OF OMANI, VIEWED FROM ABOVE (FRANKFORT PLANE).

Figure 9

6·088 HASIK, SOUTH ARABIA

SKULL OF SOUTH ARAB (HASIK) VIEWED FROM ABOVE (FRANKFORT PLANE).

Figure 8

317

examined by Captain Thomas than among the Omani, yet it does seem probable that a people with Armenoid characters has at some past period mingled its blood with that of the ancestors of the southern tribes. This admission does not mean that we assign the South Arabs to the Armenoid Caucasian stock.

Before proceeding to discuss the racial traits revealed in Captain Thomas's photographs of South Arabs it may be well to touch here on the kind of evidence which should guide us in fixing the place of a newly discovered people in any scheme of racial classification. Professional anthropologists have unconsciously given the impression that a race of mankind can be identified only by measurement of head, body, of colour of skin, of texture of hair—by calculating indices, etc. Now if we are to build up a scientific system of knowledge concerning races—a system to which every worker can add his quota, then exact instrumental measurements must be made. But we should never forget that every man and woman born into this world is an anthropologist by nature—a student of the breeds of mankind. We need no technical aid to help us to identify negro, Chinaman, European, Bushman, etc., as they pass us in the street; a cast of the eye is sufficient to weigh a hundred and one diagnostic features. Explorers and travellers become wonderfully expert at identifying at sight members of tribes and of peoples, wherever they meet them; by merely glancing at them they can often assign them to their native localities. We can never hope to make our technical methods yield us so delicate and so reliable results in racial identification as are reached by travellers dependent merely on their senses and judgment. For instance, Captain Thomas cites the opinion of the Sultan of Muscat in support of his contention that the affinities of the South Arabs are with the races of North-east Africa rather than with those of Northern Arabia. Such an opinion deserves consideration; from day to day the Sultan has to make racial identifications and has a wide experience of the peoples who live on the coastlands from Zanzibar to Bombay. It is by exercise of these natural gifts that Captain Thomas has come to the conclusion that the South Arab should be placed amongst the hamitic rather than among the semitic races of mankind. A survey of his photographs leads us to support this conclusion. The South Arab presents us with a strange blend of characters. His fuzzy hair, his face often almost beardless, his dark complexion—almost black, his small body and some of his facial features are reminiscent of races in the neighbouring parts of Africa—Somali, Danakil, Hadendoa, Egyptians—both predynastic, and dynastic and modern. But there are many other features which are Caucasian—to be more precise, Semitic Caucasian. The large luscious dark eye is met with in North Arabia as well as in the south. The facial features and expression, the nose and lips—often full—are Caucasian. And yet amongst them, especially in childhood, we come across features which recall those of the native of southern India. Some of the women are hamitic in their facial traits, and yet again, as we shall point out presently, individuals occur in the south with the same ram-faced countenance as we meet with so frequently in Persia and Afghanistan, the Pamir and valleys in the western flanks of the Himalayas. The North Arab (Badawin) to the tutored eye is wholly Caucasian or Semitic Caucasian. The South Arab in comparison is only half a Caucasian; the rest is Hamitic—or Dravidian.

Now when anthropologists meet with a people who exhibit mixed characters they are apt to at once presume that such a people is of hybrid origin. The mere fact that Armenoid traits occur in the natives of South Arabia gives support to such an interpretation. We have still, even while admitting an Armenoid admixture, to explain the hamitic traits we find in the south.

We shall now proceed to develop a new theory which helps us to understand why the people of South Arabia should resemble adjacent natives of Africa on the one hand and those of India on the other. We have also to account for the Armenoid traits. The new data placed at our disposal by Captain Thomas's daring expeditions into unknown territory lend support to the theory which we are now to put forward.

The enigma of modern anthropology is the Black Belt of mankind. It commences in Africa and peters out amongst the natives of the Melanesian Islands of the Pacific. At each extremity of the belt, in Africa as in Melanesia we find peoples with black skins, woolly hair, more or less beardless, prognathous and long-headed. We cannot suppose these negro peoples, although now widely separated, have been evolved independently of each other. We therefore suppose that at one time a proto-negroid belt crossed the ancient world, occupying all intermediate lands, Arabia, Baluchistan, India, Further India, the Philippines and Malay Archipelago. We further suppose that intermediate parts of the proto-negroid belt became transformed, giving rise to the Hamitic peoples of Africa and to their cousins the Dravidian and brown-skinned peoples of India. On our theory, the Arabian Peninsula was at one time occupied by a people intermediate to the Somalis on the one hand and to the Dravidian peoples of India on the other. Then, at an uncertain date, the great Black Belt was broken into by two great eruptions from the north. The Mongolian stock, evolved to the north of the Himalayas, broke southwards into Further India, the Malay Archipelago, and reached the islands of the Pacific, obliterating, except in isolated areas, the people of the proto-negroid belt, thus isolating the people of India from those of Melanesia. There was another racial break-through which separated—in a racial sense—India from Africa. The meagre evidence at our disposal leads us to believe that the Caucasian stock was evolved in western Asia north of the highlands which join the Himalayas to the Mountain Chains of Asia Minor. The Caucasian stock broke southwards into the Arabian peninsula and the lands which link Mesopotamia to the Punjab, Persia, Baluchistan and Afghanistan. At the time of the Caucasian break-through, probably in late pleistocene times, Arabia was a well-watered and fertile land—a land to tempt a race of adventurous hunters. If our theory is well founded then we ought to find in the extreme south—if anywhere—traces of the original hamitic population of Arabia. We may reasonably suppose that long before the Caucasian invaders had penetrated to the southern extremity of the peninsula they had absorbed native hamitic blood; or, to state the matter somewhat differently, the native peoples of the south would have absorbed much invading blood. At least such a theory helps us to explain the racial characteristics which Captain Thomas observed in the South Arabs. Only our theory was formulated before Captain Thomas's observations were at our disposal.

How are we to account for the round-headedness of the South Arab? Although he has not the flat high occiput of the Armenoid he is extremely round-headed. South Arabia is an oasis of brachycephaly in a wide desert of dolichocephaly. It is improbable that the South Arab came by the roundness of his head by independent evolution; most likely the character was introduced from the north. Were the original Caucasian invaders of the peninsula round-headed? The evidence derived from the ancient graves of Mesopotamia is against such a supposition, for the early inhabitants of Mesopotamia, so far as we yet know them, had long and big heads. It does seem possible that southern Arabia was not invaded from the northern base of the peninsula but from lands on the eastern side of the Persian Gulf and Gulf of Oman. To the north of these lands lies the chief centre of Caucasian brachycephaly. It is not to Armenia but to Baluchistan and Persia that we would seek for the originals of the round-head of South Arabia. The Yaf'i soldier squatting in the front row, the second on the spectator's left, in the illustration between pages 24 and 25, reproduces features often met with in countries to the east and north of the Persian Gulf.

We have now done with theory and must deal with anthropological matters of much greater importance—the records made of the South Arabs by Captain Thomas—particularly his measurements and photographs. The part of the report which follows has been drawn up by one of us (W. M. K.), but for the statements made both authors are responsible.

The data placed at our disposal by Bertram Thomas has proved of great value, not so much in interpreting a puzzling racial situation, as in suggesting lines of racial contact and hinting at the *modus operandi* of human evolution. Indeed, we may add that its greatest value lies in the fact that it presents important problems to be solved only by subsequent exhaustive research.

The head measurements taken have been only two in number, the *length*, taken as glabellar—inion length, and *breadth*, greatest breadth wherever found. The resultant index, the cephalic index, offering a length-breadth ratio, has long been a favourite measure of racial comparison. In this report the measurements of only forty-two subjects are considered, and of these, thirty-seven are adult and five are children. Furthermore, the forty-two subjects are divided among ten tribes: Somali (six), Yaf'i (five), Masha'i (one), Mahra (five), Qara (seven), Shahari (nine), Al Kathiri (four), Bautahari (one), Harasis (one), and Omani (three). The conclusions to be drawn, therefore, are only tentative. The important fact remains, however, that the material at our disposal is significant for the very reason that within its limited range it offers several clues to racial origins in South Arabia.

The cephalic index, objectively considered, permits of a very rough classification into long-heads and round-heads, with intermediate graduations. In doing so, however, it tends to neglect the relative proportions which have gone into its make-up. It must be self-evident that the brachycephaly of one people may not be like that of another; the first may have achieved round-headedness by a very short skull; the second by a very broad skull. The absolute dimensions, therefore, become of importance in the detailed analysis of cranial form.

With the exception of the Somali, all of the south Arabian tribes measured by Bertram Thomas are brachycephalic, confirming the earlier investigations of Professor C. G. Seligman.[1]

The average head measurements and indexes are given as follows, the tribes being grouped according to geographic location, west to east, for reasons we shall make clear later on:

LIST OF MEASUREMENTS OF SOUTH ARABIAN TRIBES MADE BY BERTRAM THOMAS

Group.	Age.	Stature.	Length.	Breadth.	Index.
Somali:					
1	20	5′ 4¾″	163	130	79·75
2	20	5′ 4½″	175	137	78·28
3	20	5′ 4½″	169	138	81·65
4	30	5′ 8½″	174	142	81·61
5	32	5′ 8½″	188	147	78·19
6	36	5′ 10″	180	144	80·00
Averages		5′ 6¾″	174·83	139·66	79·91

[1] Seligman, C. G.—*Physical Character of the Arab, J.R.A.I.*, 47, 1917, pp. 214-37.

[323]

APPENDIX I

Group.	Age.	Stature.	Length.	Breadth.	Index.
Yaf'i:					
1	20	5′ 2¼″	184	151	82·09
2	22	5′ 2½″	165	142	86·06
3	23	5′ 4″	174	137	78·73
4	25	5′ 2½″	180	141	78·33
5	28	5′ 5½″	173	144	83·23
Averages		5′ 3¼″	175·20	143·0	81·68
Masha'i:					
1	40	5′ 4¾″	174·00	150·00	86·20
Mahra:					
1	20	5′ 3″	167	148	88·62
2	23	5′ 5″	163	148	90·79
3	27	5′ 3¾″	175	143	81·71
4	27	5′ 5″	167	144	86·22
5	34	5′ 8″	172	148	86·04
Averages		5′ 5″	168·80	146·20	86·67
Qara:					
1	9[1]	3′ 11½″	158	148	93·67
2	11	4′ 11½″	163	141	86·50
3	12[2]	4′ 8¾″	168	140	83·33
4	15	5′ 7″	162	154	95·06
5	33	5′ 9″	168	146	86·90
6	35	5′ 4″	165	150	90·90
7	40	5′ 5″	168	147	87·50
Averages		5′ 6¼″[3]	164·57	146·57	89·12

[1] Mahra mother.   [2] Son of seven.   [3] 1 to 3 excluded.

[324]

MEASUREMENTS OF S. ARABIAN TRIBES

Group.	Age.	Stature.	Length.	Breadth.	Index.
Shahari:					
1	18[1]	5′ 3¾″	164	150	91·46
2	20	5′ 2″	164	150	91·46
3	24	5′ 3½″	168	148	88·09
4	30	5′ 1″	173	146	84·39
5	33	5′ ¼″	170	146	85·88
6	40	5′ 8″	181	151	83·43
7	40	5′ 4″	175	151	86·28
8	47	5′ 5″	162	158	97·53
9	60	5′ 0″	171	143	83·59
Averages		5′ 3½″	169·77	149·22	88·12

[1] Son of nine.

Group.	Age.	Stature.	Length.	Breadth.	Index.
Al Kathiri:					
1	11	5a- 4′ 6″	153	138	90·19
2	35	5′ 6″	170	148	87·06
3	35	5′ 5″	163	150	92·02
4	35	5′ 5″	163	150	92·02
Averages		5′ 5½″[1]	162·25	146·50	90·32

[1] 1 excluded.

Group.	Age.	Stature.	Length.	Breadth.	Index.
Bautahari:					
1	40	5′ 7″	182·00	144·00	79·12
Harasis:					
1	22	5′ 1½″	174·00	145·00	83·33
Omani:					
1	21	5′ 4¾″	167	144	86·23
2	26	5′ 10″	171	148	86·55
3	47	5′ 6½″	174	144	82·76
Averages		5′ 7″	170·66	145·33	85·18

APPENDIX I

TABLE I

Tribe.		Length.	Breadth.	Index.
Somali	. .	174·83	139·66	79·91
Yaf'i	. .	175·10	143·00	81·68
Masha'i	. .	174·00	150·00	86·20
Mahra	. .	168·80	146·20	86·67
Qara	. .	164·57	146·57	89·12
Shahari	. .	169·77	149·22	88·02
Al Kathiri	. .	162·25	146·50	90·32
Bautahari	. .	182·00	144·00	79·12
Harasis	. .	174·00	145·00	83·33
Omani	. .	170·66	145·33	85·18

This table permits of a more careful analysis of the south Arabian cranial types included under the general term brachycephaly. Most obvious is the transition from mesocephaly in the west to marked brachycephaly as one goes east, though at the extreme east it decreases slightly. Of more importance still is the fluctuating head length. There are three obvious groupings: a western, a central, and an eastern, the first and third of equal length, the second considerably less. It is as though from the two sides influences making for greater length were encroaching upon a possibly indigenous or earlier shorter-headed people. Breadth does not seem to have changed much, if one excepts the Somali who are clearly of different stock.

We have here the crux of the problem: the disentanglement of the several strains which may have influenced the apparent diversity in cranial form.

It is well established that the northern Arabian is long-headed or dolichocephalic, in keeping with the general Semitic type. We may well consider, then, the possibility that the southern Arabian represents a northern type influenced by a brachycephalic invader.

Through the courtesy of Mr. Henry Field we have been privileged to study his unique photographic collection of Mesopotamian types, Arabs around Kish, and a group of Baiju Badawin. With the exception of an occasional "Semitic nose," none of the southern Arabs resemble the northern types in the least detail of facial feature. More important, however, is the comparison of actual cranial measurements, which has been already illustrated by our chart (Fig. 1, page 307).

The very marked difference in the grouping of the northern and southern types has already been made (Fig. 1) evident. With but few exceptions the latter are to be found in the portion of the chart which marks off small heads. The essential difference is seen to be one of absolute size: the northern Arab is a relatively big-headed type; the southern Arab is small-

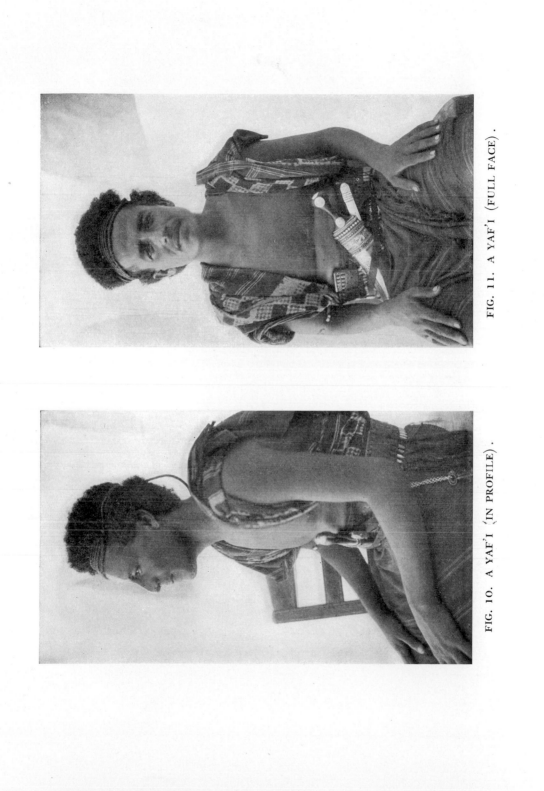

FIG. 11. A YAF'I (FULL FACE).

FIG. 10. A YAF'I (IN PROFILE).

FIG. 13. GROUP OF MAHRA.

FIG. 12. QARA AND AIBINI.

FIG. 14. GROUP OF SHAHARA.

headed. The possibility of a common origin seems remote, unless one assumes that a tendency to brachycephaly—achieved through an intermixture with a brachycephalic type—is accompanied by diminution in length. And, as we shall note, this is not the case, for the Armenoid skull, pronouncedly brachycephalic, is considerably longer than the skull of the southern Arabian.

In Table I we have noted that the more western tribes were less pronouncedly brachycephalic and that the head length was greater. It was hinted that this may be due to the impact of a longer-headed people from the west, viz. North-east Africa, or to the origin of the South Arab and Somali from adjoining parts of the original black belt. That a kinship between South Arabs and Somali exists we may infer, for not only do we have an intimation of such a conclusion in the head-form, but much more strongly so in the facial aspect of the tribes as far east as the Mahra and the Shahari; there is an unmistakable hamitic strain evident in this entire area.

A study of the photographs made by Bertram Thomas of the Yaf'i (Figs. 10 and 11), Qara (Fig. 12), Mahra (Fig. 13), and Shahara (Fig. 14), tribesman will reveal the typical hamitic "fuzzy-wuzzy" hair, black—or dark brown—pigmentation of hair and skin, as well as general facial similarities more difficult of exact definition. A comparison with the excellent photographs of the Hadendoa and Beni Amer by Seligman[1] will establish the impression of hamitic affinity. At the same time it must be observed that the southern Arabians are more fully bearded than the Hamites, though less so than the northern Arabians.

We have thus far identified one racial strain positively manifested among the tribes under consideration, viz. the hamitic. But we have noted that even though the features be of this stock, the cranial form is certainly not, for the typical Hamite is dolichocephalic. The extreme brachycephaly of the southern Arabian leads us at once—and geographical contiguity supports us—to suspect the possibility of Armenoid influence, for this people possesses an average cephalic index of approximately 85.

But again we must question the components of the index: how is it achieved? Kappers[2] gives an average length of 182·0 and width of 155·4 for 97 Armenians, both measurements being considerably larger than any of the averages for our south Arabian tribes. If there has been any influence on cranial form it must have been accompanied by an absolute decrease in dimensions.

[1] Seligman, C. G., p. cit.
[2] Kappers, C. U. A., *Contributions to the Anthropology of the Near East*, I. 'The Armenians,' Vol. xxxiii, *Proceedings*, Amsterdam, 1930, pp. 792-801.

APPENDIX I

But we may have a final check on the probability of the infiltration of an Armenoid type—the shape of the skull itself. The Armenoid skull is characterised by a greatly flattened occiput, resulting in a decreased post-auricular dimension, and a very high vault. The living are further distinguished by a prominent "Armenoid" ("Semitic") nose, which, to a lesser extent, can be discerned on the skull as a relatively prominent nasal bridge. (See Fig. 19.)

Now, the question is, do we find these Armenoid traits among the south Arabian tribes? The answer is yes, though their occurrence is limited to the extreme east and possibly south-east, among the Omani and the Harasis, the latter being doubtful. I am referring here only to the typical cranial form. The prominent "Armenoid" nose may be discerned as slightly more widespread, extending to the Mahra-Shehera-Qara group. But even then its occurrence is sporadic, infrequent, and it tends more toward prominent aquilinity rather than the curved full-winged nose typical of the Armenian.

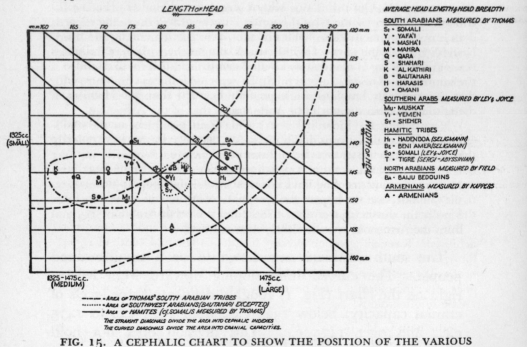

FIG. 15. A CEPHALIC CHART TO SHOW THE POSITION OF THE VARIOUS SOUTH ARABIAN TRIBES MEASURED BY CAPT. B. THOMAS.

It may be well, at this stage, to make a conspectus of the relation of one tribe to another. In Figure 15 I have plotted the average head-lengths and head-widths of the several tribes, the data for which is presented in Table I. In addition the following comparative material is offered.

TABLE II

Tribe.			Length.	Breadth.	Index.
Muscat	.	.	184·35	144·58	78·28
Yemen	.	.	180·95	145·50	81·07
Sheher	.	.	180·21	145·76	80·92
Somali	.	.	191·81	143·19	74·79
Hadendoa	.	.	189·97	145·10	76·39
Beni Amer	.	.	190·49	142·25	74·70
Tigre	.	.	192·10	143·20	74·0
Baiju Badawin		.	191·37	140·26	73·0
Armenian		.	182·00	155·40	85·38

A comparison of this Table with Table I brings out at once the interesting feature that in all of these groups the head-length greatly exceeds that of the south Arabian, whereas, except for the Armenian, the head-width is about the same. In other words, the brachycephaly of the tribes we are studying is due mainly to diminished head-length, and not to a change in head-width, such as might be expected from an admixture with a pronouncedly brachycephalic population. The round-headedness of the south Arabian seems to be quite unlike that of the Armenian.

Now what does Figure 15 tell us? First of all it emphasises the small-headedness of the groups under discussion, at the same time graphically recording their relative isolation from other groups. Secondly, we may note how the south-western Arabian tribes—the Yemen, the Sheher, and Muscat—form connecting links between the dolichocephalic Hamites on the one side, and the hyper-brachycephalic south Arabians on the other. Finally the distinctness of these tribes from the north Arabian type, and from the Armenoid type, is clearly demonstrated.

The south Arabians are shown to be a small-brained people. The curved lines sloping upward from left to right on the chart (Fig. 1) roughly delineate three levels of cranial capacity: below 1325 c.c., from 1325 c.c. to 1475 c.c., and over 1475 c.c. This division does not hold absolutely, for smallness in length and breadth dimensions

[329]

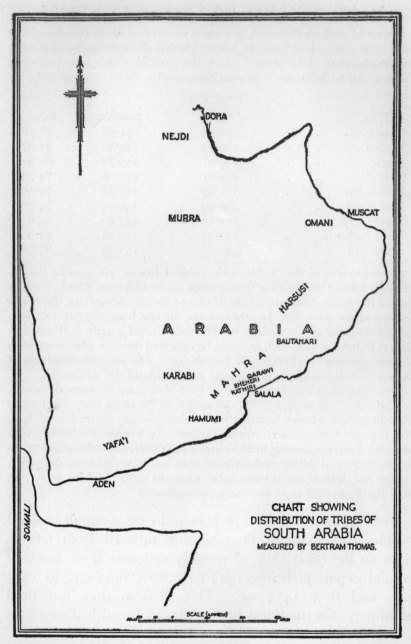

CHART SHOWING
DISTRIBUTION OF TRIBES OF
SOUTH ARABIA
MEASURED BY BERTRAM THOMAS.

A CHART TO SHOW THE DISTRIBUTION OF THE VARIOUS SOUTH
ARABIAN TRIBES MEASURED BY CAPT. B. THOMAS.

FIG. 16. HAMUMI AND KATHIRI.

may be compensated for by an increase in height, either basio-bregmatic or auriculo-vertical, or vice versa. Again, length may have been achieved by large frontal sinuses, breadth may be due in part to thickened parietal walls, and so on, so that actual cranial capacity is lessened. In general, however, the grouping holds.

The possibility of Armenoid influence in the Omani is at once admitted, but it must be emphasised that only this group possesses the typical Armenoid hypsi-brachycephaly. The other groups are brachycephalic, to be sure, but the head form is achieved by decreased length rather than increased breadth. Most important, however, is the fact that the decrease in length is not post-auricular, a trait which is so typically Armenoid.

The conclusion seems logical, therefore, that there exists in South Arabia a brachycephaly which is relatively unique; a wide, short skull of medium height, but with non-Armenoid dimensions (*i.e.* post-auricular length).

With regard to the hamitic element, its influence is to be traced as far east as the Mahra Qara-Shehera groups. The fuzzy-wuzzy hair, the chin tufts, the hair and skin pigmentation, the general facial picture, are all hamitic. In this connection it is of import, as Capt. Thomas[1] himself remarks of a Qara who looked like a Bisharin, and a Mahra who had a pronounced (Egyptian) chin.

It is, perhaps, dangerous on the strength of a few photographs, to speak of racial resemblances, yet attention must be drawn to the Masha'i (Figs. 17, 18), and to a lesser extent the Kathiri (Figs. 19, 20), who give a strong hint of the Dravidian, *i.e.* Tamil or Singhalese, also the

[1] Thomas, B., 'Among Some Unknown Tribes of South Arabia,' *J.R.A.I.*, 1929, Vol. LIX, pp. 97-112.

photographs of Shehera and Kathiri children who look strongly 'Indian' (Figs. 21, 22). The occurrence, in South Arabia, of these types raises an interesting question; have they an Eastern (Indian) origin, or have the Dravidians moved in from the west, or have both come from a common (intermediate) centre, or, finally, do both represent remnants of a once common aboriginal population, the traces of which are now largely obliterated through the impact of later waves of migration?

In conclusion we wish to thank Captain Thomas for the privilege he has accorded us in permitting us to assist him with his anthropological observations. It is clear, from what we have already written, that a full knowledge of the native peoples of South Arabia is essential to those of us who are seeking to explain the origin and distribution of the races of the Old World—particularly races which occupy countries bordering on the Indian Ocean. How are we to account for the resemblances of the Hamites of Africa with the Dravidians of India? Hitherto we have been hampered by lack of data. Dr. Seligman certainly rendered anthropologists a great service by systematising the state of knowledge concerning the native peoples of South Arabia before Captain Thomas, taking his life in his hands, succeeded in giving us a harvest of facts concerning representative tribes of the 'darkest' part of Asia. We have approached the problems concerning the racial nature of the South Arab under the conviction that the various stocks or races of mankind have evolved in an orderly way, and we presume, until the contrary has been proved, that any given race has come into existence under the working of evolutionary processes in or near the country in which we now find it. Races do extend their territory; they migrate and

FIG. 18. A MASHA'I (FULL FACE).

FIG. 17. A MASHA'I (IN PROFILE).

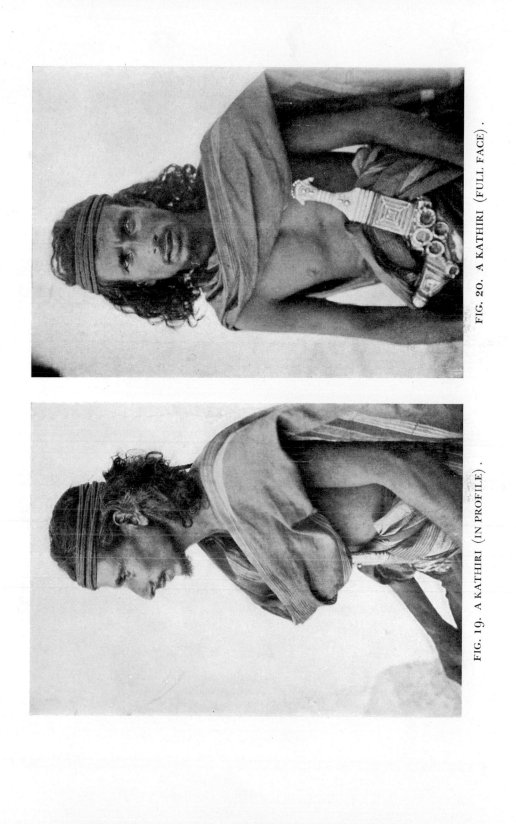

FIG. 20. A KATHIRI (FULL FACE).

FIG. 19. A KATHIRI (IN PROFILE).

FIG. 21. GROUP OF SHAHARA AND KATHIR CHILDREN.

FIG. 22. GROUP OF SHAHARA AND KATHIR CHILDREN.

colonise; new races can come into existence by hybridisation. If migration and hybridisation can be substantiated by evidence—however imperfect—we accept these factors as explanatory of the characters of a race. But we believe that 'intermediate' races rarely arise by miscegenation of two extreme types, but represent a stage in evolutionary development which is intermediate to the two extremes. It is from the evolutionist's point of view we have sought to interpret the origin of the tribes amongst whom Captain Thomas lived in South Arabia. Our final conclusion, then, regarding the racial nature of the South Arabs, is that they represent a residue of hamitic population which at one time occupied the whole of Arabia. To account for their round-headedness and certain caucasian features we have had to postulate migration and miscegenation. We are aware, however, that the anthropological facts may be explained in ways which differ radically from the solution we have offered. The dark-skinned indigenes of South Arabia may have been round-headed and, at a later date, Hamites from Africa and round-headed Caucasians may have invaded their land and their marriage beds. For aught we know many racial waves may have spread southwards or northwards in Arabia in long past times. As already said the clues to such problems lie buried in the sands of Arabia.

APPENDIX II

ZOOLOGICAL NOTE

BY W. T. CALMAN, F.R.S.

ARABIA, lying as it does on the borders of three of the great zoological provinces into which the world is divided, presents problems of particular interest to the zoogeographer. Collections of animals from this region are, therefore, of value for the light which they throw on these problems. It is for this reason, and not because of the possible discoveries of new species, that the arrival of Mr. Thomas's collections was eagerly awaited at the Museum.

Mr. Thomas's two journeys have, however, additional interest, since he traversed the unknown Rub' al Khali and the Qara Mountains, from which latter region, as far as I know, only one collection of natural history objects had previously been brought home. In 1890 Mr. and Mrs. Theodore Bent made an expedition into the Qara Mountains and brought back a collection of plants and lizards. The latter were described by Dr. John Anderson in his *Herpetology of Arabia,* 1896.

From other parts of Southern Arabia the British Museum has received a number of collections from residents and travellers. From the region of Aden we have collections made by Colonel J. W. Yerbury and Messrs. A. B. Percival and W. Dodson. In the Yemen the well-known traveller, Wyman Bury, found time to make extensive collections during his several journeys, and from further north Mr. Philby has sent many interesting specimens. From Muscat we have received collections of considerable interest from Sir Percy Cox, Surgeon-General A. S. Jayakar, Colonel S. B. Miles and Dr. G. M. Lees, while more recently, Major R. E. Cheesman has brought back a collection of exceptional interest from Hofuf and the Jabrin Oasis.

From this enumeration it will be evident that Mr. Thomas's collections go to fill up the largest blank remaining in the zoogeographic map of Arabia.

[334]

ZOOLOGICAL NOTE

In the lists that follow, my colleagues in the zoological and entomological departments of the Museum give details of the various groups of animals as far as it has been possible to work them out at present. It must be pointed out, however, that it in no way detracts from the interest or importance of a specimen if we are not yet in a position to decide finally as to its appropriate specific or subspecific name. For example, the Fennec Fox, obtained by Mr. Thomas, will almost certainly require a new name, but Captain Dollman very wisely refrains from calling it a new species or subspecies until it has been possible to bring together, and subject to critical examination, all the available material of these animals from Africa and Northern Arabia.

Perhaps the most important result of this expedition, so far as zoology is concerned, has been to demonstrate the absence of any Oriental (Indian) elements in the fauna, even in this south central region of Arabia, where, if anywhere, their presence might have been expected. Even the Indian wolf, which we knew already from Muscat and Aden, does not represent such an Oriental element, for it is a species of distinctly palæarctic affinities which extends into India from the north.

NOTES ON THE NATURAL HISTORY COLLECTIONS
by members of the Staff of the British Museum (Natural History).

These notes are made after a first examination of the specimens. Further investigation will be required before it can be decided how many new species there are in the collection, but probably some twenty or more, including a fox, a snake, and various insects, will have to be described.

A. BIRDS. By N. B. Kinnear, M.B.O.U. (With acknowledgments to *The Ibis*).

Mr. Bertram Thomas, in the beginning of 1930, made a preliminary journey into the Rub' al Khali as far as the edge of the sands of Al 'Ain. During this journey he was accompanied by his secretary, 'Ali Muhammad, who had been taught to skin, and

[335]

fifteen birds were collected, besides a number of mammals and specimens of other orders.

Unfortunately, on his final journey this year, Mr. Thomas had no one with him who could skin birds, and, although he brought back interesting collections of other orders, birds were only represented by two eagle's eggs which he took from a nest at Hadh, Mazarig (Central Sands). These eggs I have carefully compared with those of all the likely birds of prey in our collection, and though identification by eggs alone is very risky, I think that they probably belong to the Abyssinian Tawny Eagle, *Aquila rapax raptor*.

Corvus corax ruficollis. Brown-necked Raven.

Apparently the Brown-necked Raven was not common, and the only specimen brought back was an abnormally coloured example from Ramlat Mugshin on the edge of the sands on 31st January.

Rhinocorax rhipidurus. Fan-tailed Raven.

On 19th January a female Raven was shot by Mr. Thomas at Hailat ash Shisur (1080 feet). The skin was hurriedly removed and a perfectly formed egg was found in the oviduct. As there was no time to skin out the head and wings, this was delayed till the next camp was reached, but in the absence of a lamp for the night's operations, and the need to make an early morning start, the feathers began to slip before it could be attended to and the skin had to be thrown away. The egg, however, was kept, and this I have compared with others in the Museum Collection, and consider that in all probability it belongs to the above species. Furthermore, when I showed Mr. Thomas skins of the Fan-tailed Raven and the Brown-necked Raven, he assured me that the former was the bird that was met with oftener than the latter.

Argya squamiceps squamiceps. Brown Babbler.

The true *squamiceps* came from Akaba in North Arabia, and it is also found in Palestine, Muscat (Mills, Jayakar and Cox), and the Oman Peninsula (Lees).

[336]

The single female in the collection was collected by Mr. Thomas at Shaiba on the north side of the Qara Mountains, amongst some scattered frankincense trees at an elevation of 2000 feet.

Pynconotus xanthopygos xanthopygos. Arabian Bulbul.

A male was obtained amongst some acacia and palm trees near Bin Ju'ai (1500 feet) on the north side of the mountains.

After examining the series in the British Museum from different parts of Arabia, I am unable to distinguish the race *reichenowi* of Lorenz and Hellmayr from South-west Arabia.

Ammomanes cinctura pallida. Arabian Black-tailed Sand-Lark.

The Arabian Black-tailed Sand-Lark was originally described from Qunfuda on the Red Sea in 1850, and seventy-nine years later Cheesman obtained four during his expedition to the Jabrin Oasis. Mr. Thomas obtained a female at Hailat Bil Rizaz (1060 feet) in some scrub in open country, about 18° 2′ N.

Motacilla alba subsp.? White Wagtail.

A single example of a white Wagtail, resting on migration, was shot by the water-hole at Al 'Ain on 28th January, but is not in sufficiently good plumage to enable the race to be distinguished.

Phoenicurus ochruros phoenicuroides. Kashmir Redstart.

A male of the Kashmir Redstart, also on migration, was obtained at the water-hole of Al 'Ain in the Mugshin district on 28th January. Cheesman met with this Redstart at Hofuf in January, and saw several in South Hasa in March.

Oenanthe deserti atrogularis. Indian Desert-Chat.

These Chats I identified at first as *oreophila,* and as such recorded them in the *Geographical Journal.* On further examination, however, I think they are undoubtedly Indian Desert-Chats.

Two males are in the collection, one on 28th January at Al 'Ain water-hole, on the edge of the sands, and the other at Sa'atan (2065 feet), on the north side of the Jebel Qara on 11th February.

Cheesman met with both of the eastern races of this migratory Chat in the Hasa and Jabrin Deserts.

[337]

Falco tinnunculus tinnunculus. Kestrel.

On 2nd January a female was shot near Bu Matahan, 3070 feet, in the Qara Mountains.

Circus macrurus. Pale Harrier.

A male in first winter plumage was obtained at Mistan in the Qara Mountains (north side), at an elevation of 1650 feet, on 15th February.

This migratory species has been recorded at various times from Arabia; Cheesman met with it at Hofuf in November and December, in the Jabrin Oasis in February, and off the Hadhramaut coast on 11th April.

Burhinus capensis dodsoni. Arabian Stone-Curlew.

There is a female in the collection which was shot on 11th February amongst some 'Tishgaut'-trees (*Boswellia* sp., from which frankincense is obtained) at Al Qatan (2500 feet), just north of the divide on the Qara Mountains.

This Stone-Curlew was hitherto known only from the Aden hinterland (Dodson, Meinertzhagen), the Abdali district of the Yeman (Bury) and the north Somali coast (Zedlitz), so that this new record is a considerable extension to its range.

Pterocles senegallus. Senegal Sand-Grouse.

At Al 'Ain in the Mugshin district, on the edge of the sands, there is a spring which Mr. Thomas describes as 'a green shallow water-hole a yard or so in diameter,' and 'a few yards distant beyond some bushes there was another water-hole which spread out into a shallow pool.' This apparently was a great attraction for migrating birds as Mr. Thomas saw several there, and early one morning, while he was waiting, a flock of 150 Sand-Grouse came to drink, and he secured a male and female on 28th January.

Ammoperdix heyi intermedia. Arabian See-See.

A pair of the Arabian See-See were shot on 11th February at Saig Hawar, about 2000 feet, on the north side of the Qara Mountains. The Arabian See-See is now known from Aden to Muscat.

MAMMALS

B. MAMMALS. By Captain J. G. Dollman, B.A.

Asellia tridens. Leaf-nosed Bat. From cave of Sahaur (Qara Mountains) on previous journey.

Taphozous nudiventris, Cretzschmar. The Naked-Bellied Tomb Bat. 'Ain, 1500 feet. Collected 8th November 1930.

The genus *Taphozous* is found over a considerable part of Africa (except the north-western portion), Southern Asia and the East Indies eastward to Australia, New Guinea, and the Philippine Islands. This species, together with the Babylonian form (*T. babylonicus*), has been placed by some authorities in a genus distinct from *Taphozous* called *Liponycteris. Taphozous nudiventris* extends across tropical Africa from Nigeria to the Sudan and Tanganyika Territory, and spreads eastwards into Arabia.

Paraechinus dorsalis. Two hedgehogs from the fringing sands of Umm al Hait.

Hyaena hyaena L. The Striped Hyena. 'Ain, Qara Mountains, 1500 feet. Mairbon, 2800 feet. Collected November 1930.

Two of these specimens are males and the other one a female. With the latter specimen are two foetuses which show to advantage the marking of the coat in this species. These Striped Hyenas may eventually prove to differ from Asiatic and African specimens of *Hyaena hyaena.* The species is one of several carnivores common to Africa and Asia: its range extending throughout northern and eastern Africa, through Syria and Arabia to Asia Minor and India. In Africa a number of different races have been distinguished, but they are all very alike and doubtfully distinct.

Canis pallipes, Sykes. Indian Wolf. 'Ain, Qara Mountains, 2500 feet. 9th November 1930.

This specimen represents the western limit of the species.

Vulpes vulpes arabica, Thomas (Arabian Fox). 'Ain, Qara Mountains, 1500 feet, 7th November 1930. Khiyut, 1750 feet,

[339]

12th November 1930. Jurbaib, 30 feet. 18th November 1930. Khor Salala, sea-level. 24th November.

These specimens all appear to be rather blacker on the ventral surface than the typical *Vulpes vulpes arabica*. The type of this race comes from Muscat, and the Museum collection possesses a series of specimens from various localities in Arabia, as well as specimens from Persia and Egypt which probably belong to the Arabian race.

Fennecus sp. Arabian Fennec Fox. One specimen.

This Fennec would appear to represent an Arabian race of the Egyptian Fennec which is found in North and North-east Africa. The Museum possesses one specimen from the desert of Al Kuwait in Arabia, which may be useful to compare with the present specimen when the time comes for working out these interesting foxes.

Mellivora ratel Sparrm. Ratel. Sha'ab Fuzul, 250 feet. 18th November 1930.

The Ratel is found over a very great part of Africa south of the Sahara and extends eastward into India. Very little variation in colour or size can be found between the African and Indian forms, and at the most they would appear to be merely geographical races.

Gerbillus arduus, Chees. and Hint. Arabian Gerbil. Three specimens.

The sub-family Gerbillinae contains the African and Asiatic Gerbils, in which the incisor teeth are grooved and the hind-feet elongated. The Common Gerbils of Africa are placed in two genera, *Taterona* and *Gerbillus,* the species of which are usually bright buff or sandy in colour above and pure white below.

Arvicanthis testicularis, Sund. Field Rat. One specimen.

The common Field Rat of Africa, *Arvicanthis testicularis,* is divisible into a very large number of local races, and possibly, when more material is available for examination, it will be found that the Arabian Field Rat is a pale race of the typical African Field Rat.

Lepus omanensis cheesmani, Thos. Cheesman's Arabian Hare. Yadil, 1000 feet. 22nd December 1930. Ramlat Urba, 900 feet. 25th December 1930. Shanna, 1000 feet. 5th January 1930.

These four specimens would appear to represent the hare that was recently named after Major R. E. Cheesman.

Oryx leucoryx. The Arabian Oryx. A rare antelope of which the distribution is imperfectly known.

Gazella muscatensis, Brooke. Muscat Gazelle. 'Ain al Rizat, 220 feet. 30th October 1930. Jurbaib, 50 feet. 24th November 1930.

This gazelle is closely allied to the Arabian Gazelle, from which it is distinguished by its rather smaller dimensions; the tips of the horns are usually turned sharply inward instead of forward.

Procavia syriaca jayakari, Thos. Arabian Coney. Ilha'az, 1800 feet. 12th November 1930. Deriyot, 1750 feet. 13th November 1930.

This race was described by the late Oldfield Thomas from Dhufar in Southern Arabia. It is a close relation of the typical *Procavia syriaca syriaca,* originally described by Schreber as 'Hyrax syriaca' in 1784.

C. REPTILES AND AMPHIBIANS. By H. W. Parker, B.A.

The reptiles and amphibians collected by Mr. Bertram Thomas are sharply divisible into two groups, corresponding with the two contrasting climatic and vegetational zones which he visited. Only one species is common to the two regions, and that has a distinctive subspecies in each. The conditions of life in the arid Rub' al Khali demand a degree of specialisation not required for life in the forested Qara Mountains and Dhufar littoral, but this does not appear to have been the sole factor at work in producing such marked differentiation. The paucity of snakes in the desert (where only 3 species were found as compared with 8 in Dhufar) and the relative abundance of lizards (14 species compared with 5 in Dhufar) may reflect the adaptability of the two groups, but meteorological conditions can scarcely be invoked to account for the absence from Dhufar of such a plastic family as the Lacertidae. A critical examination of the lists given below shows that the Dhufar fauna has a strong Ethiopian element, whereas that of the desert has a decided Palæarctic facies; genera such as *Psammophis*, *Atractaspsis* and *Bitis* are essentially Ethiopian, but *Alsophylax*, *Phrynocephalus*, *Acanthodactylus* and *Malpolon* are scarcely known outside the Palæarctic region. It is difficult to avoid the suggestion that in Dhufar there is a relic of the former population of Arabia, persisting from the epoch when the Indian and Ethiopian regions were faunistically one; desiccation destroyed this primitive fauna over a large area, and the dry region was subsequently re-populated from the north.

The species collected, and the approximate geographical ranges of each are:

Qara Mountains and Dhufar Littoral.

Lizards: Geckoes (1) *Pristurus rupestris*, Blanf. Shahari: Ichera, Ijeroh. Arabia, and Socotra to Sind. (2) *Pristurus carteri tuberculatus*, Parker. Shahari: Budh. This species ranges from Aden to Muscat, but three geographical races are recognisable, one in the north-east, another in the south-west, and the third, discovered by Mr. Bertram Thomas, from the southern slopes of the Qara Mountains.

Agamas. (3) *Agama sinaita*, Heyden. Shahari: Zedakhait, Sidahait. From Libya and the Sudan to Syria and Muscat.

Skinks. (4) *Chalcides ocellatus ocellatus* (Forsk.). Shahari: Gemsh. Algeria to Egypt, Syria, Cyprus, Crete, Greece, Arabia, Persia, and Baluchistan.

Chameleon. (5) *Chamaeleon calcarifer*, Peters. Shahari: Shahabel. Aden to Muscat.

Snakes: Colubrids (Harmless). (6) *Coluber rhodorhachis* (Jan). Shahari: Difen, Ojem, or Shalthum. Egypt to Somaliland, Arabia, Syria, Persia, Baluchistan, Transcaspia, and Northwest India. (7) *Coluber thomasi*, Parker. Shahari: Shalthum, another of Mr. Thomas's discoveries; it is allied to *C. variabilis* of the Aden hinterland and *C. somalicus*. (8) *Spalerosophis*

[342]

diadema (Schlegel). Shahari: Fe'e de'e. Africa north of the Sahara to Turkistan and North-west India.

Colubrids (slightly venomous). (9) *Psammophis schokari* (Forsk.). Shahari: Ishor, Inshor. Africa north of the Sahara to Persia, Afghanistan, and North-west India.

Cobras (venomous). (10) *Naja haje* (Linn.). Egyptian Cobra. Shahari: Haut; juveniles Difen or Ojem. South-east Arabia to the Transvaal and Zululand; westwards, north of the Sahara, to Morocco; the present is the most northerly record. (11) *Atractaspis andersoni,* Boulenger. Shahari: Disos. Hitherto known only from the extreme south of Arabia.

Vipers (venomous). (12) *Echis carinatus* (Schneid). Shahari: Ojem. Africa north of the Equator to Transcaspia and India. (13) *Bitis arietans* (Merrem), Puff-adder. Shahari: Dololat. Africa, except the Rain Forest regions, and South Arabia; the present is the most northerly record.

Amphibians: Frogs and Toads. (14) *Bufo dhufarensis,* Parker. Shahari *aqaqet.* Discovered by Mr. Thomas and apparently most closely allied to the North-east African toad, *Bufo dodsoni,* Boulenger.

Rub' al Khali.

Lizards: Geckoes. (1) *Alsophylax blanfordii* (Strauch). Arabic: Nagas Milh, Alaghaybis, or Dhatur. Egypt and South Arabia. (2) *Ceramodactylus major* Parker. Arabic: Dhatur. Hitherto known from only two specimens, both collected by Mr. Bertram Thomas on an earlier journey to the Rub' al Khali. (3) *Pristurus carteri carteri,* Gray. Muscat to Dhufar hinterland.

Agamids. (4) *Phrynocephalus arabicus,* Anderson. Arabic: Abu Tahay or Bu Tahaihi. Hadhramaut to the Persian Gulf. (5) *Phrynocephalus maculatus,* Anderson. Arabic: Fakhakh, Bu Radhaima or Sharaihi. Persia, Baluchistan, and East Arabia as far south as Dhufar. (6) *Agama jayakari* Anderson. Arabic: Fakhakh. Muscat to the Dhufar hinterland, northwards to El Qatar. (7) *Uromastix thomasi,* Parker. Arabic: Bu Kurdifat or Bu Qursh. Previously known from two specimens, both collected by Mr. Thomas. (8) *Uromastix microlepis,* Blanf. Persia and Iraq to Dhufar hinterland.

Monitors. (9) *Varanus griseus* (Dand.). Grey Monitor. Arabic: Wural or Ruwal. Morocco to the Sudan, northwards to the Caspian and North-west India.

Lacertids. (10) *Acanthodactylus cantoris,* Gunther. Arabic: Asa-wada or Sauwedda. The distribution of this species, as hitherto known, was discontinuous, no specimens having been recorded between Persia and the Aden-Wadi Hadhramaut district of South Arabia. The specimens in the present collection bridge the distributional gap, but do not link the northern and southern races in morphological characters. (11) *Acanthodactylus scutellatus* (Audouin). Arabic: Dhubdhuba. Africa, north of the Sahara, from Cape Verde to the Sudan, Palestine and Iraq. (12) *Eremias brevirostris* (Blanf.). Arabic: Nagas Milh. Punjab, Baluchistan, Persia, Iraq, Syria; not previously known so far south. (13) *Eremias adramitana,* Boulenger. Arabic: Suwayda. Hitherto known only from the Hadhramaut.

Skinks. (14) *Scincus mitranus,* Anderson. Arabic: Damusa or Bihalaklak. Sind and South-east Arabia.

Snakes. Boas. (15) *Eryx jayakari,* Boulenger. Arabic: Difen. Muscat and Yemen.

Colubrids. (16) *Malpolon moilensis* (Reuss). Arabic: Zaraq. Algeria to the Sudan, northwards to Iraq and South Persia.

Vipers. (17) *Cerastes cornutus* (Linn.). Egyptian Horned-viper. Arabic: Kabsh (male). Algeria to the Sudan, Arabia, Iraq.

D. LOCUSTS, GRASSHOPPERS, MANTIDS, etc. By B. P. Uvarov.

The collection of *Orthoptera* made by Mr. Bertram Thomas represents a valuable contribution to our knowledge of the fauna of Arabia, which remains very little studied.

The following list of species is a preliminary one and full notes on the collection, as well as descriptions of new species, will be published elsewhere:

Cockroaches (*Blattidae*):

1. *Blattella mellea*, Kr. Previously known only from Aden, but found by Mr. Bertram Thomas in several places in the Qara Mountains.
2. *Pycnoscelus surinamensis*, L.
3. *Dorylaea rhombifolia*, St. These two species are associated with man and practically cosmopolitan.
4. *Hololampra* sp. Probably new.

Mantids (*Mantidae*):

5. *Eremiaphila* sp. Specimens immature and indeterminable.
6. *Tarachodes obtusiceps*, St. Qara Mountains. Known previously only from the Sudan, Somaliland and Erythraea, and belonging to a purely African genus.
7. *Microthespis dmitrievi*, Werner. Qara Mountains. Known from the Somali coast, South Persia and Palestine.
8. *Sphodromantis* sp. n. Qara Mountains. A fine new species of a purely African genus.
9. *Empusa* sp. A young larva, indeterminable.

Stick-insects (*Phasmidae*):

10. *Leptynia* sp. n. 'Ain al Rizat, Qara Mountains. A very interesting new species allied to L. *attenuata*, Pantel, occurring only in Portugal.

Crickets (*Gryllidae*):

11. *Liogryllus bimaculatus*, Deg. Qara Mountains. A species common in tropics of the Old World and in the Mediterranean countries.
12. *Gryllodes* sp. Rub' al Khali. Probably a new species, but exact determination impossible from a single female specimen.

Long-horned grasshoppers (*Tettigoniidae*):

13. *Conocephalus iris*, Serv. Qara Mountains. Known only from Africa and from its islands (Madagascar, Mauritius, Rodriguez, Seychelles).
14. *Conocephalus* sp. n. South Arabian desert.

[345]

APPENDIX II

Short-horned grasshoppers and locusts (*Acrididae*) :

15. *Acridella grandis,* Klug. Qara Mountains.
16. *Acridella* sp. n. Qara Mountains.
17. *Aiolopus thalassinus,* F. South Arabian desert.
18. *Stenohippus mundus,* Walker. South Arabian desert.
19. *Morphacris fasciata sulcata,* Thunb. Qara Mountains and South Arabian desert. Widely distributed in Africa and South Asia.
20. *Pycnodictya dentata,* Kr. Qara Mountains and South Arabian desert. Not previously represented in the British Museum.
21. *Genus* and sp. n. South Arabian desert. A single specimen of a remarkable wingless grasshopper of the subfamily *Oedipodinae.*
22. *Sphingonotus balteatus* sbsp. n. South Arabian desert.
23. *Sphingonotus* sp. n. South Arabian desert.
24. *Acrotylus insubricus* sp. n. South Arabian desert.
25. *Trilophidia* sp. South Arabian desert.
26. *Tenuitarsus* sp. Rub' al Khali. (Recorded in the preliminary list as *Leptoscirtus* sp.)
27. *Chrotogonus* sp. South Arabian desert.
28. *Cyrtacanthacris tatarica,* L. South Arabian desert.
29. *Anacridium arabicum,* Uv. Qara Mountains.
30. *Schistocerca gregaria,* Forsk. South Arabian desert. This is the Desert, or the Bible, Locust.
31. *Patanga succincta,* L. South Arabian desert. A common Indian species, never yet found so far west.
32. *Catantops saucius,* Burm. South Arabian desert. An African species.
33. *Cataloipus* sp. n. South Arabian desert. Belongs to an essentially African genus.
34. *Thisoicetrus continuus,* Walk. South Arabian desert. Previously recorded only from Sinai and Palestine.
35. *Euprepocnemis* sp. n. Serv. South Arabian desert.
36. *Acorypha glaucopsis,* Walk. South Arabian desert. An Indian species.
37. *Acorypha* sp. South Arabian desert. Another Indian species.

[346]

It will be seen that out of the total thirty-seven species, not less than seven are new to science, with possibly two or three more, which have not yet been determined. The discovery of a new genus of grasshoppers makes the scientific results of the expedition most noteworthy, as regards this particular group of insects.

E. DRAGONFLIES. By Miss C. Longfield.

Of sixty-two specimens received, the following nine species have been determined: 6 *Libellulinae*, 1 *Coenagrionine*, 1 *Aeschnnine*, which are all common African species, and one new species of *Urothemis*.

1. *Pseudomacromia torrida*, Kirby. 3 males, 1 female. Milwah al Aud. 30th October. 'Ain al Rizat. 31st October. Found in South, West and East Africa. The dimensions of these four specimens run small, and the wings are exceptionally deeply saffroned in both sexes.

2. *Pantala flavescens*, Fabr. 1 male, 1 female. Sahalnot. 4th November. Common nearly all over the world.

3. *Trithemis annulata*, Beauv. 12 males, 1 female. Milwah al Aud. 30th October. 'Ain al Rizat. 31st October. Sahalnot. 4th November. Khiyut. 11th November. Common in North and East Africa and Arabia.

4. *Crocothemis erythraea*, Brulle. 10 males, 5 females. Sahalnot. 4th November. 'Ain (Qara Mountains). 9th November. Khiyunt. 11th November. Has a wide range over South Europe, all Africa, and parts of Asia.

5. *Orthetrum chrysostigma*, Burm. 13 males, 8 females. 'Ain al Rizat. 1st November. Sahalnot. 4th November. 'Ain.' 5th November. Khiyut. 10th November, 11th November, 13th November. Milwah al Aud. 30th October. Iu. 14th November. Has a wide range over South Europe and Africa.

6. *Diplacodes lefebvrei*, Ramb. 1 male. Sahalnot. 4th November. Has a wide range over Africa to Arabia.

7. *Hemianax ephippiger*, Burm. 2 males. Sahalnot. 4th November. Farajja (Sanam). 21st January. Found in North and East Africa, Arabia, Persia and North India.

8. *Ceriagrion glabrum,* Burm. 3 males, 2 females. Khiyut. 11th November, 13th November. Has a wide range over North, South, East, and West Africa. The wings of these five Arabian specimens are extra deeply saffroned.

9. *Urothemis* sp. n. 1 male. 'Ain al Rizat. 31st October.

F. BUGS. By W. E. China, M.A.

The collection contains eleven bugs representing ten species and genera. Of these species three are apparently new, three are of wide distribution in the Eremian sub-region, one is recorded only from Turcomania, two are of Indian origin, and one is widely distributed in the Ethiopian and Oriental Regions and the Mediterranean sub-region. Two of the Eremian species have previously been recorded from Arabia, and one extends into the Mediterranean sub-region.

On the whole, the collection corroborates the belief that Arabia faunistically forms part of the great Eremian sub-region which extends from Senegal and North Nigeria in the west, across the Sahara to the Sudan, across Arabia and Persia to the Punjab and Turkistan. There is no evidence from this group of the existence of a true Ethiopian element in the Arabian fauna.

1. *Macroscytus brunneus* F. Fuzah, 1350 feet. 14th November. Local name, Adhayrite. Widely distributed in the Mediterranean, Ethiopian, and Oriental Regions.

2. *Cydnus* sp. nov. near *pilosulus.* Fuzah, 1350 feet. 14th November. Local name, Adhayrite.

3. *Amaurocoris orbicularis,* Jak. Hadh al Mazariq, 570 feet. 17th January. Recorded only from Turcomania.

4. *Chroantha ornatula,* H. S. Bahat al Jamal, 550 feet. 15th January. Hadh al Mazariq, 570 feet. 17th January. Recorded from Spain, Dalmatia, Sicily, Greece, Algeria, Tunisia, Egypt, Syria, Persia, Turcomania and Arabia.

5. *Adria parvula,* Dall. Fuzah, 1350 feet. 14th November. Local name, Adhayrite. Recorded from North India and South Persia.

6. *Carbula insocia*, Walk. Fuzah, 1350 feet. 14th November. Local name, Adhayrite. Recorded from India, both North and South.

7. *Centrocoris* sp. nov., near *degener* Put. Suwahib, 600 feet. 14th January. Local name, Tassaiyah.

8. *Cosmopleurus fulvipes*, Dall. Hamr al Ain Abn Genin. 21st December. Siddat al Harsha, 900 feet. Recorded from Algerian Sahara, Egypt, Sudan, Nubia, and Persia. Recorded food plant: *Calotropus procera.*

9. *Dieuches* sp. nov. 'Ain al Rizat, 250 feet. 31st October. Local name, Digadig. There are in the British Museum collection specimens from Mesopotamia.

10. *Laccotrephes fabricii,* Stal. 'Ain al Rizat. 31st October. Local name, Sinortami (water-cat). Recorded from Arabia, Suez, Sudan, Abyssinia and Senegal. Also doubtfully from East Africa, South Africa and India.

G. BUTTERFLIES. By Captain N. D. Riley.

Fifteen species of butterfly were obtained, two of which are new to science, and belong to the genus *Charaxes*. The species are strongly African in their affinities, as the following rough analysis will show:

(a) Species occurring throughout Africa

    1. and to Australia,
        Danais chrysippus
        Precis orithya

    2. and as far as India,
        Teracolus calais (India only)
        Teracolus danae (India and Ceylon)
        Azanus jesous (India, Ceylon and Burmah)

    3. but not found East of Arabia,
        Charaxes varanes bertrami
        Leuceronia buquetii
        Herpaenia eriphia
        Sarangesa eliminata
        Myrina silenus

[349]

APPENDIX II

(*b*) Species found only in the African Savannah region (W. Africa to Sudan, Somaliland, etc.)

Charaxes hansali arabica
Teracolus evarne

(*c*) Mediterranean species:

Tarucus theophrastus (which also reaches India).
Apharitis myrmecophila (known only from Tunisia and Transjordan).

(*d*) Almost cosmopolitan:

Pyrameis cardui (The Painted Lady).

The absence of certain species taken by Cheesman at Hofuf and of others known to occur in the Aden district is striking, but further collecting will probably bring some of them to light. Cheesman's most remarkable find at Hofuf consisted of the two essentially palæarctic species *Papilio machaon* (the Swallowtail), and *Colias croceus* (the Clouded Yellow), neither of which was obtained by Mr. Bertram Thomas. Several other species, notably the *Citrus*—frequenting Swallowtail *Papilio demoleus,* which is not uncommon at Muscat, might reasonably have been expected.

On the other hand the occurrence in some numbers of the two species of *Charaxes* and of the brilliant blue *Myrina silenus* is very unexpected. All three are truly African insects, only the *Myrina* having been recorded from any part of Arabia hitherto.

This collection, and the smaller one made by Mr. Bertram Thomas on his expedition into the desert north-east of Salalah, details of which are here included, show that the coastal region, at least, of Southern Arabia is to be reckoned, as far as butterflies are concerned, quite definitely as part of the Aethiopian faunal region. The only butterfly obtained in the Great Southern Desert itself was the small Lycaenid, *Apharitis myrmecophila,* Dumont, belonging to the Mediterranean sub-region, which provides the next strongest element in the fauna. There is no purely Oriental derivative present. There exist several accounts of the butterflies of Aden (Butler, A. G., 1884, 1886, etc.), but the only attempt at a comprehensive treatment of the Lepidoptera of Southern

Arabia yet published is by Rebel (Denk. Kais. Akad. Wiss. Wien, LXXI—issued as a separate publication in 1907).

Danaidae

  Danaida chrysippus L.

    1 ♂ Ain al Rizat, 250 ft., 1. 11. 30 (No. 104).
    2 ♀ Mitsaib, 1000 ft., 5. 11. 30 (Nos. 168, 169).
    1 ♀ Khiyunt, 1500 ft., 11. 11. 30 (No. 232).
    7 ♂ 3 ♀ Hamirar Road, 1500 ft., 14. 11. 30 (Nos. 291, 293, 295-302).
    1 ♂ In, 1350 ft., 15. 11. 30 (336).
    1 ♂ Fuzul, 1350 ft., 17. 11. 30 (No. 354).

Of this series, 7 ♂ 5 ♀ are f. *chrysippus*, 3 ♂ 1 ♀ f. *dorippus*. The latter is often the predominant variety in arid regions. The species occurs throughout Africa and Southern Asia to the Far East and Australia, and is everywhere common.

Nymphalidae

  Pyrameis cardui L.

    1 ♀ Ain, Qara Mountains, 1500 ft., 9. 11. 30 (No. 212).

Almost cosmopolitan. The single specimen obtained is unusually small.

  Precis orithya

    1 ♀ Milwah al Aud, 220 ft., 30. 10. 30 (No. 35).
    1 ♂ Ain al Rizat, 250 ft., 1. 11. 30 (No. 106).
    1 ♀ Sahalnot, 350 ft., 4. 11. 30 (No. 141).
    1 ♀ Ain, Qara Mountains, 1500 ft., 8. 11. 30 (No. 198).

These four specimens are, unfortunately, in such poor condition that it is difficult to decide to which subspecies they should be referred. It is clear, however, that they are distinct from the African subspecies *boöpis* Trimen, and from the isolated subspecies (*cheesmani*, Riley) hitherto only met with in the oasis of El Hofuf. They appear to agree best with subspecies *here*, Lang, which flies throughout Mesopotamia, and to which also specimens from Aden are doubtfully to be attributed.

P. orithya has a range extending from West Africa to Australia; the affinities of the South Arabian specimens appear to be in the direction of the race occurring in the Mediterranean sub-region rather than with either the African or the Oriental race.

Charaxes varanes bertrami, Riley (Entom., 64, 279, 1931).

Wadi Arbot (In), 500 ft., 14. 11. 30, 3 ♂ (Nos. 319, 320, 321); 15. 11. 30, 1 ♂ (No. 337).

Gurgaz, North-east Salalah, 400 ft., 11. 1. 30, 1 ♀.

This handsome subspecies of *Ch. varanes* can be distinguished at once from all others in that the fore-wing is entirely fulvous, there being no trace of the white basal patch common to them. On the hind-wing also the white basal patch is very much reduced in size and does not extend outside the cell, except towards the inner margin and (less prominently) the costa. The pale fulvous spots forming the marginal and submarginal rows (especially the latter) on the fore-wing are noticeably paler and therefore more conspicuous than in other subspecies, and the margins of the wings are more strongly dentate.

The upper side in this interesting new race, except for the white hind-wing patch, bears a striking resemblance to that of the Socotran *Ch. balfouri*, Butler; the under surfaces are, of course, very different. The two species are clearly closely related.

Ch. varanes occurs throughout Africa south of the Sahara, but has not been recorded hitherto from any part of Arabia.

There is so little left of the single female obtained by Mr. Bertram Thomas (on his earlier expedition) that I hesitate to describe it; it does not appear to differ in markings at all, however, from the male.

Charaxes hansali arabica, Riley (l. c.)

6 ♂ 3 ♀ Hamirar Road, 1500 ft., 13. 11. 30 (Nos. 290, 202, 294); Fuzul, 1350 ft., 15. 11. 30 (No. 340); Sahalnaut, 350 ft., 4. 11. 30 (No. 141); Sa'arin, 1400 ft., 5. 11. 30 (No. 170); Ain, Qara Mountains, 1500 ft., 9. 11. 30 (No. 211); Khiyunt, 1750 ft., 11. 11. 30 (No. 231); Gurthurnut, 2950 ft., 11. 2. 30.

♂ ♀. Rather smaller than typical *hansali,* darker and with narrow pale bands. On the upper side the basal thirds of both fore-

and hind-wing are not grey-brown but black like the remaining ground-colour, and there is no pale spot at the apex of the cell of the fore-wing. On both wings the yellow band is little more than half as wide as in typical *hansali,* and on the fore-wing it tends very noticeably to become macular. On the underside the white-ringed dark markings of the proximal areas are smaller, and, instead of being dark olive-green or greyish, they are definitely black; also, the wide, dark marginal border on the hind-wing is wholly deep olivaceous (except for the usual markings) with strong purplish reflections, and devoid of the chocolate-brown inner border which occurs in typical *hansali,* and also in the subspecies *baringana* Roths.

With the exception of the types these specimens are all in very poor condition.

Ch. hansali Felder, is a species of very limited range, being so far known only from Abyssinia, Somaliland, South Sudan and the northern parts of Kenya Colony. This, and the preceding species are the first *Charaxes* to be recorded from Arabia.

Pieridae

Teracolus calais calais Cram.

1 ♂ (No. 58), Ain al Rizat, 250 ft., 31. 10. 1930.

This solitary female is very much damaged. It is, however, quite definitely referable to the African subspecies and not to *T. calais carnifer,* Butler, which inhabits the coastal districts around the Persian Gulf and extends eastwards to Sind. Typical *calais* is common at Aden, along the shores of the southern Red Sea and in many parts of Africa.

Teracolus danae eupompe Klug.

3 ♂ Fuzul, 120 ft., 18. 11. 30 (380, 386), 19. 11. 30 (402).
2 ♂ Wadi Nihaz, 250 ft. 18. 11. 30 (364, 365).
1 ♂ Salalah, sea level, 25. 11. 30 (416).
1 ♀ Ain al Rizat, 250 ft., 1. 11. 30 (109).

In the preliminary account of these specimens (*Geog. Journ.,* 78, 232, 1931), written before they had been set up, it was indicated that they showed a close approach to Indian *danae*. This is not confirmed upon closer examination. The shape and relative size of the red apical patch on the fore-wing appear to afford the best guides as to racial affinities, which lie in the case of these rather ragged specimens in the direction of ssp. *eupompe* of Western Arabia and the Red Sea region.

The species occurs throughout Africa (south of the Sahara) and eastwards through Western India to Ceylon.

Teracolus evarne Klug.

1 ♂ Milwah al 'Aud, 220 ft., 30. 10. 30 (34).

1 ♂ 2 ♀ Ain al Rizat, 250 ft., 31. 10. 30, 1. 11. 30 (♀) (48, 49, 108).

16 ♂ 6 ♀ Fuzul and Wadi Nihaz, 150-250 ft., 18-19. 11. 30 (361, 362, 366, 371-9, 381-5, 387, 400-1, 403-4).

These specimens are all distinctly small and pale. Except in size they agree best with the form described by Butler as *phillipsi*, being much less heavily marked than typical *evarne*, but not so nearly immaculate as form *citreus*, Butler.

The species occurs only in North-east Africa, being common in Kenya Colony, Abyssinia, Sudan and Somaliland, but hitherto it has been recorded only once from Arabia, namely by Rebel, whose specimens were captured at Ras Fartak in March. It is apparently absent from the Aden district, but has been taken in some numbers by Major Philby at Jidda in December.

Herpaenia eriphia Godt., form *tritogenia* Klug.

1 ♀, Wadi Nihaz, Qara Mountains, 250 ft., 18. 11. 30 (No. 360).

Klug's typical specimens of *tritogenia* were collected at Ambu-kohl on the Nile. The species has not hitherto been recorded from Arabia, where, however, it has quite recently been met with also by Squadron-Leader E. B. C. Betts at Dhala and As Sauda to the north of Aden, and apparently in exactly the same form as that found by Mr. Bertram Thomas in the Qara Mountains. It occurs commonly throughout Africa except in the tropical rain-forest areas.

[354]

Leuceronia buqueti arabica Hopf.

   1 ♂ Wadi Arbot, 500 ft., 14. 11. 30 (No. 322).
   1 ♂ Fuzul, 1350 ft., 15. 11. 30 (No. 335).
   1 ♀ Wadi Nihaz, 200 ft., 18. 11. 30 (No. 363).

L. buqueti occurs throughout Africa south of the Sahara, except the rain-forest areas. In Arabia it has been recorded from the Aden district, and from Gaul esch Schech on the route from Ba-el Hauf to 'Azzan in the Hadhramaut.

Lycaenidae

Tarucus theophrastus F.

   3 ♂ 2 ♀: Milwah al Aud, 220 ft., 30. 10. 30 (No. 32); Ain al Rizat, 220 ft., 31. 10. 30 (Nos. 53, 54); Khiyunt, 1750 ft., 11. 11. 30 (No. 258); Fuzul, 120 ft., 18. 11. 30 (No. 370).

This is an essentially Mediterranean species which extends, however, to Abyssinia, Somaliland and Aden, and also India. Identification is based on an examination of the genitalia of the three males.

Azanus jesous Guér.

   3 ♂ 2 ♀ Ain al Rizat, 250 ft., 31. 10—1. 11. 30 (Nos. 51, 56, 60, 61, 107).

Quite typical. The species ranges throughout Africa and a great part of Southern Asia; it also occurs in parts of the Mediterranean region, *e.g.* Syria, and is common at Aden.

Apharitis myrmecophila Dumont.

   1 ♀: Shenna, 1000 ft., 8. 1. 31 (No. 458).

This is the only butterfly taken actually in the Rub' al Khali. It belongs to an essentially deserticolous genus, and the species it represents has so far been recorded only from barren sand districts in Tunisia and Transjordania. Dumont met with it first in 1919 in the former district, where he found the larva feeding at at night on *Caligonum comosum*, L'Hérit, and resting by day in the galleries about the roots formed by the ants *Catoglyphia bicolor* L. and *Cremastogaster auberti* Sm., which appear to tend them most carefully. A species of *Cremastogaster* was obtained by Mr. Bertram Thomas in the Rub' al Khali at Bahat-al-Jamal on 15th January.

Myrina silenus F.

7 ♂ 2 ♀: Milwah al Aud, 220 ft., 30. 10. 31 (No. 32) ; Ain al Rizat, 250 ft., 31. 10. 30 (No. 50, 52, 55, 59) ; 1. 11. 30 (No. 105) ; Ain (Qara Mountains) , 1500 ft., 8. 11. 30 (No. 199) ; Al Ain, 1500 ft., 10. 11. 30 (No. 225) ; Khiyunt, 1750 ft., 13. 11. 30 (No. 256) .

This species is distributed practically throughout Africa south of the Sahara, in both dry and wet zones. It is not known from Aden, but there seems very little doubt that the reported occurrence (by Rebel) of *Myrina ficedula,* Trimen, a very closely related species, at Ras Fartak on the South Arabian coast, is really based upon this species. Rebel draws attention to the restricted form of the blue area of the upper side of the hind-wing in the female, a feature which, in fact, provides the easiest means by which to distinguish *M. silenus* from *M. ficedula* in that sex. The wings of the only females obtained by Mr. Bertram Thomas are unfortunately almost entirely denuded of scales.

Hesperiidae

Sarangesa eliminata Holl.

1 ♂: Khiyunt, 1750 ft., 13. 11. 30 (No. 271) .

This species occurs throughout the drier parts of Africa south of the Sahara. In Arabia it is known from Aden, Ras Fartak and a few other parts of the southern coastal region. Arabian specimens (var. *deserticola,* Rebel) are not distinguishable from typical *eliminata* Holl.

H. MOTHS. By W. H. T. Tams.

The moths, which are not so numerous as the butterflies, include:

Euproctis sp.

Bryophilopsis tarachoides Mab.

Arcyophora longivalvis Guen.

Achaea catella Guen.

Pandesma anysa Guen.

Anumeta cestis Ménét.

Anumeta hilgerti Rothsch.

Somatina virginalis Prout.

Cossus cheesmani Tams.

Bombycopsis hyatti Tams.

Zygaena simonyi Rebel.

Ommatopteryx ocellea Haw.

Bradina admixtalis Walker.

Like the butterflies, the Moths are more closely allied to the African than to the Oriental fauna.

1. COLEOPTERA (Beetles). By K. G. Blair, B.SC.

The beetles collected by Mr. Bertram Thomas amounted to fifty-three specimens distributed among twenty-five species, as under. Of these rather more than half are to be assigned to the dominant family in a desert fauna, the *Tenebrionidae*. These are generally bulky insects of a uniform black colour, and though some of them bury themselves in the sand by day or hide away under stones and clods of earth, yet many run actively in the hottest sunshine.[1] In a few cases the black body-colour is concealed, sometimes by a white exudation that covers the whole surface, sometimes, as in the *Leucolaephus* of this collection, by a dense covering of closely lying white hairs. In a few instances these desert-dwelling beetles are of a reddish-yellow colour approximating to that of the sand on which they dwell, but these are nocturnal in habit and very difficult to detect, looking like shadows moving over the sand.

The collection as a whole is eminently characteristic of the palæarctic deserts, some of the species ranging right across North Africa to Northern India and Central Asia, but their affinities

[1] Buxton, P. A., *Animal Life in Deserts*, 1929.

are with the African element rather than with the Asiatic. A large proportion are confined to the region including Egypt, Arabia, South Persia and Baluchistan, others form the eastern fringe of a population extending across North Africa. One of the new species, *Pterolasia multicostata,* appears to belong to a genus wholly West African without known intermediate links. The Longicorn, *Batocera rubus,* on the other hand, appears to be a western colonist from an Indian source.

In the following list the native name of the insect is given immediately after the scientific name. References to literature have been omitted as they will be found in the respective parts of Junk's *Coleopterorum Catalogus;* the new species are described in the *Entomologist's Monthly Magazine* for December 1931.

Family *Tenebrionidae.* Desert Beetles.

1. *Erodius (Dirosis) octocostatus* Peyerimh. (Ga'aid al Banat) Rub' al Khali; No. 461; Gusman, 900 ft. 12. 1. 31 (1 ex.) n. Described from Sinai, this handsome species was not represented in the British Museum.

2. *E. (D.) Reichei* All. (Ga'aid al Banat) Rub' al Khali; (Nos. 457, 464) . Shena, 1000 ft. 5. 1. 31 (2 ex.)

3. *Tentyria thomasi,* sp. nov.
Rub' al Khali; Nos. 438, 439, Ramlat Shu'ait, 1000 ft., 23. 12. 1930, Bu Ragaiba; Shena, 1000 ft., 5. 1. 1930; Umm al Gharaiba; No. 487, Muneffar Sanam, 650 ft., 18. 1. 1931; Umm Raghaiba, No. 499; Auda, 400 ft., 24. 1. 1931. Bu Raghaiba (5 ex.) .

4. *Oxycara subcostata* Guér. (Handhot, Dhiyat.)

5. *Adesmia cancellata* Klug. (Handhot.)
Qara Mountains; No. 69, Ain al Rizat, 250 ft., 31. 10. 1930. (3 ex.) ; No. 120, 2. 11. 1930 (1 ex.) Tingifer.

6. *Adesmia (Oteroscelis) khaliensis,* sp. nov. (Yahma.)
Rub' al Khali; Nos. 434-437, Ramlat Shu'ait, 1000 ft., 23. 12. 1930.

7. *Leucolaephus arabicus,* sp. n. (Ga'aid al Banat.)
Rub' al Khali; Nos. 520, 521, Jaub Safiya, 200 ft. 31. 1. 31 (2 ex.) .

The genus *Leucolaephus* has hitherto been known only from North Africa, two species occurring in Algeria, two in Tripoli and one in Abyssinia. The extension of its range to South Arabia is of considerable interest, particularly as the remaining genera of the subfamily to which it belongs, the *Platyopinae,* are all Asiatic in distribution, ranging from Asia Minor, through Turkestan to Siberia, or, as a more southerly branch, by Mesopotamia to Persia.

8. *Prionotheca coronata* Oliv. (Yahma, Fasaiya.)

9. *Ocnera philistina* Reiche (Hatata.)

   Rub' al Khali; No. 534, Qatar Steppe, 130 ft., 4. 2. 1931. Known from Egypt and Syria, Arabia (Yemen and Hadhramaut) to Persia and Karachi.

10. *Pimelia arabica* Klug. var. *thomasi* nov. (Fasaiya.)

   Rub' al Khali; No. 461, Shena, 100 ft., 5. 1. 1931.

   This example differs from the typical form from Yemen and Hadhramaut in having the tubercles of the costae long and sharp, and the intervals between the costae more hollowed, with few and small granules. An example collected by Mr. Thomas on a former journey at Mug ug tayg, 18. 1. 1930, forms an intermediate stage between this and the type.

11. *Pimelia hirtella* Sénac (Hatata.)

   No. 535, Qatar hinterland, 130 ft., 4. 2. 1931 (1 ex.)
   Recorded from Egypt, Syria and Arabia.

12. *Pterolasia multicostata,* sp. n. (Handhot.)

   No. 87, Milwah al Aud, 220 ft., 1. 11. 1930 (1 ex.).
   No. 119, Am al Rizat, 250 ft., 2. 11. 1930 (1 ex.).

13. *Blaps Wiedemanni* Sol. (Fasaiya.)

   No. 511, Jaub Kharit, 350 ft., 29. 1. 1931 (1 ex.).
   Occurs in Egypt, South Arabia, Sinai and South Palestine.

Family *Buprestidae.* Metallic Beetles.

14. *Steraspis arabica* Waterh. (Kidamair.)

   No. 420, Qara Mountains, Wadi Hauf, 1150 ft., 15. 12. 1930, 1 ex.

The type was from Muscat, and the species had been previously found by Mr. Thomas at Ba Rizaz, 4. 2. 1930, and Hailat as Shisur, 19. 1. 1930. It is closely allied to the African *S. speciosa* Klug.

15. *Capnodis excisa* Ménét., var. *aericolor* nov. (Sha'ar.)
16. *Lampetis mimosae* Klug (Sha'ar).
17. *Lampetis catenulata* Klug (Tinkifa, Feuzūz.)

Family *Cerambycidae*. Long-horned Beetles.

18. *Batocera rubus* L. (Zayror.)
    No. 193, Qara Mountains, Ain, 1500 ft., 8. 11. 1930; Nos. 313, 314. Fuzul, 1350 ft., 14. 11. 1930.

Family *Chrysomelidae* (*Galerucinae*). Plant Beetles.

19. *Aulacophora* (*Rhaphidopalpa*) *foveicollis* Luc. (Idhi Bir.)

Family *Curculionidae*. Weevils.

20. *Ammocleonus hieroglyphicus* Ol. (Tuwaysha.)

Family *Scarabaeidae* (determined by G. J. Arrow.)
Coprinae. Dung Beetles.

21. *Scarabaeus sacer* L. (Bhaban.)
22. *Heliocopris gigas* L. (Ga'ayla, Sa'al.)
23. *Onitis alexis* Klug.

Melolonthinae. Cockchafers.

24. *Phalangonyx arabicus* Arrow, n. sp.
    Rub' al Khali, Jaub Sufaiya, 200 ft., 31. 1. 31.
    Not known from elsewhere than Arabia; an allied species has been found at Baghdad.

Cetoniinae. Rose Beetles.

25. *Pachnoda spreta* Bl.

    Qara Mountains, 'Ain al Rizat, 250 ft., 2. 11. 1930.
    Known only from Arabia. The species was not previously represented in the British Museum Collection.

F. BEES, WASPS, etc. The bees have been identified by R. B.
Benson, M.L., the wasps by R. E. Turner, and the ants by
H. Donisthorpe. The report on this Order has been com-
piled by Hugh Scott, Sc.D.

Fourteen species of *Hymenoptera* were collected, and it has
been possible to name ten (the remaining four can at present only
be referred to their genera). The most noticeable fact is that
their affinities are as much with Africa as with the Orient, or
even more so. Four species are common to the northern part of
Africa and Southern or South-western Asia; one species, a common wasp (*Polistes hebraeus*), is a widely spread Oriental form
not occurring in Africa; and one species has previously been
taken only in Southern Arabia. Apart from these, no Asiatic
element is apparent. The remaining named species comprise one
that occurs in the Mediterranean Region and all over Africa; one
that is widely spread in the northern and central parts of that
continent; and two that are widely distributed in tropical Africa.
The case of one of these last is very remarkable, namely the ant
Messor barbarus sub-species *galla;* the species is widely distributed
in southern Europe, Africa, and parts of Asia as well, but the
sub-species *galla* has hitherto been known only from Africa
(where it occurs in Abyssinia, East Africa, Somaliland, the Sudan
and Senegambia), and the addition of the Qara Mountains to its
known range is of considerable interest.

Bees: *Xylocopa aestuans* L. Qara Mountains: Fuzah, 120 feet,
19th November; Khiyut, 1750 feet, 12th-13th November; 'Ain
al Rizat, 250 feet, 31st October; Milwah al Aud, 220 feet, 30th
October. Dhufar: Salala, sea level, 25th November. Northern
Africa, Sudan, etc., West and South Asia.

Xylocopa fenestrata F. Qara Mountains: Khiyut, 1750 feet, 13th
November; Fuzah, 1350 feet, 15th November; 'Ain al Rizat,
250 feet, 1st November. Northern Africa, Southern Arabia,
India, etc.

Anthophora sp., not in the British Museum Collection. Rub' al
Khali: Shanna, 1000 feet, 5th January.

[361]

APPENDIX II

Wasps: *Polistes hebraeus* F. Dhufar: Salala, sea level, 25th November. Widely distributed in the Oriental Region and Pacific.

Cyphononyx bretoni Guér. Qara Mountains: 'Ain Qara, 1500 feet, 8th November. North and Central Africa, including Mediterranean and Cape Verde Islands.

Hemipepsis heros Guér. Qara Mountains: Fuzah, 1350 feet, 14th November. Tropical Africa.

Trogaspidea sp., not in the British Museum, possibly new. Qara Mountains: 'Ain al Rizat, 250 feet, 30th October and 2nd November.

Solitary fossorial Wasps: *Sceliphron spirifex* L. Qara Mountains: Fuzah, 1350 feet, 14th-15th November; 'Ain Qara, 1500 feet, 9th and 16th November. Mediterranean and Ethiopian Regions.

Tachysphex aemulus Kohl, *var*. Qara Mountains: 'Ain al Rizat, 250 feet, 2nd November. Southern Arabia ('Abd el Kuri and Ras Fartak, 1899, Expedition of the Vienna Academy of Sciences).

Sphex heydenii Dahlb. Qara Mountains: Milwah al Aud, 220 feet, 30th October. Mediterranean and West Asia.

Bembex dahlbomi Handl. *var*. Rub 'al Khali: Banaiyan, 300 feet, 28th January. North Africa and South-west Asia.

Ants: *Messor barbarus* L., sub-species *galla* Em. Qara Mountains: Khiyut, 1750 feet, 11th November. Three soldiers. Abyssinia, Somaliland, Sudan, East Africa and Senegambia.

Camponotus (Tanaemyrmex) compressus L. sub-species *thoracicus* L. Qara Mountains: Milwah al Aud, 220 feet, 30th October. One soldier. Deserts and oases of Algeria and Tunisia.

Crematogaster (Sphaerocrema) sp. (indeterminable from female sex alone). Rub' al Khali: Bahat al Jamal, 500 feet, 15th January. Two queens, one winged, with the venation of the forewings abnormal, the other dealated.

[362]

K. TWO-WINGED FLIES. By F. W. Edwards, sc.d., m.a., and Miss D. Aubertin, m.sc.

The Diptera include very few species, but among them is the mosquito *Anopheles mauritianus*, taken in Jurbaib Qara littoral, of which there is no previous Arabian record, although the species occurs in Egypt and South Palestine, and also throughout tropical Africa. The Bee-flies (*Bombyliidae*) include *Bombylius analis*, a common African species, also found in Palestine, and a species of *Exoprosopa* new to the Museum. Other flies of Ethiopian affinities are a species of *Promachus* (a robber-fly), *Eristalis taeniops* (a hover-fly), three species of blow-fly, and *Hippobosca maculata*, an ectoparasite of the camel.

L. SHELLS. By G. C. Robson, m.a.

The *Mollusca* obtained by Mr. Thomas at Farhud are represented by thirty-five specimens and thirteen species, all of which are marine. Forms like the *Potamides* and *Cardium* are probably euryhaline, *Potamides* being usually considered a brackish water or estuarine genus.

    Retusa turrigera Melville.
    Murex (Chicoreus) anguliferus Lamarck.
    Drupa margariticola (Broderip).
    Potamides cingulatus (Gmclin).
  Pirenella conica (Blainville).
    Cerithium moniliferum Kiener.
  *   ,,   *scabridum* Philippi.
    Glycimeris pectunculus (L.), var.
    Cardium (Trachycardium) rubicundum Reeve.
    Asaphis deflorata (L.)
    Psammotaea elongata (Lamarck).

Two Lamellibranchs, perhaps a *Paphia* and a *Chama*, indeterminable.

All the above species, which were identified by Mr. J. R. le B. Tomlin, are living in the Indian Ocean at the present day, the two marked * extending also into the Mediterranean. The specimens of *G. pectunculus* differ somewhat in shape from any recent ones we have, but it is a variable species.

M. FOSSILS. By L. R. Cox, M.A.

The fossils collected by Mr. Bertram Thomas in his traverse of the Rub' al Khali, like those obtained on his previous expedition (see *G. J.*, 77, 1931, p. 31), are all from a white limestone of Middle Eocene age. They come partly from the southern part of the Rub' al Khali interior and partly from the low-lying plain beyond Misaimir, in the hinterland of Doha, on the Persian Gulf. The Eocene limestone thus seems to be the most widespread sedimentary formation in this part of Arabia. The following species are represented; all those identified specifically are forms discussed in a recent paper by myself on mollusca from the Eocene of India (*Trans. R. Soc. Edinb.*, vol. lvii, pt. 1, No. 2, 1931).

From the Rub' al Khali Interior: *Ostrea brongniarti* (Bronn), thick depressed left valve (near Ramlat Ubaila); *Lucina pharaonis,* Bellardi, two internal casts (Kharaimat Fasad); *Hippochrenes,* cf. *amplus* (Solander), internal cast (Kharaimat Fasad).

From the Plain beyond Misaimir, Doha hinterland: *Ampullospira,* cf. *oweni* (d'Archiac and Haime), *Gisortia* sp., *Campanile* sp., all internal casts.

The above determinations confirm a preliminary report on the age of the fossils made by Dr. J. A. Douglas, palæontological adviser to the Anglo-Persian Oil Co., Ltd.

From the earlier collection mentioned above, also:

Gastropoda: *Campanile* sp. (Wadi Dhuhair); 'Natica' cf. *longa* Bellardi (Wadi Dhuhair, Bin Ju'ai and Sa'aten); *Gisortia murchisoni* (d'Arch. and Haime), (Wadi Dhuhair).

Lamellibranchia: *Lucina pharaonis* Bellardi (Hanfit); *Lucina nokbaensis* Oppenheim (Adhabugh); *Lucina* cf. *quadrata,* Leymerie (Wadi Furum); *Cardium* sp. (Bin Ju'ai).

N. METEORITE, ROCKS, AND MINERALS. By W. Campbell Smith, M.A.

By far the most interesting specimen in Mr. Bertram Thomas's geological collection is a stone picked up on the sand at Buwah, Suwahib, on January 14th, 1931, which proves to be a meteorite. The stone is of irregular form with quite sharp angles measuring 9 x 4½ x 4 cm. and weighing before examination 241 grammes. It is coated with limonite glazed by the wind, and quartz grains are firmly cemented in little patches in the hollows on its surface. This limonite glaze completely disguised the true nature of the stone, and it was at first passed by as a fragment of 'iron pan.' Subsequent re-examination showed it to contain a high proportion of magnetic nickeliferous iron, and when a thin section was prepared for the microscope it showed the chondrules cemented by a metallic matrix typical of many stony meteorites. None of the original crust seems to be preserved, and the stone is probably an inner portion of a much larger meteorite burst into pieces in its passage through the atmosphere. A complete examination of this stone is necessary before it can be fully described, but it appears to be, in Brezinas's classification, a black spherical chondrite. Its density is 3.52.

The only other known meteorites from Arabia are the famous stone preserved as a sacred relic in the Ka'ba at Mecca, of which the history goes back beyond the seventh century, a grey bronzite-chondrite which fell at Et Tlahi in the Hejaz in 1910, and a meteoric iron found in 1863 in Nejd, of which two masses weighing 131 and 137 lb. were found in the Wadi Bani Khaled. These were said by the agent who sold them to have fallen during a thunderstorm, but it seems probable that they were not actually seen to fall.

The Hejaz meteorite was described by J. Couyat (*C.R. Acad. Sci.*, Paris, 1912, 155, 916). The Arabs who brought it him said it fell on a night in the spring of 1910 and that four pieces were found in an area about 15 km. across. One of them came from Et Tlahi, about six days' journey (by camel) from the coast at Doba (?Dhaba) in Madian (?Midian). The fragments of this meteorite in the British Museum are much lighter in colour than the Suwahib meteorite, and chondrules described by Couyat in the Hejaz stone are much larger.

Gypsum was found at Hadaba Dhibi at 250 feet (No. 45, January 30th, 1931) forming clear cleavage plates (selenite), and farther north as rounded fragments of pink alabaster at Lizba at sea level (No. 48, 1st February 1931). At this locality it was associated with a fine-grained pink sandstone, a compact, pale-pink limestone, and an apparently recent cemented shell-sand. In a quite different form gypsum was found with the highly saline sand associated with the marine, recent shells from Farhud (see note on shells by Mr. G. C. Robson). Here the gypsum occurs in small crystals of approximately hexagonal outline and lenticular section, a habit which is unusual, but is found in the gypsum deposited in some South African salt-pans at Uitenhage in Cape Province, and at Riverton near Kimberley. The peculiar habit is caused by a rounded development of the pyramid faces (111), so that the crystals are flattened parallel to the dome face (101). Curiously enough a similar form is developed by gypsum crystals in vesicles of some lavas at Aden.

Salt (Halite) was collected at Sabkhat al 'Amra. An analysis made in the Anglo-Persian Oil Company's laboratory gave 86.7 per cent of sodium chloride and 9.25 per cent of sodium sulphate. It is present in appreciable quantity in two sand samples from Buwah and Sanam (Nos. 33 and 40), and in abundance with the gypsum in the shell-bearing sand at Farhud just mentioned.

Another mineral of some interest is aluminite, found at Turaiga Sanam (No. 39, 20th January 1931), in the form of flakes of irregular form resembling whitened fragments of bone.

With the fossils identified by Mr. L. R. Cox as Eocene from Kharaimat Fasad were found red flints and hollow chalcedonic concretions lined with quartz crystals which, when loose, rattle about when the stone is shaken. They are almost certainly of the same kind as the quartz geodes described by G. E. Pilgrim (*Mem. Geol. Surv. of India,* 1908, vol. 34, pt. 4, p. 116) as occurring in great abundance in a soft white marl and in the limestones of Eocene age in the Bahrain Islands. These stones, known locally as *gilgil,* were not credited by the Arabs with any special powers, except that of absorbing warm milk if immersed in it.[1] It seems probable, however, that stones of this kind are one of the many varieties of Aetites, or Eagle-stone, mentioned by Pliny. The name *Aetites* seems to have been applied to various hollow concretions within which some loose stone rattled about. The lore of these eagle-stones is curious. The best kind were supposed to be found in the nests of some species of eagle and were believed in some way to help them to lay. For human beings they were regarded as a powerful charm assisting the birth of children, preserving children from harm, conferring sobriety, increasing riches, and bringing victory and popularity.

Other concretions found by Mr. Thomas at 1000 feet, ten miles south-west of Shanna (Nos. 13-17, 4th January 1931), are calcareous sandstone concretions which bear a superficial resemblance to fossil bones. One of these is nearly 2 feet long and like a rib bone, another, remarkably symmetrical, 1½ feet across, bears some resemblance in outline to the pelvic girdle of some reptile. The concretions consist of quartz sand-grains cemented with calcite. With the bone-like large ones were others, small and spherical, or in odd shapes like Lösspuppen or fairy-stones.

The sand in the district from which the first Eocene fossils came is surprisingly rich in grains of limestone. Sand-dune gravel from 'Uruq Mitan, consisting of white and brown grains up to 3 mm. in diameter, consists entirely of limestone pebbles. A greenish sand noticed below the surface of red sand about Dhahiya 'Uruq consists mainly of minute grains of limestone, along with many other minerals, among which green glauconite is common. About Shanna were also found two pebbles of white quartz, one about 3 cm. in diameter. A similar sand is that from Shanna at 1000 feet, and from Gusman at 900 feet is a sample resembling the finer-grained portion of the sands of 'Uruq. Lighter in colour, but still containing abundant grains of pink-and-white limestone,

---

[1] One of these concretions, 7 cm. in diameter, did not absorb cold water, but it took up about 30 cc. when the water was gently heated up to about 90° C.

are the sands from the southern Sanam border, Jadida, and Tarega. The larger grains in these sands, about 1 mm. in diameter, are well rounded, and the majority are of quartz. The smaller grains, averaging 0.1 mm. in diameter, are sub-angular. No detailed analyses of the heavy minerals in these sands have yet been made.

Farther north in Sanam and Jaub the composition seems much the same, with the addition of grains of black rhyolite and other rocks similar to those which occur in the gravel plain in the Jaub area, north of Banaiyan.

The pebbles collected in northern Sanam consist of buff-coloured limestones with small dendritic markings, and showing etching and wind polish; quartz, pale yellows to the colour of carnelian; olive-green epidosite; black and very dark red rhyolite, somewhat vesicular; brick-red quartz-porphyry; and a rough flattened nodule of chalcedony.

These are similar to the pebbles collected by Major R. E. Cheesman from the gravel plain which he found between the limestone areas of Hufuf and Jabrin. The assemblage of pebbles is similar and some of the kinds are identical, for example, the buff-coloured limestone, the black rhyolite, and the epidosite, and yellow quartz. In that area the immediate source of the pebbles appeared to be a bed of conglomerate which lies below the gravel plain in the Jafura desert and outcrops in the bed of the Wadi Sahba. It is possible that the steep outcrops in sand noticed by Mr. Bertram Thomas at Banaiyan may be due to a similar formation.

O. ANALYSES OF WATER, SAND, AND SALT. By Mr. B. K. N. Wyllie, Anglo-Persian Oil Co., Ltd.

The salinity of all the samples is many times (50 to 100 times) greater than that of normal river or lake waters. In every case the acid radicles determined exceed the bases; and some 2-4 gms./litre of sodium are presumably present—that is to say, the waters contain relatively large proportions of alkali sulphate and chloride, with subordinate amounts of alkaline earths (calcium and magnesium) . One might perhaps guess that gypsum or gypseus strata underlie a good part of Mr. Thomas's route. To attempt a complete analysis of any of the water samples would have been impossible, because of the extremely small quantities available. The largest sample, No. 22, contained 250 ccs., a quantity much too small for complete analysis.

Of the sand samples, two contained an appreciable quantity of sodium chloride, two a heavy trace, three a trace, and two none.

The salt sample consisted of sodium chloride, 86.7 per cent., sodium sulphate, 9.25 per cent., water, 4.2 per cent.

The values obtained are detailed below:

	Khor Dhahiya.	Shamma.	Bchat Al Jamai.	Bansiyar.	Sufsiya.	Hakwair.	Khafus.	Al Ain Mueshin. *(Earlier Journey.)*	Harun. *(Earlier Journey.)*
Total solids dried at 110° C.	6·0	6·7	10·8	7·9	8·2	5·0	10·0	—	—
Calcium (Ca)	0·48	0·7	0·72	0·36	0·56	0·25	0·61	3·5	1·9
Magmesium (Mg)	0·36	0·08	0·24	Less than 0·01	0·13	0·19	0·32	2·9	1·05
Sulphate (SO$_4$)	2·84	1·06	3·2	1·6	2·2	1·6	2·24	4·2	1·22
Chloride Cl$_2$)	0·24	2·6	2·8	1·9	2·4	not estimated		4·0	2·5

All quantities are expressed in gms./litre. In no case was the water alkaline to phenolphthalein.

APPENDIX III

REGIONAL SANDS AND WATER-HOLES OF THE RUB' AL KHALI

Sand Region and Water-holes.	Average depth in fathoms.	Location.	Length and breadth in days' marches.	General direction.
I. EASTERN SAND REGIONS				
Al Hamra Zuraitan, Zaharani, Abu Ghar, Halib	4-5	Middle of eastern edge of sands; long. 55°: lat. 23°	3×3	—
Ghasaiwara Sweet water: fall of W. Aswad	½	South of Al Hamra; long. 55°: lat. 22°	2×1	N.—S.
Ghafa One brackish water-hole, Khor Naqa	—	South of Ghasaiwara; long. 55°: lat. 21°	3×2	N.—S.
Ghanim Much water in West Khasfa, Ablutan, Bughara, Lahus Mansa, Abu Dhur, Dhirib, Tuwaifal	Varying between ½-3, but average 1	South-eastern corner of sands;long.54°:lat.20°	4×2	N.E.—S.W.
Batin Brackish Khiran many holes	1-2	Due south of Liwa and west of Al Hamra; long. 54°: lat. 23°	4×1	E.—W.
'Uruq Al Marakiha **'Uruq Ash Shaiba** **'Uruq Bin Tamaisha** **'Uruq al Mijora** None	—	Due south of Batin heavy dune country running north and south dividing habitable sands of centre from those of eastern borderlands; long. 54°: lat. 23°-20°	—	N.—S.
Sabkhat Mijora Umm Sahud	5	West of Ghanim; long. 54°: lat. 20°	2×1	E.—W.

[370]

II. CENTRAL SAND REGIONS

Qidan

Abu Qutub, Al Khubba (sweet), Garaini, Khor Tuwairish, Khor Bin Ham, Qara, Bil Hanna, Umm al 'Amad, Abu Ruwawil	4-5-6	South-west of Qidan; long. 53°: lat. 22°	5×3	N.E.—S.W.

Al Hamra
No sweet water

	—	South of Qidan; long. 53°: lat. 21° 30′	4×2	N.N.E.—S.S.W.

Hibak
Plentiful but brackish —Haraim, Zaghain, Gardhum, Khor Jarub, Khor Saif, Manthur, Khor Shiban, Khor Saba'in, Bu Istam, Khor Tar'uza, Khor Bin Tamaisha

	2-3	South of Hamra; long. 53°: lat. 20°-21°	5×2	N.N.E.—S.S.W.

Suwahib
Plentiful but generally extremely brackish (in parts Khiran, undrinkable by man or camel)

	Generally ½-1 fathoms	West of Hibak; long. 51°-52°: lat. 19° 30′-21°	10×6 marches	N.E.—S.W.

(i) Hadh Buwah
Bahat Faris(s) Bahat Salama, Bahat Jumal, Bahat Najran

	1	long. 51°: lat. 20°	3×1	E.—W.

(ii) Hadh Libda

Hadh Ajman
Khiran

	2	long. 52°: lat. 20°	2×2	—

(iii) Umm Malissa (Western)
Sabkhat 'Ali Mahsin

	—	long. 51°: lat. 20° 30′	2×1	E.—W.

Umm Malissa (Eastern
Fida, Sabkhat Njrah

	—	long. 52°: lat. 20°-21°	3×1	N.—S.

(iv) Karsu'a
Khiran

	2-3	long. 52°: lat. 20° 30′	1½×1	E.—W.

(v) Wasa'
Khiran

	2-3	long. 52°: lat. 21°	1½×1½	—

Hadh Mazariq
Hadh Nuwasif

Hadh Munajjar Minjorat Mahayub, Minjorat Hadi	5	West of Karsu'a and Wasa'; long. 51°: lat. 21°	3×2	N.—S.
Hadh Abu Suraifa Khiran (Abu Suraifa)	½-2	West of Hamra; long. 52°: lat. 21°	4-5×2	N.—S.
Al Maharadh	—	West of Qidan; long. 52°: lat. 22°	5×1	N.—S.
Hadh Mahiqiq Mijhut, Habaran, Bani Qadhai, Bu Mahaqiq, Abu Faris	2-3	West of Maharadh; long. 51° 30': lat. 22°	4×1	N.—S.
Sanam Al 'Ubaila, Umm al Hadid, Umm Quraiyan, Safif, Turaiga, Farajja, Ibrahima, Fijafil, Umm al 'Amad, Asaila, 'Auda, Duwairis, Umm Raqa, Khalak, Al Hirra, Waiya, Banaiyan (Western water-holes of exceptional depth are called Tuwal), Bir Fadhil is said to be in Murbakh al Faris to West.	10-12	long. 51°: lat. 21°-23°	6-7×4	N.—S.

III. SOUTHERN SAND REGIONS

Ramlat Mugshin **Ramlat al 'Aradh** **Umm Dharta** **Fasad** **Mitan** **Shu'ait** Dune-country and well-less	—	The edging sands of south taking names from Wadis of same name that fall into them (except Umm Dharta, where sands emit wheezing noise when walked upon); between long. 52°-55°: lat. 18° 30'-19° 30'	1-2 days' depth	E.—W.

'Uruq Ar Raqa'at Raqa'a Ash Shamailiya, Raq'a al Janubiya	2-3 fathoms	South of Hibak, north of Fasad; long. 53°: lat. 19°	4×4 marches	—
'Uruq al Miniyur	—	West of Raqa'at, north-west of Mitan; long. 52°: lat. 19°	2×2	—
'Uruq adh Dhahiya Khor Dhahiya, Bi Dhiyab, Bin Hamuda	—	North-west of Shu'ait; long. 51° 30': lat. 19°	2×2	—
Kharkhir Kharkhir	2	Edging sands south-west of 'Uruq adh Dhahiya; long. 51°: lat. 18° 30'	3×3	—
Umm Gharib	—	Edging sands west of Kharkir; long. 50°: lat. 18°	2×2	—
Ga'amiyat Said to be waterless	—	West of Umm Gharib; long. 49°-50°: lat. 18°-19°	8×5	N.E.—S.W.
Dakaka Bil Ashush, Sabla, Mashruma, Bil Afen, Turaiwa (15), Zuwayra, Shanna (11), Khudhifiya (6), Bir Hadi, Al Harsha, Wughawak, Bin Waraiqa, Umm Dasis, Tuwaiyal, Al Bahaisin, Ga'ada Mifatih, Khor Shiban, Abu Madaiyin, Ga'aimi Sigani, Gham Ghim	Eastern wells, 3; western, 15	Central southern sands just within edging sand-dune country; long. 50° 30'-52° 30': lat. 18° 30'-20°	7×3	W.S.W.—E.N.E.

IV. NORTHERN SAND REGIONS

Mijan, Sabkhat Matti, Dhafra, Liwa, Qufa, Taff, Bainuna, Khatam, Jafura		As shown already on Hunter's map.	
Zibda and Sha'ala	15		
Mijan	2		
Bainuna	4-6		

[373]

APPENDIX III
TOPOGRAPHICAL TERMS

al hūta: A gorge or belly between sand-hills or ridges—generally with vegetation.

shagga or *sarūg:* A gorge or belly between sand-hills or ridges—generally with vegetation.

makhtūm: A wall of sand lying transversely across a *hūta.*

raidfa: A gentle curving slope of a sand-ridge in *hūta.*

rākib: A flat roof of elevated sand.

rubādh (pl.) *rubabīdh,* or *rubāl* (pl.) *rubābīl,* or *argāb* (pl.) *arāgīb:* sand-banks (drift).

kharaiyim: Steppe corridors within southern fringing sands.

nukhdat: An offshoot of a wadi, emptying into sands.

hazm (pl.) *huzūm:* Stone outcrops.

masīla: Soft, sandy wadi bed in steppe.

raga'a: Small patches of gypsum.

hissi: Depression in stony outcrop, where water will collect after rain.

ga'aida: Large sand-dune.

ga'īda: Largest sand-dune.

tar'ūza (Murri) : Largest sand-dune.

sinīn: Sand-dune with conical peak.

shansuba: Lofty sand-dune.

hugna: Horseshoe-shaped sand-hill.

urūq: Sand-dune ridges.

zibāra: Hard sand (good going).

ath-ath or *beth-beth:* Soft sand (heavy going).

gāra (pl.) *guwār:* (in north) ridge or hills.

burga: (in north) peak.

al afja: (in north) Grazing ground in the Jaubs.

raudha: (in north) Sandy patches in the stony steppe of Qatar.

sabkha: Salt plain.

asfila: The fall of the wadi where it is lost on edge of sands.

APPENDIX IV

FLORA

Mountains:

Libaniferous trees: (1) Frankincense, three varieties—Negedi (Nejdi), sh'abi (or somali), and shazari tree of mughur. Negedi is the famous tree of the three. It grows on the intramontane wadi-slopes, between 2250 feet and 2500 feet. (2) Mulukh: a tree growing on the plains along lower wadi beds at 500 feet. Gum exudes naturally from the branches and is of an edible kind. (3) Tishgāut: found on the Divide (2750-3000 feet). A low, bushy tree, in numbers from a distance resembling vineyards of Syria. Its gum is flattened into cakes and sometimes exported.

Vegetation in the mountains from 600 feet to 3000 feet: Mushta, thamar, la'ilāub, al khaimur, mughalif, hurāum, mitān (this provides a heavy wood which is said not to float in water and is used for making *ghatrifs*), subāra, and khafāut.

On the Divide (Qatan), 2750-3000 feet: Tikidauhaut, laifit, zurfit, ra'i zintirāut, tishgāut, gushar, qarhahaur, and dhubdhubaut.

Steppe:

In the *masīla* of wadis or plains: Samr (acacia), Sheheri—Saidhna, the most important camel fodder. This is the predominant intramontane vegetation between 2000 feet and 1200 feet: none below 1200 feet. Markh and hardhai trees, almost equally important for fodder, become predominant at about 1200 feet, and remain so during these mid-courses of intramontane wadis. Dha'uwut, hailaima, dha'a bushes, or scrub, are next in importance, though they do not survive rainless periods so well as the first three. They thrive in Sih at 1500-1000 feet. Ragus, al gha (b), alithal (tamarisk, met first time at 1200 feet, where the samr acacia was left behind), gutufa (wadi hill slopes), al 'usfa, raka, qilqa (dh), 'arad, jinn tree, qarada or qaraira, dumdum, dur'ma, hisham, gandra, baluk, aigail, fani, 'utib, hauwai, saaban (lubdi

[377]

thail) , dhanuna or ma'anum, asaf or ghadaf (palm bushes which provide material for rope-making) , tanfit, kaithi, dhuwaila, harmel, eshriq, ilisunam, and rimram. The last seven named have medicinal uses. Jhamam, turfa' (generally at heads of wadis and salt plains) , huguba, arad, shaukhir, rusris, mailuh, laibid, iskud, khurais-shabah.

In sandy soils on the verge of the Sands at 500 feet: Ghaf (acacia) , tarthuth (resembling the head of a bulrush) , basul, al ashera (the al ashkhara of Oman; first isolated example found at 1050 feet at Hailat Shisur on edge of sands, predominant vegetation at 500 feet, last example at Maraha) , thurmid.

Sands:

Al Abala (whose fruit is khuri) , zahara, barkana, gusais, hadh, gadha, shinan, 'angud, zaraiga, thurmid, haram.

Appendix V

CAMEL BRANDS MET WITH IN CENTRAL SOUTH ARABIA

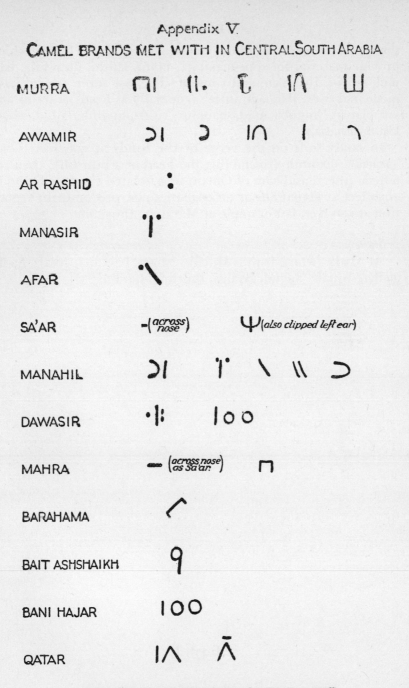

MURRA

AWAMIR

AR RASHID

MANASIR

AFAR

SA'AR   -(*across nose*)   Ψ(*also clipped left ear*)

MANAHIL

DAWASIR

MAHRA   ━ (*across nose as Sa'ar.*)

BARAHAMA

BAIT ASHSHAIKH

BANI HAJAR

QATAR

CAMEL BRANDS IN SOUTH ARABIA ARE FOUND ALMOST
INVARIABLY ON THE NEAR SIDE — CHEEK, NECK, or QUARTER

APPENDIX VI

ARAB CHANTS

'Every neck is a hairy trombone
(Rtt-ta-ta-ta! is a hairy trombone)
And this is our marching song.'
                    KIPLING, *The Jungle Book.*

The full list of

'camelty tuncs of our own
to help us trollop along'

that I met with in South Arabia is given on the following
pages.

[381]

APPENDIX VI   ARAB CHANTS (SOUTH ARABIA & RUB AL KHALI)

SHALLA (JANABA)

CAMELS OVER WATER JANABA

BRINGING CAMELS TO WATER JANABA

LOADING CAMELS JANABA

OVER WATER JANABA

LOADING CAMELS JANABA

TAQRUD (TROTTING) AWAMIR & YAL WAHIBA

HAMBAL OR RAZFA (WALKING) AWAMIR & YAL WAHIBA

HAMBAL OR RAZFA AWAMIR & YAL WAHIBA

LUTE SONG & DRUMS DHUFAR TOWN

SLAVE SONG DHUFAR

MURRA CHANT

MURRA CHANT

LOADING UP CHANT (RASHID OR MURRA?)

RAGAZAIT OF MAHRA TRIBE ~ HAY DANADON

HIBOT OF QARAMTS:

MINSHA AIR OF QARAMTS: (WOMEN)

INDEX

[389]

INDEX

INDEX

INDEX

INDEX

INDEX

INDEX

Umm —*continued.*
  al Laisa, dune, 156
  ar Ru'ūs, 156
  ash Shadīd, water-hole, 130
  as Samīm, quicksands, 184
  at Tabbākh, 143
  Dharta, region, 154, 170, 199
  Ghārib, 181
  Malíssa, sands, 230
  Quraiyin, water-hole, 242
Umr, Bait (Qara), 46
Umran, Nabi, 85
Unicorn, 134
Ur, 309
'Urba, wadi, 140
Urine, camel, use of, 224
'Uruq adh Dhahiya, 164, *sqq.*, 181
'Urūq Mijōra, region, 181

V

Vaginal blowing, 81
Valley of Remembrance, 126
Vegetation, desert, 265
Venus, 129, 229
Viper, 148, 238
Von Wrede, 184
Vulture, 147

W

Wabar, 161
Waraiga, water-hole, 199
Wāris, 209
Wāsa', 230
Wasps, 147, 361
Water-holes, 370
Week, lucky and unlucky days, 218
Whales, 3
Wild-cat, 146, 236, 237

Wilson, Sir A. T., xxii
Witchcraft, 87
Wolves, 60, 105, 237, 293
Women, position of, 32, 98, 101
Wood, *mitain,* heavy, 68
Wrede, von, cited, 184
Wyllie, Mr. B. K. N., 368

Y

Yadīla, dunes, 164
Yāfa', Yāfa'i, 26, 323
Yahām, tribe, 86
Yahar, Ahl, 26
Yal Wahiba, 182
Yam, tribe, 273
Yaqūt, cited, 161
Yazīd, Ahl, 26
Yemen, xxiii, 123, 161
Yerbury, Col. J. W., 334
Yibaila, 164
Yin Minīyōr, 164
Yusif, brother of Bu Zaid, 246, 277

Z

Zahair, shrine, 85
Zairutun, 140
Zaiyān, Bait, 41
Zart (Shahara), 46
Zenaitī, 161, 277
Zoology, Notes, 334 *sqq.*
Zuferōl (Shahara), 46
Zuftair, Ai, 46
Zughain, water-hole, 199
Zurbaig, Air, 46
Zurgha, water-hole, 298
Zuwa, frankincense grove, 123
Zuwaira, water-hole, 223

Date Due

5356	Jan 30		
5579	Mar 25		
6163	Oct 21		
7010	Apr 15		
8585	Dec 3		
JAN 2			
MAR 1			
MAR 18			